PETER KNOWLES
GOD'S FOOTBALLER

PETER KNOWLES
GOD'S FOOTBALLER

STEVE GORDOS

First published in Great Britain in 2009 by
The Breedon Books Publishing Company Limited
Breedon House, 3 The Parker Centre, Derby, DE21 4SZ.

ISBN 978-1-85983-720-7
Printed and bound by Gutenberg Press Ltd, Malta.

CONTENTS

For Lindsay

Foreword

The story of Peter Knowles has fascinated football fans for some 40 years. A good-looking, highly-talented footballer turned his back on fame and fortune because of his religious beliefs. He preferred knocking on doors and trying to convert people to Christianity rather than knocking the ball into the net and converting pinpoint centres from the likes of David Wagstaffe in a more-than-useful Wolves team in the late 1960s. Players and fans who gave little credibility to the sincerity of his beliefs came to admire him for his faith as much as they admired him for his undoubted football talent. That his glorious potential was never fulfilled will continue to rankle with those who idolised him, but Knowles, on the rare occasions he has spoken about his headline-making decision, has expressed no regret. He is certain he did the right thing.

As the 40th anniversary of Knowles's decision arrives it seems appropriate to trace the career of a special player. It is the story of a young man who had the courage of his convictions back in 1969, and a story which continues to intrigue all who happen upon it. Singer-songwriter Billy Bragg came across the Knowles story many years later and was so moved by it that he wrote the song *God's Footballer*. Bragg was happy to lend that same title to this book, and Knowles will forever be known by that soubriquet.

In compiling this biography, I have been greatly helped by many people. Jane Stack's scrapbooks, lovingly compiled during the years Knowles wore the gold and black of Wolves, have been an invaluable source of information, as have the writings of my late former *Express & Star* colleague Phil Morgan. Other ex-sports desk pals, John Dee, David Harrison and David Instone and that doyen among West Midlands freelances, Ron Warrilow, have also provided help and encouragement, as has Clive Corbett, a fan whose 2007 book *Those Were*

The Days is a must read for all Wolves fans. Clive has also proofread this book and pointed me in the right direction on several factual matters.

Jim Heath, one of the stalwarts of Wolves' fanzine *A Load of Bull*, has also been a more-than-useful source of information, comments and cuttings from his Wolves scrapbooks and memorabilia. The facilities and helpfulness of the staff at Wolverhampton Council's archive department are also much appreciated, along with the splendid programme collection of Molineux regular Kevin Jones. Extremely useful also was the collection of football memorabilia that belonged to Andy Donkersley, a former *Express & Star* reporter whose death in 2008, at the age of 52, greatly saddened his many former colleagues and friends. My thanks also to long-serving Wolves photographer Peter Harrington.

Knowles has always fought shy of interviews with journalists and did not wish to be involved with this book. I hope that, without his direct input, it will still do him justice. It seeks not to judge him but merely to recount his story, to detail the games in which he played and to place on record the gratitude of those of us who saw him play football, coupled with a lasting admiration for a man of faith.

Football 0, God 1

The Beatle-haired footballer trotted quickly off the pitch and down the tunnel to the home dressing room in Molineux's ageing Waterloo Road stand. Peter Knowles had vowed never to play professional football again, but most Wolverhampton Wanderers fans on a crisp September afternoon in 1969 were more concerned with the fact that their side had let slip a three-goal lead to draw 3–3 with Nottingham Forest. 'He'll be back' was the general opinion as they reflected on a Forest rally which brought three goals in nine second-half minutes.

Knowles had decided that after becoming a Jehovah's Witness he could not remain a footballer and be true to his religious beliefs. Teammates and fans alike thought Christianity was just his latest fad. He would, they believed, realise he could not do without football and would return to Molineux desperate to resume his career.

He did not come back.

All were proved wrong. Knowles, not quite 24, was done with the game that had made him a local hero and was starting to make him a national one. He had found something far more important. His beliefs were deep and sincere. As the years passed, those who had doubted him came to admire him for his faith in the same way they had admired him for his skilful feet and astute football brain. On the rare occasions he has talked publicly about his decision he has maintained it was the best thing he ever did. He has even gone so far as to say he wished he had never played football. Yet he has also said how much he admired Manchester United's George Best and how he wished he could have played just one match in the same team as the Irish footballing genius. You can take the man out of football, it would seem, but you cannot take football out of the man.

While accepting that Knowles genuinely believed he had good reason to turn his back on the game, Wolves fans who saw him mature to the brink of stardom in a six-year first-team career wish he could have waited perhaps another six years or so before calling it a day. Knowles, they feel, could have been the difference between the Wolves team of the early 1970s being a great one rather than just a very good one. A squad who included Mike Bailey, Derek Parkin, Frank Munro, Jim McCalliog, Derek Dougan, John Richards, Kenny Hibbitt and Dave Wagstaffe brought Wolves close to major honours. Though they did win the League Cup in 1974 and reached the UEFA Cup Final in 1972, they needed just a little extra to make them a real force to rival Arsenal, Liverpool, Derby and Leeds who were the big guns at that time. Knowles could have provided it.

Without a doubt, the legend of Knowles's ability has grown over the years, and no one can say for certain whether he would have fulfilled his potential. No one, though, can deny he had that potential. Wolves fans who saw him believe he was on the brink of great things. He had been somewhat unpredictable once he had established himself in the Wolves side. There was also a petulance that often reared its head and threatened his progress, but by the time the 1969–70 season arrived he seemed to be reaching football maturity. He was freely being talked of as a future international, and England manager Sir Alf Ramsey was aware of his blossoming talent. He seemed to have every chance of making the squad who would defend the Jules Rimet trophy at the World Cup Finals in Mexico. In a useful Wolves side, he was admired by fans young and old.

Yet the truth was that by then he had made Ramsey aware of his plans to turn his back on the game. The public might think he was on the brink of football stardom, but it was suddenly the last thing Knowles wanted.

Knowles had come a long way since signing for Wolverhampton Wanderers in the 1960–61 season. Born in Yorkshire on 30 September 1945, a job as a miner seemed the most likely life mapped out for him. His home village was Fitzwilliam, which boasts England cricketer Geoff Boycott as its most famous sporting son. It owed its very existence to the coal industry, being built to house miners working at Fitzwilliam Main, which later became Hemsworth Colliery. Talking about his boyhood in an interview with Rogan Taylor for BBC Radio Five in 1994, Knowles recalled he had come from a hard background. 'The village was round the pit, and my dad was a miner. He used to be a rugby player for Wakefield Trinity and York. Me and Cyril [one of Knowles's brothers who would play for Spurs and England], we liked our sport. My dad died when he was 42, so that left my mother. She was only 36, and she had to bring six of us up. When my father died my mother had only just a few weeks earlier had a baby and it was a Down's Syndrome child. About four weeks later that child died as well. So it was hard. Like a lot of kids in those days who had not got a father, we had free meals at school and passed our clothes down.'

Rogan Taylor wondered if religion had played a part in Knowles's life at that time. 'Not at all,' Knowles told him. 'We never discussed it because of what happened to my father and my two sisters – I lost another sister with pneumonia. We never discussed God. We never asked why, we just thought it was bad luck.'

If religion did not loom large in Knowles's early life, neither did thoughts of a career as a professional footballer. 'When I left school I was going to go down the pit. I was going to be a miner like my father and my brother. Then I was playing football for the school, and a Wolves scout came to look at a player on the other side and I happened to take his eye. He came to my house the same night and asked me if I'd like to go to Wolves and sign for them. I said "No." I said I wasn't interested in going to Wolves. I had just watched Wolves play Leicester in the Cup, and I thought it was very boring, yet he persisted and kept coming, and I met Stan Cullis, the manager. He wanted me to come, and he was an honest person so I decided to sign there and then. Yet on that day I was supposed to have gone down the pit.'

Ironically, his brother Cyril, who was 14 months older, was rejected by Wolves. While working at Monkton Colliery, he had a trial with the club as a winger but did not do enough to impress the Molineux staff. He was later discovered by Middlesbrough, where he made his name as a full-back. He signed for Boro in October 1962.

Confirmation that the young Peter was a talented sportsman came from Peter Crawshaw, who attended the same school, Kinsley Secondary Modern. 'If you gave him the ball at cricket and said he could bowl 12 in a row he would bowl them all out. He was that fast,' recalled Crawshaw. 'When he batted you just could not get him out. He was not brilliant academically, sport was his thing. I think he got into the school football team when he was much younger than the rest. He was that good. I have a feeling he played at centre-half because he was a big lad. But he could get the ball and run through everybody and score. When he got the ball you could not get it off him. His dad, who was also called Cyril, being an ex-rugby league man, would take Peter and his brothers on to the local playing field, and he would kick the rugby ball as high as he could, and you'd see the boys trying to catch it.'

Crawshaw has fond memories of Knowles, 'He was a very likeable lad. He always had a smile, but he could be rough and would occasionally give you a playful backhander. We had some good times. I remember once when Peter, me and another lad were told to report for a football trial. It might have been Yorkshire or Wakefield District. It was at a school about five miles away, but you walked in those days so we set off over the fields in our kit and football boots, but when we got there we found it was a cross-country running trial. So we had to walk all the way back.

'There were four main estates at Fitzwilliam – the City, Little Wigan, Council Houses and Wimpey's. Peter's family lived in First Avenue on the Council Houses estate. It's all very different now. The pit is long gone. You would not know it had been there. It's all landscaped. We had a reunion a few years back in a pub in Fitzwilliam, and only a few people turned up, but Peter came. He wore a sort of trench coat, black, and he had on little glasses. He wasn't the Peter I knew as a lad. He was still very pleasant, very nice but much quieter, and we chatted for a long time. He was very articulate and is still a lovely lad. He said he was going to speak at a Jehovah's Witnesses' meeting in Hemsworth the next day.'

Another old school pal who can testify to Knowles's sporting prowess as a child is Jim Harrison. 'I was in infants, juniors and secondary school with him, and he was always very sports orientated. You could see he was going to be a sportsman from junior school. It was any sport: cricket, football, rounders, even tiddlywinks – he'd be good at it. I remember once when he was about 15 he hit this shot from almost the halfway line and it was a goal, but we had no nets and the ball hit the building behind the goal. It was a library, a wooden structure with a brick base, but Peter hit that shot so hard it smashed the wood. I've never seen anything like it.

'Peter liked a laugh and was just one of the lads. Once, four of us were smoking after a gardening lesson. We were behind the compost heap with one cigarette, passing it around, and suddenly Peter and the rest of us were covered in water. Mrs Betts, the deputy head, had thrown a bucket of water over us. She said, "I thought the compost heap was on fire", but she knew what she was doing. We always used to have a really good laugh. My wife Pat, who was Pat Jackson in those days, was in the same class in the infants and junior school, and we both remember him. He was a good lad, was Peter. The last time I met him when he was still a footballer was when he came up to the Fitzwilliam Hotel – it's gone now, flattened – but he was well-dressed, in a smart suit and arrived in his sports car. He had all the trappings of a football star, and the next we heard he had become a Jehovah's Witness. It was a big surprise because I thought he would go on to be even better than George Best. That's how good he was in my opinion. The one today who most reminds me of Peter is Cristiano Ronaldo at Manchester United. Peter had all the same tricks and the same skill.' Harrison added, 'I was also at that school reunion. Peter had a Bible with him, and he would not have a drink or anything to eat because we were in a pub.'

Harrison also reckons Knowles did not leave school straight away at 15, which you could do at that time. 'He should have left at Christmas, but Mr Buchanan, the games teacher, arranged for him to stay on because he knew Wolves would not sign him until he was 16. He probably thought Peter would just be messing about if he left or else get a job down the pit.'

Knowles signed for Wolves in 1961, and one wonders whether his reference to the Cup match with Leicester was the occasion the teams met in the sixth round at Leicester's Filbert Street ground in March 1960. It was a dour match, which Wolves won 2–1. In those days only edited highlights were shown on TV, but it still seems to have influenced Knowles. Despite the impression that game left on Knowles, the persuasive powers of Stan Cullis won the day in getting him to pursue a career in football. Though Knowles was not a committed Christian in those days, Cullis was. The manager ruled Molineux with discipline but did so with fairness and without ever swearing. In later life he took great pride in the fact that his son Andrew became a member of the clergy. So one can well understand how Cullis's basic honesty persuaded Knowles to sign and cut his teeth with their famous Wath Wanderers nursery side in Yorkshire. It should also be remembered that in 1961 Wolves were still among the top three teams in the land. They had established a tradition of finding young players and bringing them through the ranks. Yorkshire had proved a fertile ground in that respect with players like Roy Swinbourne, Ron Flowers, Jack Short and Barry Stobart making the grade at Molineux.

'When I went to Wolves I was 16 years old. I was so impressed with the manager Stan Cullis,' Knowles recalled in 2007. 'He showed me into the trophy room and at the end of it said "Wolves are the greatest team in Europe, and you can be part of it." I signed straight away. Stan Cullis slept, ate and breathed Wolves, and one of the things I will never forget about him was he never swore.' The youngster soon learned that without swearing Cullis could still demand strict behaviour. 'One of the things that struck me straight away at Wolves was the discipline. We were not allowed to look at the pitch until Saturday. My first job was cleaning the reserve dressing room out each day. I was there six months before I was allowed in the first-team dressing room – just to clean it. The respect and fear was tremendous in those early days.'

Yet when he was allowed to show what he could do, Knowles obviously convinced the Wolves staff that he had what it took to make the grade. He soon became a member of a very useful youth squad at Molineux and in 1962 helped them reach the FA Youth Cup Final. Producing their own players was one of the strengths of Wolves in the 1950s, as their team rivalled Manchester United as the country's best. Having begun Cullis's reign by winning the FA Cup in 1949, Wolves were First Division champions in 1954, 1958 and 1959 before neatly rounding off the most successful spell in the club's history by again winning the FA Cup in 1960. That was why fans found the struggles of the early 1960s difficult to stomach. They had become used to their side being the best in the country.

Times were changing in English football. For years players had been limited in their earning power by a maximum wage rule. It was a leftover from a bygone age, and the fight by the players' union, the PFA, to get it abolished was to prove a success. By the time Knowles decided on a football career, the battle was won and a man expected to be paid according to his talent. Fulham and England captain Johnny Haynes in 1961 became the first player to be paid £100 a week, and others would follow. It was a far cry from the sort of money players could earn by the end of the 20th Century, but suddenly football was an attractive profession, and footballers themselves were about to become superstars.

It has become a cliché to describe the '60s as 'swinging', but it was without doubt a decade of change where youngsters were more determined than ever to enjoy themselves and to find idols or role models. It was the age of the Beatles and Rolling Stones, and some of the musical magic rubbed off on football. George Best, the gloriously talented Manchester United teenager, blazed the trail and created a new kind of football hero – adored by teenage girls, money to spend and the world at his twinkling feet. Knowles fell easily into the Best mould. He was a handsome young man of undoubted soccer skill. He would not be content to take the bus to Molineux. For him a sports car would eventually be the chosen mode of transport, and he would enjoy his status as a local hero. Even in his early days, Knowles had a touch of arrogance about his play. It was not an arrogance that stemmed from conceit or was assumed to mask a lack of true talent. His was that arrogance which many great footballers have possessed – a complete belief in their ability. One saw it in Denis Law and George Best. One saw it many years later in Eric Cantona.

Knowles saw it that way, too. Looking back in 1994, he said, 'I was a quiet player and then when I got into the first team it changed. The arrogance came out. I could see there were other players around me that had flair. Best, Marsh, Bowles – they were flair players, and that's what I wanted to be, an individual who'd got flair. But to do that you'd got to have this kind of arrogance. It was getting into the first team that totally changed me.'

Former Wolves boss Sammy Chapman's perception of players like Knowles is that their talent is natural and therefore taken for granted by them. They have not had to work at it, they can do things other players cannot do but do not regard it as anything special. 'People like Peter are wonderful players,' says Chapman, 'and it's a God-given talent, easy for them, nothing's difficult. It's like picking up a glass. You say bend that ball and they just do it. The only problem you have with talented players is that they cause you trouble. Those with less talent have to work hard – they don't cause you trouble. Those that have the real talent are your biggest problem because they don't understand why someone has difficulty, say, with crossing. They say "Didn't he see me? What's wrong with him?" The unfortunate thing is it is also very easy for them to give it up because they've never thought that much of it.' That Chapman thesis may explain why Knowles could just walk away from football.

Knowles would, in his early years, often be his own worst enemy. He would overdo the fancy tricks and lose possession or would lose his temper and get his name into the referee's notebook. By the time he decided to turn his back on the game, however, Knowles had learned when to turn on the clever stuff and when not. He was almost the finished article, a key member of the Wolves side with his talent ready to blossom. Yet even in those days he would try the sort of things that have fans drooling when many years later they see them done by Cristiano Ronaldo or Chelsea's Joe Cole. Sadly, matches then were not routinely recorded as they are now, and glimpses of Knowles in action are few. However, on the BBC video celebrating *25 Years of Match of the Day* there are two cameos which sum him up. First he is seen robbing Spurs maestro Jimmy Greaves and then passing the ball to a colleague but not in an orthodox way. He chooses to swing his right leg behind his left and execute the sort of flicked pass rarely tried in those days. Secondly, there is a glimpse of Knowles in the same game being penalised for a foul. Instead of walking away he slams the ball down in anger in front of the referee and is promptly booked. John Motson's 'voiceover', with more than a hint of understatement, recalls that petulance was a feature of Knowles's game.

How good was Knowles? At the time of his voluntary retirement he was close to football maturity. The flair was still a big part of his game, but the losses of self control were far fewer. He could beat an opponent with a swivel of the hips, he could pass the ball sweetly and could score goals. He was a player for the 1970s – an all rounder, not tied to a particular role. Most reckoned he had every chance of making England's World Cup party to defend the trophy in Mexico at the end of what proved to be Knowles's farewell season. If he did not make Mexico he would surely win a full cap in due course. He had the tricks of Joe Cole, the passes of David Beckham and could score goals like Wayne Rooney. Phil Parkes, who in 1966 also broke into Wolves' first team as a teenager, confirms Knowles's ability. 'Peter was a naturally gifted athlete. He was a six-handicap golfer, he was a great cricketer, he could play table tennis, tennis – just about anything.'

Parkes also provides a glimpse of what the 21-year-old Knowles was like. 'My first away game in the first team was at Portsmouth and I shared a room with Peter. He was mad. He didn't drink, but he was just daft – anything for a laugh. As it was my first away trip, my mum had put an apple and an orange in my bag. He said, "Can I have that orange?" I said yes, and anybody else would peel it, but he bit it. He'd got two false teeth at the front and pulled one of the teeth off his plate. So he said, "I can't play tomorrow with a gap in my teeth." So Jack Dowen, the old trainer, came up the next morning and Peter said: "You'd better go and tell Ronnie [Allen] I can't play" and Jack says, "What d'you mean?" He said, "Look, I can't play like this – it's on *Match of the Day* tonight." So Ronnie Allen and Jack Dowen stuck his tooth back on with chewing gum, I think, and he played. He scored the equalising goal that day and ran into the net, picked the ball out and kicked it over the stand. And they made him pay for the ball. That was Peter – I tell you, he wouldn't have played without that tooth. That's the way he was.'

Frank Munro, who established himself in the Wolves team during Knowles's last full season at Molineux, also recalls his antics on the field – 'He was the first player I saw sit on the ball during a match at the corner flag' – and remembers one particularly bizarre incident against Coventry. The Sky Blues, who would pip Wolves for the Second Division title in 1967, had one of the game's true hard-men in their defence – George Curtis. Says Munro, 'I had to laugh, I had the ball on the halfway line and I tried to play it to Waggy [Dave Wagstaffe], but I played a bad ball. I sliced it, and it was going towards the corner flag, but Knowlesy was through on to it. But he could hear the "hooves" behind him – George Curtis! So he runs behind the corner flag and Curtis kicks the ball up the pitch. Peter just ran off the pitch and left the ball, yet he was through.'

It came as a big surprise to the team when Knowles became interested in religion. Full-back Derek Parkin remembered, 'He just comes in one day, and he's got a Bible in his hand.' Munro recalls, 'I thought he'd be back in three months.' They, like so many others, admit they were proved wrong and admire the way he stuck to his decision. Parkin adds, 'I played in a testimonial match with him. He had never played in any benefit matches, except his brother's, but he turned up. This was years after, and I remember talking to him after the game, and I had tremendous admiration for him because he was such a brilliant talented player, and I remember saying "Do you miss it all, Peter? You must miss the training, even I miss the training and the patter with the lads." And he said, "The only regret I have is ever having played."'

Despite his sense of fun and tendency to do the unusual, Knowles was very serious about his football. Parkin backs that up, 'He used to love it. He was a great trainer. He used to come back afternoons, doing extra – but yet he said that to me at that testimonial game. I couldn't believe it.'

It is difficult all these years later to try to convey the shock caused by Knowles's decision to quit football. Nothing like it had happened before and nothing since. To those who had seen Knowles as a typical lad out to enjoy himself while still young, it was a bolt from the blue. Most of his teammates thought it was just a passing fancy, and though they came to realise he was serious about his faith, Knowles reckoned they had little to say to him at the time he played his last match in September 1969. Looking back in his Radio Five interview in 1994, Knowles said 'Not one of them took it seriously. They just thought it was a joke. They just thought "Give him six months." Like my brother, my brother said the same. I can always remember the last game I played, against Nottingham Forest, not one of them came and said "All the best, cheerio." They just thought, "After a couple of weeks, he'll be back again." I think what made it strange was being a Jehovah's Witness. I think if it had been Church of England or Catholic, but the fact I was giving up to become a Jehovah's Witness, I think that puzzled a lot of people.'

It should be noted that what Knowles said in this interview was at odds with what appeared in the *Sunday Express* newspaper the day after his last game. The paper quoted him thus: 'In the dressing-room all the players shook me by the hand and wished me all the best.'

Skipper of Wolves at the time was Mike Bailey, and he was one of many who tried to persuade Knowles not to give up the game. 'I think we all tried to have a word with him,' said Bailey. 'We had a chat on the coach going to one game, but he was more interested in trying to recruit us. He tried to turn us. I said, "It's up to you, but bear in mind you are giving up a lucrative profession, albeit a short one." I liked Peter, he was a nice lad. He loved life. He was a Jack the Lad, the last one you thought would do that, but you can't knock him. He has proved a lot of people wrong. I think we all thought he'd come back.'

News of Knowles's conversion to Christianity, and the possibility he might quit was broken exclusively in the *Daily Mail* by their staffman, the late Mervyn Thomas, towards the end of January 1969. It seems Thomas may have used a little subterfuge to get the story his rivals were all after. Ron Warrilow, a freelance reporter in Wolverhampton for nearly 50 years, reckons Thomas led Knowles to believe that he, too, was a Christian. 'That's how he got in with Peter,' recalled Warrilow. 'I'm not sure whether he told him he was a Jehovah's Witness, but he certainly gained his confidence and got the story to himself.'

Warrilow, still a regular in the Molineux press box in 2009, was as surprised as anyone when Knowles decided to turn his back on football. He remembered the young man with the white sports car who had an eye for the girls and a passion for the game. 'He loved that car. He had his initials put on it in red. It was all part of the image that helped him chat up the girls. He liked to enjoy himself, but I'm sure he took his career seriously.'

Knowles has in recent years worked at Marks and Spencer's store in Wolverhampton town centre. 'I still see him occasionally,' says Warrilow, 'helping people load their shopping into their cars. He'll always speak and despite what he has said about football he usually asks me about Wolves, asks me how they are playing. There is definitely some affection still there.' Warrilow has also asked him how he now spent his time, and Knowles said he read the Bible daily and continued his work for the Jehovah's Witnesses. It is a simple, uncomplicated life and one that has brought him contentment and happiness. Alas, Knowles was not so happy to learn from Warrilow that I was writing his story. He still has a distrust of journalists, so I hope he will not judge me too harshly if he should chance to read this book. It would have been good to have some direct input from him, but he declined Warrilow's offer to set up a meeting between us.

When it became known, via that *Daily Mail* story, that Knowles was a Jehovah's Witness, Wolves manager Bill McGarry tried to play down any possibility of the player giving up football. The truth, however, was that Knowles was certain he would not carry on much longer. His was no shock decision, and no one could dissuade him. I cannot place the exact date, but, as a young sports sub-editor, I recall Knowles being in the Wolverhampton head office of the *Express & Star* one day. He was talking to John Dee, who was at the time a sports reporter who also wrote a weekly feature in the Saturday night football paper, the *Sporting Star,* affectionately known as 'the Pink' because of the colour of the paper it was printed on. Knowles had a regular column in the Pink which Dee ghosted for him. A Knowles visit to our office usually saw Dee and he having a fairly light-hearted conversation. I did not pay much attention to their chatter on this occasion until I saw Dee look over to me and indicate, without Knowles knowing, that I ought to eavesdrop as Knowles was telling him something important. Unfortunately, I could not hear every word but got the definite impression that whatever it was Knowles had told Dee, he was adamant about it. I seem to recall Dee asking him if his mind was made up and Knowles saying that it was. After Knowles had left, Dee explained to me that Knowles had told him he was definitely going to give up football. He had asked Dee to keep it quiet as he wanted to sort a few things out before finally packing up the game. Knowles had stressed he was speaking off the record and, like all good journalists, Dee respected that fact.

I refer to this incident because it is evidence that Knowles's decision had been carefully considered. People at Molineux thought they could make him think again and were unhappy when news of his intentions finally leaked out, feeling it may have forced his hand. They believed they could work on him and make him reconsider. Manager Bill McGarry was among those who thought that all was not lost. They were mistaken. Knowles had thought long and hard about it, had discussed it with his wife, who shared his faith, and was adamant that he could not be a footballer and a Jehovah's Witness. Football or his faith? One would have to go – and his Christianity was what mattered to him.

The *Express & Star* respected Knowles's wishes and 'sat' on the story, but as the weeks passed rumours grew that he was about to turn his back on football. It was feared one of the national newspapers would break the news first. Knowing this, the *Express & Star* ran a story – not written by John Dee – which suggested Knowles was wrestling with his conscience about whether he could be both a footballer and a Jehovah's Witness. As I recall it, Bill McGarry was far from happy that the *Express & Star* had carried such a story. He felt he was getting somewhere with trying to dissuade Knowles and thought the article was hardly helpful to his mission. McGarry was wrong. No one could have made Knowles reconsider. That conversation with John Dee in the *Express & Star* office had made it clear that his mind was made up. It was just a matter of tying up a few loose ends. His intentions were certain, it was only a question of when.

Dee's recollection coincides with mine. 'There was no question about it,' Dee told me. 'He said that day at the *Express & Star* that he was finishing and that was that. He decided his last game would be on the Saturday after Wolves faced Spurs in the League Cup because his brother, Cyril, was in the Spurs team, and he fancied one more game against him. I know McGarry was not very pleased with us when we carried that story, but nothing would have made Peter change his mind.'

For many years now a distinguished writer on snooker as well as greyhound racing and football, Dee shares the views of others on Knowles's talents. 'He was the missing link' is how Dee sees it. 'That Wolves team of the early '70s was a very good one. They just needed that little bit extra to have made them not just a good team but a great one, and I think Knowlesy would have made the difference. He was just coming into his prime.' Though no one could have made Knowles have a re-think, Dee recalls that McGarry always lived in hope. 'I think the nearest he got was a few weeks after his last game. Derek Dougan had just been banned, and McGarry thought he'd got Peter to say he'd play again, but at the last minute Peter changed his mind.'

Dee has fond memories of Knowles both on and off the field. He recalled an occasion when he had to cover a Wolves game because veteran *Express & Star* Wolves correspondent Phil Morgan had been taken ill. Says Dee, 'We used to travel with the team in those days on the coach. We were playing at Chelsea, and it was very cold, and I said to Peter as we were getting off the coach, "It's going to be freezing in that press box today." Well he'd just bought himself a sheepskin coat – they were all the rage in those days – and he said, "Here, have my coat, that'll warm you up." And he insisted I borrow it, and I got a lot of envious glances from the other press lads. It was virtually a brand-new coat, but that gesture was typical of Knowlesy.'

At the time of Knowles's decision, both Dee and Phil Morgan said his main reason was that he would have to try to foul people if he was to be a successful footballer. Morgan, in the *Wolverhampton Wanderers Football Book*, wrote, 'He had got it into his mind this business about the need to "clog" people – not that he was ever one of the more notable of the game's "cloggers" – and nothing would change his view that he could not be a "clogger" and a Christian.'

The argument that players like Stanley Matthews, Tom Finney and Bobby Charlton had managed to reach the very top of their profession without resorting to dubious methods seemed not to count with Knowles. The interview he gave to BBC TV at the time of his retirement is indicative of the way he was thinking, even though some of the logic seems a little over the top. He said, 'I know the personality that I am, the flair I've got, that I could one day break somebody's leg. No matter how long I play football, no matter how long I'm a Jehovah's Witness or how near to perfection I come, I know for a fact, the personality I am, and I'm imperfect, that I could break somebody's leg. And I'd hate this on my mind. It's not the thought of breaking somebody's leg, it's just the thought that that person could be out of work, that person could be a cripple for the rest of his life. And when you're a cripple for the rest of your life and when you've been earning £100 a week you come down in wages. And that's going to be a big drop, especially if a footballer's got four or five kids. And also, when you've broken your leg you're hanging about the house, you start being niggly with your wife and it could easily break a marriage up. People say this is rubbish, but it has happened and I don't want this on my conscience. I know that, the personality I am on a football field, I could do this.

'I found that when I started reading the Bible and when I started trying to be a Christian I found that after Wednesday, the nearer we got to Saturday, I was dragging myself away from my wife and I was dragging myself away from religion. I was building myself up as nearer I got to Saturday. I was starting to be on my own, and I was thinking about the game, and I was thinking how I was going to play and what happened if somebody kicked me or what happened if somebody was going to score, what would I do? I was really getting involved in the game. From Wednesday until Saturday I might as well not be married. I might as well have been on my own. But this is wrong because the Bible expects you to be a Christian seven days a week. I think sport's gone out of football, myself. It's getting a big business, and there's that much at stake, well, anything can happen. It's the same with crowds. At one time women would never go to a football match, but now there's all women in the crowds. There's people getting smashed over the head with bottles, and there's people getting stabbed, and I can see that it's going to come to a big climax in one game.'

While one might think Knowles was being melodramatic about the injuries he might do to other players and the possible consequences, his final remarks are startling, bearing in mind he was speaking in 1969. In view of some of the awful tragedies that occurred on football grounds in the latter half of the 20th century, Knowles's words seem almost prophetic.

If not wanting to be a 'clogger' was what did not fit in with his religious views in 1969, some 25 years later he was presenting a slightly different version of what had been troubling his conscience – it was the hero-worship. In his interview on Radio Five Live, he told Rogan Taylor, 'When I got more into the Bible, it started to mention about idolatry. I began to notice that people began to worship me, idolise me, and I realised that this wasn't right. I can remember playing against United at Molineux. I remember the crowd chanting my name and I always remember going over to pick the ball up and can remember these people screaming and shouting and I thought, "Well, this isn't right. I'm just an ordinary fella like anybody else yet here I am being worshipped by these people, and the Bible says it's not right." So it just grew more and more, you see. You look at all players who have got flair and arrogance, they are all temperamental – in any sport – and I was that kind of person.'

Although Knowles played the first nine games of the 1969–70 season, it is clear the idea to quit had been formulating during the latter part of the previous season. He had impressed in a couple of England Under-23 matches and was undoubtedly rated by Sir Alf Ramsey as full cap material. He clearly felt he ought to let the England boss know what was on his mind. In his 1994 interview he recalls approaching Ramsey after Wolves had played Ipswich in Ray Crawford's testimonial match at the end of the 1968–69 season. 'I went up to Ramsey. I can picture him now, he was talking to Bobby Robson, the Ipswich manager. I can remember going up to him in the boardroom and I said to him, "Alf, I expect you've heard that I'm a Jehovah's Witness" and he said, "Yes." I said, "There's been rumours going around that I'm thinking of giving up football" and he said, "Yes." And I said, "Well, I don't think I could go on the trip to Portugal with the England team." And I always remember, he turned round to me and he said, "What you're really saying, lad, is you don't want to play for your country." I said, "That's it." And I can picture him now, he just turned his back on me and left me standing, looking at the back of his collar. I thought, "That's it, Peter, your football career now is finished. You don't want to play for your country any more" and from that day on I just got things moving to give up football. When anybody mentions Alf Ramsey to me, that's what I always remember about the man.'

Once the news broke that Knowles planned to quit, pleas for a change of mind were futile. A couple of Wolverhampton girls wrote out page after page pleading 'Peter, don't go', or words to that effect. We did a story about their petition in the *Express & Star* and I was detailed to call at Knowles's home on the outskirts of Wolverhampton. Though he must have been fed up of being bothered by press, local and national, he still answered the door to me. While he asked me to say thank you to the girls, he stressed their petition would make no difference. It was over.

It is difficult to convey the disbelief and desperation felt by the fans at the time of Knowles's departure, especially the younger ones. Such a supporter was Clive Corbett whose book, *Those Were the Days*, a superb recollection of the Wolves from 1964 to 1977, was published in 2007. Corbett told me, 'Although others saw it coming, it came as a total shock to me, and I was utterly convinced that he would be back. I genuinely hated the Jehovah's Witnesses for what I saw as luring him away against his will to join some Moonie-like sect. It must be remembered I was a very immature 12-year-old at the time. I even blamed his wife. Peter was seen at the time by some as being a very shallow and selfish young man who was walking out on his responsibilities and letting us all down. How wrong we were – we were losing a hero, a pop star, our Beatle or George Best, but what a man! What strength of purpose and what dedication to a way of life! Who were we to dare to say that this was the wrong choice? In terms of quality of life and personal happiness, Peter got it absolutely right.'

More confirmation of Knowles's place in the younger fans' affections came from Jim Heath, a regular contributor to the Wolves fanzine, *A Load of Bull*. Heath recalls, 'Peter Knowles was one of the main reasons I started supporting Wolves. The biggest star of the day was, of course, George Best, but Wolves, I reckoned, had their own genius in Peter. He seemed to be cut from a similar cloth to Best. He had the haircut, he had the skills and he had that rebellious streak that made him different from his contemporaries. And he played just down the road! My first Wolves scrapbooks are adorned with pictures of Knowles. He must have been a photographer's dream, what with his pop star looks, his cheeky grin and a pout that punk rocker Billy Idol would be proud of – and, boy, could he pose! Even for stills and portrait pictures he would put on some sort of show for the lensman. One of my favourites is Knowles in mid-air with the ball seemingly stuck to his boot and an outrageous smile that suggests "Look how easy this is."'

Bob Blower, now living in Perton, just outside Wolverhampton, was a teenage fan when Knowles came to prominence and sums him up simply, 'I thought he was fabulous. It was just everything about him. He was arrogant, he had style, he had skills – he even had a graceful way of running that was all his own. I just thought he was a special player, and so did my pals. We were shattered when he gave up, but we've all come to admire him for having the courage of his convictions.'

In The Beginning

No one could possibly have predicted the abrupt end to Knowles's football career, which had begun with such enthusiasm for the game. Knowles joined Wolves in the early 1960s, first having a spell with their Yorkshire nursery side, Wath Wanderers, where so many future Wolves stars were nurtured by ex-player Mark Crook. Knowles would serve under no fewer than four managers and see Wolves relegated and promoted. His was a steady progress, virtually from day one, as it became clear that he had a special football talent. One man who remembers an early encounter with Knowles is Reg Summerfield, now a theatrical agent of some repute in the West Midlands. Summerfield, who lives in Bilston, recalled, 'Wolves used to field a lot of teams in those days, and I played against probably their fifth team in a Wolverhampton Amateur League game, possibly for Ettingshall Holy Trinity or Highway Rangers. There was this young lad in the Wolves team, and I just could not get near him. It was like Billy Wright against Puskas. Afterwards I was talking to one of the Wolves coaches, and he said the lad was one of the best prospects they had ever had. That was the first time I came across Peter Knowles, and everything that coach predicted for him proved right.'

Summerfield's encounter with Knowles is confirmation that the youngster was soon sent down to Wolverhampton, such was his obvious promise. Wolves fielded their fifth team in the Wolverhampton Amateur League, a side who consisted of apprentice professionals like Knowles and the occasional trialist or two. Next step up was the Worcestershire Combination team, and the first record of Knowles playing in that side is from 8 April 1961 when he was at inside-right and scored one of the goals in a 3–0 win over Walsall side, Shelfield. His star was in the ascendant, and in the programme for the opening home game of the 1961–62 season his name appeared among the club's list of their playing staff. His height was listed as 5ft 10.5ins (1.75m) and his weight 9st 9lbs (61.29kg). By the time he started his last season, Knowles was listed as 5ft 11.5ins tall (1.82m) and 11st 2lbs (70.8kg).

The name of Knowles really came to prominence at Molineux during that 1961–62 season as part of the side who reached the FA Youth Cup Final. He was on target twice when they beat Villa 4–1 at Villa Park against a side who included future Arsenal star George Graham, who should have opened the scoring. He rounded Wolves 'keeper Jim Barron who promptly grabbed his legs. In those days a 'keeper did not get sent off for such an action, and to add insult to injury he then saved the resultant penalty taken by Alan Baker. Wolves made Villa pay and earned a semi-final meeting with Chelsea. A goal from inside-right Alan Attwood 12 minutes from time was enough to win the first leg at Stamford Bridge, where Knowles saw a shot hit a post. It was Knowles who paved the way for a 3–0 second-leg win to clinch a place in the Final. Phil Morgan took a look at the youngsters and described Knowles as 'an inside-forward prospect if ever there was one' and was impressed by the way Knowles, with not much space, had still managed to get in his shot to open the scoring. Morgan's final words, 'After allowing for a certain amount of hurry in the Wolves front line there was still much to admire, particularly in the work of Knowles, the outstanding performer, with a hint of maturity in the way he frequently used the ball.'

Word of the promising youngsters in gold and black had spread by the time the Final against Newcastle United arrived, and there were 13,916 fans at the first leg which ended 1–1. John Galley's shot was deflected in by David Turner to give Wolves a lead after 34 minutes. Knowles went close with a flying header, and full-back Bobby Thomson had two shots narrowly off target. Wolves paid for their misses when the Geordies' right-half Clive Chapman resisted three tackles to fire home an equaliser in the second half. The second leg gave Knowles a taste of the big time as 20,688 were at St James' Park to see the Final decided when a corner was headed home on 58 minutes by Bobby Moncur, a future defensive kingpin for Newcastle but in those days an inside-forward. Galley thought he had equalised when he seized on a poor backpass from a free-kick and beat goalkeeper Stan Craig. The referee said 'no goal' and explained afterwards that he had refused it because he had not signalled the free-kick to be taken. There may have been no winners' medal for Knowles, but now he was being talked about as a player to watch, as were several other members of the team. The Final line up was:

Wolves: Barron, Rickerby, Thomson, Goodwin, Woodfield, Knighton, Povey, Attwood, Galley, Knowles, Calloway.

Newcastle: S.Craig, D.Craig, Clish, Chapman, Markie, Turner, Gowland, Suddick, Watkin, Moncur, O' Neill.

In the second leg, Kemp replaced Attwood, but Newcastle fielded the same team.

Of that Wolves team, Jim Barron, Bobby Thomson, Fred Goodwin, David Woodfield, Ken Knighton, John Galley, Fred Kemp and Knowles would all have successful first-team careers, though not all at Molineux. For seven members of a youth side to progress to greater things is a considerably high percentage. As well as the Youth Cup exploits, Knowles was a regular in the Midland Intermediate League side, also making the occasional appearance in the Worcestershire Combination. The next step on the ladder would be a game with the reserves in the Central League, and that came early in the 1962–63 season. He played inside-left in the team who beat West Bromwich Albion reserves 3–0 on 6 October 1962. He was just past his 17th birthday and lined up in the following side: Finlayson, John Harris, Gerry Harris, Durandt, Slater, Knighton, Read, Stobart, Ford, Knowles, David Thompson. He was mixing with experienced professionals in that team, including four of the victorious 1960 Cup Final side – Malcolm Finlayson, Gerry Harris, Bill Slater and Barry Stobart. Before that debut in the reserves Knowles had hit a hat-trick in a 6–0 win over Boldmere in the Worcestershire Combination and another in a 9–1 defeat of Notts County in the Midland Intermediate League.

It was in October 1962 that Knowles signed professional forms, and by the end of the season he was established in the reserve team. In those days he was in digs in Wolverhampton in Newhampton Road, within walking distance of Molineux. At some stage he also shared digs with winger Terry Wharton in Waterloo Road, even closer to Molineux. Wharton, a Lancastrian, and Knowles, a Yorkshireman, got on well. 'He was always cheerful,' Wharton remembered. 'He was always up to some tricks. He could act a bit daft now and then, but there was no real harm in him. He was never a boozer either. He liked to enjoy himself but that was all. He was just a very pleasant lad.' Knowles would later move to the Warstones Estate, a sprawling network of mostly council houses and flats, in the Penn district of the town.

Towards the end of the 1962–63 season Knowles again sparkled in Wolves' youth team. Manager Cullis and his staff must have seen something in him in addition to his obvious talent and entrusted him with the captaincy of the team who reached the semi-final of the FA Youth Cup that season. A campaign made longer by the severe winter weather saw Knowles catching the eye as it finally drew to a close. In late April a 1–0 win over Chelsea in the FA Youth Cup fourth round had Knowles described in the *Express & Star* as being 'much in evidence'. A week later he was in the reserve side who hammered Albion 8–3 in a Central League game at Molineux. Centre-forward Ted Farmer hit four goals, and Knowles was also on target. Still the games came thick and fast for the youngster. In the home FA Youth Cup quarter-final with Arsenal he was played at half-back because of injury problems and, according to the match report, 'brought the house down with a waist-high, right-foot volley which rocketed into the net.' His opposite number in the Gunners line up, Peter Simpson, equalised with a 30-yard effort. Two days later Knowles was stepping out in the first leg of the Midland Intermediate League Cup Final against Walsall at Fellows Park. He scored twice, one direct from a free-kick, as Wolves won 4–0. The scoreline was the same a week later when Knowles helped his side beat Arsenal in the FA Youth Cup quarter-final replay at Highbury. That Arsenal team included future members of their 1971 Double-winning team – Peter Storey, John Radford and Simpson.

This was clearly a young man of great promise. Stan Cullis and his coaches must have felt Knowles's progress would benefit from being with the senior players in the party to tour the US and Canada. With Ron Flowers, Alan Hinton and Bobby Thomson on England close-season tours, Knowles, Ken Knighton and John Galley were named for the trip. Knowles then sported a swept-back hairstyle – the advent of the Beatles, which would spawn new fashions and new haircuts, was still some months away – and the Knowles quiff and broad smile were much in evidence when he posed for a picture with the club's tour party as they prepared to board a coach to start them on the trip to North America.

Before he set off on what was a big adventure for him, however, Knowles provided evidence in the FA Youth Cup semi-final of the type of play that would come to infuriate Wolves fans during his early years. Wolves were held 2–2 by West Ham at Molineux, paying the price for trying to waste time when they led 2–1, rather than add to their lead. Knowles was the ringleader, it would seem, and earned a reprimand from Football League referee Ken Stokes, who was in charge of the game. Yet, after Clive Ford had volleyed Wolves into a 12th-minute lead, it was Knowles, still captain of the side, whose perfectly-timed through pass enabled left-winger John Holder to fire home the second on 23 minutes. The Hammers reduced the lead six minutes later through Trevor Dawkins. The London youngsters eventually snatched a draw late in the game through Martin Britt, as Wolves paid for their time-wasting tactics. Because he had teamed up with the senior tour party, Knowles could not play in the Upton Park replay when Wolves went out 4–2.

In Wolves' opening tour game Knowles featured as they beat Montreal Cantalia 5–1. He was one of several substitutes used as the tourists cantered to victory thanks to goals from

Chris Crowe (two), Ted Farmer, Terry Wharton and Gerry Harris. Back in Wolverhampton the following day, Wolves announced they were granting a free transfer to former skipper Bill Slater. The man who had won three First Division Championship medals with Wolves and captained them to victory in the 1960 FA Cup Final had always been a part-time professional. During his years with Wolves he had been employed by Birmingham University but had just been appointed deputy director of the National Recreation Centre at Crystal Palace. Slater wished to carry on playing and, in view of his stalwart service, Wolves were happy to enable him to do so. As it turned out, he made only five more Football League appearances – for Third Division Brentford, where he had played in his amateur days, and managed a couple of goals for them.

The second game of the summer tour saw Wolves beat West German side Schalke, the club they had met in their first-ever European Cup tie. Wolves beat them 4–2 in New York. Jimmy Murray (two), Terry Wharton and Peter Broadbent hit the goals. Knowles did not figure in that match but was at inside-left when they beat Ukrainian Nationals 3–2 in Philadelphia. Ted Farmer struck twice after an own-goal had given Wolves a fifth-minute lead. Knowles had to be content merely to watch as the tourists announced their arrival in New York with a 5–0 win over an American Soccer League XI at Randall Island, then beat a Catholic Youth Council XI 6–0 in St Louis and a Mexico City XI 3–0 in San Francisco. Knowles was among the substitutes when Wolves' winning run finally came to an end in Vancouver as they were held 2–2 by Brazilian side Bangu. With goals from Chris Crowe and Jimmy Murray, Wolves led 2–1 but had to play the second half with 10 men after centre-half David Woodfield was sent off for a bad tackle. After beating Victoria All Stars 2–1 and Vancouver All Stars 4–1, Wolves wound up the tour on Sunday 23 June by making no errors this time against Bangu, winning 4–1 in Toronto, with Farmer, Barry Stobart (two) and Gerry Harris the scorers.

Evidence that Knowles was still little known came in the programme for the Victoria All-Stars match – he was listed as 'Fred' Knowles. There was also a Freudian slip in the programme for the match against the Catholic Youth Council side, Chris Crowe being listed as 'Christ' Crowe. The party returned home to prepare for the new season, with Knowles still regarded as a reserve. Yet he had made much progress and was ready to push for first-team recognition.

Another outcome of the trip was the beginning of a friendship with young Canadian footballer Les Wilson which would continue when Wilson finally joined Wolves a year later. Wilson recalled, 'When I was scouted by Stan Cullis and Joe Gardiner in Vancouver in 1963,

I was invited to the Wolves training session in Vancouver when they were on tour. That is where I first met Peter, along with Terry Wharton, Freddie Goodwin, John Galley and Ken Knighton. My aunt, uncle, and my mom and dad had them all over for dinner. At the Wolves training session in Vancouver, I think that I impressed Stan Cullis with my enthusiasm and running ability when he saw me play and train. Peter came over to my mom and dad's home in 1963. We then went to English Bay Beach in Vancouver on two occasions with the girl who lived next door to me. Mr Cullis wanted me to go back with the Wolves team in the 1963–64 season, but my parents would have nothing to do with this idea until I had finished schooling and education in Vancouver on the university graduation programme.'

Wilson also remembered that Bangu match which saw Woodfield get his marching orders. 'Stan Cullis was incensed at the sending off, so after the final whistle he chased the referee all over the field at Empire Stadium. After returning to the dressing room after chasing the ref Stan locked the dressing-room door and refused to give the media a post-game press conference, which did not go down too well with the local association and the press. This game was a friendly, but Stan Cullis still had that passion and determination to win. Along with his high standards, this was the attitude that I liked and admired.'

Wolves began the 1963–64 season still expected to be a force in English football. They had finished the previous season in fifth place in the First Division, having begun the campaign in fine style with an 8–1 defeat of Manchester City and having topped the table for a while. They had not won a major trophy since 1960, and the days when they and Manchester United were the two best teams in the country were long gone. Yet the gold shirts still had a touch of magic about them.

It certainly looked that way when they opened the new season at Highbury. Arsenal, managed by Wolves legend Billy Wright, had Ian Ure, the former Dundee and Scotland centre-half, making his debut but were beaten comprehensively 3–1. The most pleasing aspect of the Wolves side that day must have been the number of home-grown players in the line up – only Chris Crowe had cost a transfer fee. Knowles probably thought himself well down the pecking order when it came to getting his chance in the first team. Crowe and the experienced Jimmy Murray were the inside-forwards for the Arsenal game, while in reserve were Barry Stobart and former England international Peter Broadbent.

Wolves were quickly brought down to earth four days after their Highbury triumph as North London's other giants, Tottenham, came to Molineux and outclassed the home side in a 4–1 win. After beating Stoke at home the following Saturday, Wolves did a little better in the return game with Spurs, losing 4–3 in a thriller, but a worrying slump was under way.

They were beaten 3–0 by Nottingham Forest at the City Ground, then lost 3–1 at home to Liverpool and followed this with an even more embarrassing home defeat, 5–1 at the hands of Blackburn Rovers. It was clear that Stan Cullis, so well served by home-grown players in the past, needed to dig into the Molineux coffers to bring in some new players. He had done so early in 1962 when he paid big fees for Crowe and Peter McParland and their arrival helped keep Wolves in the First Division. This time he spent a club record £55,000 on Ipswich's former England centre-forward Ray Crawford. Cullis got his man on 16 September in time for the trip to play their return fixture with Liverpool, and what a debut it proved – the Reds romped to a 6–0 win.

As one Wolves career began, another one ended. Malcolm Finlayson, a fine goalkeeper who had won two Championship medals and an FA Cup-winners' medal in successive seasons, deputised for the injured Fred Davies. With Liverpool, who would end the season as champions, four goals up, Finlayson damaged his left hand so Jimmy Murray was in goal as Gordon Milne and Roger Hunt added further goals to those scored earlier by Alf Arrowsmith, Peter Thompson, Ian Callaghan and Hunt. In those days, of course, there were no substitutes.

Murray had been in the number-eight shirt for that game, but he gave way to Barry Stobart for the next three games as Wolves arrested their slide by winning 2–1 at Blackpool – Crawford scored two that day – then 4–1 at home to Chelsea followed by a goalless home draw with Albion and a 1–1 draw at West Ham, where Stobart made way for the recall of Broadbent. Clearly, Cullis, who at the time he was signing Crawford was also chasing Nottingham Forest half-back Calvin Palmer, was not happy with his forward line. Cue Knowles…just two weeks past his 18th birthday, he was given the number-eight shirt for the game against Leicester at Filbert Street on Monday 14 October 1963. City had been FA Cup finalists the previous season when they had been in contention for the League and Cup double and were a good side. In their defence they had England goalkeeper Gordon Banks and Scot Frank McLintock, the man destined to lead Arsenal to the double in 1971; however, it was veteran Colin Appleton who would mark Knowles. He was an experienced, tough defender, but that mattered little to Knowles who grabbed his big chance as Wolves won 1–0. The game had been postponed from the previous Saturday because City had two men on international duty – Banks for England and inside-left Dave Gibson for Scotland.

Knowles was far from overawed. That was a view confirmed by Phil Morgan in his match report in the *Express & Star*: 'Those who thought manager Stan Cullis took a risk in using this hard game to blood the youngster in the First Division need not have worried. He acquitted himself splendidly. His first three kicks at the ball produced finely judged through passes to Crawford, and his coolness in such a lively baptism was greatly to his credit. The occasional mistake was understandable, but he is entitled to be encouraged and, in any event, he showed lots of real ability and the temperament for the big occasion.'

That was a glowing endorsement from Morgan, who had covered Wolves during their greatest years and who did not lightly heap praise on players. Many years later when I joined the *Express & Star* sports desk I was fortunate enough to work alongside Morgan. A lovely man, who retained his Hampshire accent despite many years working in the Midlands, Morgan was a church-going Christian. Little could Phil have realised that a few years hence he, among many others, would try to persuade Knowles that it was possible to be a footballer and a Christian.

However, back to that rainy night in Leicester, a night which saw the only goal scored after nine minutes. Chris Crowe, playing on the right wing, fired in a cross shot which Banks could only push into the path of Crawford, who scored. From then it was Leicester who controlled the game, only to find Fred Davies in the Wolves goal in top form. A header from Ken Keyworth landed on the bar, but that was the closest City got. Wolves continued their battling rearguard action with Ron Flowers, who had lost his place in the England side the previous season after a run of 40 games, marshalling his troops well, aided by fellow veteran George Showell and the youngsters Bobby Thomson, Fred Goodwin and David Woodfield. So it was a winning start for Knowles.

The fact Knowles's selection came at the expense of Broadbent meant much to him. A superb passer of the ball, a goalscorer and a goalmaker with an outrageous bodyswerve, Broadbent was the man on whom Knowles modelled his style of play. Knowles readily admits he wanted to emulate Broadbent. When I wrote a biography of Broadbent, sadly by then suffering with Alzheimer's Disease, Knowles provided me with his views on the much-loved Molineux hero. Wrote Knowles, 'His skill and talent were something I could only scratch the surface of. I was 16 years of age when I first met Peter. I used to clean his boots and often, when I cleaned the first-team dressing room out, I would listen to Peter and the other first-team players talk about playing for England and the great floodlit matches at Wolves. As I got to know him I watched his kind of play very closely – his body swerve, his long passes, his touches on the ball. To me, he was like a ballet dancer on grass. He used to glide over the pitch. Yes, Peter was the man I modelled myself on.'

Recalling his debut, Knowles added, 'When I was told by Stan Cullis I was in the first team to play at Leicester I asked him whose place I was taking. When he said Peter's, what a shock! The man I was modelling myself on, played for England, a gifted footballer, and I was taking his place. It was so embarrassing for me, and I found it difficult to look at Peter but, just like the person he was, he was very kind to me and wished me all the best.'

I was fortunate enough to see Knowles's debut – very fortunate indeed. Making the journey with me were three pals, John Dove, Tony Moran and John Bates. We had all left school, Tettenhall College, a few weeks earlier. We were late setting off for Leicester and it was in the days before the vast motorway network so our progress was not rapid as Bates, in his mother's Ford Anglia, piloted us towards Filbert Street. Nothing should have sidetracked our driver as we strived to make up for lost time, but when a rabbit crossed our path Bates instinctively swerved to avoid it. Though the car left the road it miraculously did not turn over. We were – amazingly – shaken but not deterred and just made it in time for the kick-off. In view of Bates's reluctance to mow down one of God's creatures it should have come as no surprise to me that he later became a Methodist minister. The Reverend Bates, who now lives in Stoke, remembers more about the encounter with the rabbit than any great detail about the game, apart from a general recollection that Knowles did well.

John Bates became a firm admirer of Knowles in the ensuing years, though he remembers an early tendency for showmanship. 'I would say to my father that Peter could be a clot, but my father was a huge fan of his and would always defend him. He would say that if you took away that side of Peter then you would take away his creativity. Anything silly he did my father used to excuse on those grounds. He may well have had a point.' Bates Snr, Norman, ran a well-loved shoe shop in Dudley Street Wolverhampton and came from a family of staunch Wolves fans. He knew his football and ranked Knowles with the best the club had seen. John Bates shares his father's view, 'Peter had the vision for the game, the flair which sometimes was ahead of the people he was playing with. The bodyswerve was akin to Peter Broadbent at his height, the way he would stand sideways on with the ball at his feet and then with a twist of the shoulders be gone, leaving his opponent standing. I'm sure he would have become a regular in the England team.'

Malcolm Finlayson confirms the similarity between Knowles and Broadbent. The superb Scottish goalkeeper had been asked by manager Stan Cullis to prolong his career as cover for Fred Davies and so saw the raw Knowles when he first broke into the reserve team. 'He was a very brash, confident player, and he had the same ability as Peter Broadbent,' Finlayson confirmed. 'Unlike Broadbent, he could be quite an aggressive player, but he had the same attributes – all the ability under the sun. He would have become the complete player.'

Five days after the Leicester game, Knowles made his home bow and marked it with a goal against Bolton Wanderers after just 14 minutes. Broadbent had earned a quick recall – at inside-left – and so Knowles was able to play in the same team as his idol. Destined to be relegated at the end of the season, the Lancastrian Wanderers proved quite a handful on this occasion and were close to winning a match which eventually ended 2–2. Knowles started the move from which he scored, first finding Alan Hinton on the left with a pinpoint pass. Hinton's cross dropped awkwardly for Chris Crowe, but he managed to push the ball back to Knowles. He hit it first time, and it rocketed into the net. It was the sort of strike to make the fans sit up. Those who had not seen Knowles before suddenly realised that here was a player of natural talent and one who could score spectacular goals.

The home side missed many chances after that and almost paid for it as Francis Lee went close late on. Right-winger Dennis Butler had wiped out Knowles's goal when he struck with a speculative shot after 25 minutes only for Broadbent to head Wolves ahead again five minutes from half-time. Ten minutes into the second half, former Burnley and England winger Brian Pilkington put Bolton on terms once more. As for Knowles, he again impressed Phil Morgan; though the *Express & Star* man tempered his praise, saying the youngster still clearly had a lot to learn about maintaining contact with the game. Morgan added, however, 'Here he is not alone.'

Broadbent had returned to the exclusion of Jimmy Murray, who, it turned out, had played his last game for Wolves. Only just 28, and Wolves' leading League scorer during their Championship successes of 1957–58 and 1958–59 as well as in 1959–60, Murray was sold to Manchester City in November for £27,000, having hit 166 goals in 299 first-team games. Murray would make an immediate impact, hitting 13 goals in his first nine League games for City. He ended the season with 21 from 19 League matches in a forward line which also included ex-Albion and England striker Derek Kevan and a young left-winger who would become a Molineux idol – David Wagstaffe. Murray's departure meant one rival fewer to Knowles for the inside-forward spots.

Next stop for Knowles, who had clearly done enough in those first two outings to warrant an extended run in the side, was a trip to St Andrew's which had proved a happy hunting ground for Wolves. Birmingham City had not beaten them there in nine League games but must have thought they were going to end the hoodoo when they led 2–0 after only 16 minutes. David Woodfield, who had missed the Bolton game through injury, could only turn a cross from right-winger Mike Hellawell into his own net after five minutes. Then he deflected the ball into the path of Scottish centre-forward Alex Harley, who volleyed it past Fred Davies. Woodfield more than atoned for his early errors as Wolves, fired by skipper Ron Flowers, battled their way back. Terry Wharton was recalled to partner Knowles on the right wing and started the revival on 32 minutes. Crawford set the chance up after beating the Blues' former England centre-half Trevor Smith on the right. Wharton's shot went in despite the last-ditch efforts of full-back Stan Lynn to clear the ball off the line. On the left wing, Alan Hinton was given a tough afternoon by the redoubtable former Villa man Lynn, but Hinton had the last word 15 minutes from the end when he drove in the equaliser from 25 yards. Knowles was desperately close to scoring his second League goal soon after Wharton's effort when a Broadbent pass sent him clear. His shot beat Colin Withers in the Blues goal but scraped the upright.

The biggest test of Knowles's burgeoning top-flight career came a week later, on Saturday 2 November, when Manchester United visited Molineux. Matt Busby's side would eventually finish runners-up but were having something of a blip, having managed only one point from their previous three games. Knowles could hardly have come up against a tougher opponent – left-half Maurice Setters. The crew-cutted former Albion man, who would later be Jack Charlton's number two with the Republic of Ireland side, took no prisoners; however, Knowles still managed another useful performance as Wolves sprung a surprise by winning 2–0. Knowles even had a hand in the move which saw Wolves go ahead on 48 minutes. George Showell brought the ball out of defence and Knowles and Alan Hinton created the chance for Terry Wharton to score. Ten minutes later a poor backpass by United inside-right Phil Chisnall saw Ray Crawford nip in to collect the second. Phil Morgan, in his *Sporting Star* report, noted that Knowles had acquitted himself well in distinguished company and 'once had the temerity to get the better of [Denis] Law in a spot of ball-juggling.'

Games with United were what Knowles relished, and he faced them more times than any other side during his brief career. This, though, was the only occasion he tasted victory in nine meetings with the Manchester giants.

After eight games without defeat, Wolves' revival came to a halt at Turf Moor, though it was only four minutes from time when Burnley's England winger John Connelly scored the only goal of the game with a cross-shot which went in off the far post. Knowles had his moments and had almost broken the deadlock, only to see his powerful shot well saved by the Lancashire side's Scottish goalkeeper Adam Blacklaw. Knowles, according to Phil Morgan, ought to have learned at least one footballing lesson – the quickness with which things happen in the First Division compared with the bit of grace that is possible in the Central League.

A week after the Burnley game, it was Knowles's turn to win a match late on. He did so with a spectacular goal against Ipswich Town at Molineux. The East Anglians, champions just over a year earlier, were at the time entrenched at the bottom of the table with only one win from 17 matches. But Wolves made hard work of it. They missed first-half chances and were handicapped when left-winger Hinton was injured and returned with his left leg strapped to limp on the right wing. Terry Wharton switched to the left, and it was he who set up the opening goal on 60 minutes for Ray Crawford against his old club. Wharton beat two opponents before centring and Crawford back-heeled the ball past the visiting goalkeeper Roy Bailey. Crawford's old Portman Road goal partner Ted Phillips equalised 10 minutes later. Fred Davies could only push out a shot from Doug Moran, and Phillips was on the spot to drive the ball into an open goal. Phillips went very close to a second when he and Danny Hegan, who would join Wolves in 1971, got away on the left. The move ended when a Phillips shot hit the bar and the ball bounced down almost over the line. Ipswich shouts for a goal were ignored, and Wolves immediately went to the other end for Knowles to win the match. He resisted a tackle from veteran John Elsworthy before moving forward to beat Bailey with a perfectly struck, right-wing cross-shot.

Four days later came a special moment for Wolves' young full-back Bobby Thomson, Knowles's former youth-team colleague. Still just short of his 20th birthday, Thomson won his first full England cap. He was drafted in for the injured Ray Wilson of Huddersfield for the game against Northern Ireland at Wembley. It was a fairly comfortable baptism for the Wolves man, even though his side conceded three goals. At the other end the rampant England forwards, in a new-look Alf Ramsey side, scored eight. Southampton winger Terry Paine hit three while Jimmy Greaves went one better.

Knowles found himself at inside-left in an injury-hit Wolves side on Saturday 23 November 1963 for a visit to Sheffield Wednesday which brought a 5–0 drubbing. George Showell and Peter Broadbent were down with colds while Chris Crowe and Alan Hinton were injured. In defence Gerry Harris returned at left-back, with Bobby Thomson switching to the other flank. Barry Stobart got a recall on the right-wing, while Ted Farmer played at inside-right. Farmer had had a marvellous start to his First Division career; however, the man who could easily have become the Steve Bull of his day was dogged by injury. Knowles and a fully-fit Farmer would have been a dream ticket in the eyes of Wolves followers but the game at Hillsborough was the only occasion he and Knowles would appear in the same Wolves first team. Sadly, Farmer would make only one more appearance in the First Division before he had to hang up his boots. Wolves' re-shaped team held Wednesday until 42 minutes, but then Alan Finney scored a lucky opener. He beat Harris and sent in a cross-shot to which Fred Davies got his hands only to see the ball spin out and cross the line just inside the near post. The floodgates opened just after the hour when Wednesday scored three times in 14 minutes. It was scant consolation for Knowles that he was rated Wolves' best forward. He was unlucky in the first half when his shot struck the feet of Ray Crawford. He also set himself up well when his side were four down, only to fire wide.

Knowles was in the company of four other members of the 1962 FA Youth Cup Final line up when Wolves entertained champions Everton a week later. As well as Fred Goodwin, David Woodfield and Bobby Thomson, there was a place for 20-year-old goalkeeper Jim Barron. With Fred Davies injured in training, the Durham lad was given his First Division debut. At the other end of the pitch was an even younger goalkeeper, 19-year-old Andy Rankin, who had made his debut a week earlier, keeping out costly Gordon West in the Everton goal. Both youngsters could reflect on a satisfactory afternoon as the match ended goalless.

For the second successive away game, Wolves were brought down to earth, as they lost 4–1 to Fulham at Craven Cottage. Knowles had little chance to shine, and the limelight was taken by another inside man – former England skipper Johnny Haynes. The Fulham inside-left opened the scoring when he beat Fred Davies with a 25-yard drive after five minutes and generally ran the proceedings. Another long-range effort, from Maurice Cook, made it two on 34 minutes. Ray Crawford reduced the arrears five minutes from the break when he tapped home a Terry Wharton centre; however, late goals from John Key and Graham Leggat, the Scottish international winger playing at centre-forward, sealed Wolves' fate.

Billy Wright's Arsenal were next up for Wolves, but the match at Molineux, on Saturday 14 December 1963, proved to be Knowles's last for a while. He found it hard going against a team riding high at third in the table. Their twin strikers Joe Baker and Geoff Strong had scored 39 goals between them already that season. And it was Strong who came to the rescue after Wolves had taken a two-goal lead. Ron Flowers had a shot deflected for a rare goal on 14 minutes, after being put through by Knowles, and Chris Crowe hit a spectacular second 12 minutes later. Terry Wharton cut inside to give Crowe a reverse pass which the inside man hit home on the run. Strong reduced the arrears on 31 minutes, bringing the ball down with his right foot and hitting it home with his left. Arsenal had Baker carried off with a bruised ankle 22 minutes from time. That did not deter Strong, however, and George Eastham set him up for an equaliser 11 minutes from time. Strong might then have won the match. A mix-up among Wolves' forwards led to an Arsenal breakaway but David Woodfield caught Strong up and stopped him at the expense of a free-kick, just short of the penalty area. Under today's laws, Woodfield would have been sent off. Liverpool-born and Scottish bred, Baker had been the first player with a Scottish club chosen for England when he was capped in 1959. He was with Hibernian at the time.

Despite making Flowers's goal, Knowles had struggled, and, though his initial run in the side had proved highly promising, Cullis obviously felt he needed a rest. Knowles was dropped for the trip to Stoke the following Saturday as Wolves recalled Peter Broadbent to the attack and won 2–0, both goals coming from Ray Crawford. Wolves' Christmas games saw them held 3–3 by Villa at Molineux on Boxing Day after being 3–0 up and draw 2–2 at Villa Park two days later after leading 1–0 and 2–1. The Molineux goal rush played its part in an historic day in English football. No fewer than 66 goals were scored in the First Division on 26 December 1963, the highest total in the top flight on a single day. Fulham led the way with a 10–1 home win over Ipswich, while Blackburn won 8–2 at West Ham. It was not a full programme, either. Only 20 of the 22 clubs were in action.

Before Knowles was given another chance, a newcomer arrived at Molineux. Stan Cullis decided to let left-winger Alan Hinton go to Nottingham Forest in exchange for Channel Islander Dick Le Flem. Many felt Hinton had been given a hard time by the home fans. They gave him a fair bit of stick in the game against Forest at Molineux early in 1964, when the visitors came from two down to win 3–2. Hinton was given a rough ride by Forest's rugged right-back Joe Wilson, who came to Wolves a year later and for one memorable season became a cult figure at Molineux. As for Hinton, he was a hit at Forest, adding to the England cap he had won with Wolves in 1962 and then moving to Derby County and proving a key figure in their Championship triumph under Brian Clough in 1971–72.

Le Flem made little impact at Molineux, but he was a scorer when Knowles was recalled to the side for the trip to Chelsea in early February. It was hardly a happy return for Knowles, even though his side won 3–2 to end a run of five games without a win. Chris Crowe orchestrated the visitors' attack, and Knowles hardly figured. In a rare note of criticism, Phil Morgan wrote in the *Express & Star*: 'Unfortunately, the swift action left young Peter Knowles right out of his depth – the play just surged around him – and it was left to Crowe to do it single-handed.'

Ray Crawford set Wolves on their way, heading home Le Flem centres in the fourth and 30th minutes before Le Flem fired home a right-footed shot on 32 minutes. High-riding Chelsea rallied in the second half with late goals by Bobby Tambling and Bert Murray, but

Barry Bridges, their centre-forward, was right out of touch, missing a succession of chances. Another feature of the game was the use of Peter Broadbent at right-half and he took to it as if to the manner born.

Despite his low-key display at Stamford Bridge, Knowles kept his place for the game against West Ham at Molineux on Monday 17 February. It was a dismal night for Wolves who lost 2–0 to a Hammers side fresh from a 3–1 win at Swindon in the fifth round of the FA Cup. The Londoners were on their way to winning the Cup and looked far ahead of Wolves. The attendance was well below 15,000, but there were still enough Wolves fans there to give the home side a lot of stick as error followed error. There were shouts of derision, boos and whistles for Wolves, with the chief target Crowe, who had a bad night in stark contrast to his display at Chelsea. Geoff Hurst (23 minutes) and Johnny Byrne (66) hit the goals. Before the Hammers took the lead, Knowles's through pass to Terry Wharton brought a short centre from the winger which left Crowe with an open goal. Alas, Crowe fired the ball high up the terraces, and that miss set the pattern for the rest of the match. Knowles did get in a couple of useful shots in the second half, but the visitors, with England's Bobby Moore well in control, were worth their victory.

England Glory

The West Ham game was one to forget, and Knowles was able to do just that. It was his last League action for a few weeks – the call of his country took precedence. He was earmarked for the England squad to play in the international Youth tournament in Amsterdam. England had won the competition, dubbed by some 'The Little World Cup', in 1963 and the Football Association were determined to do well again. Over 300 players were nominated as possibles for the squad. These were whittled down to 100, and from them a party of 30 played in practice matches against Football League sides. After all that, 16 were chosen to go to Spain and Tenerife for a warm-up before the tournament itself. Knowles was one of the lucky ones. The warm-up trip, which saw Knowles make his Youth international debut in a 2–1 win against Spain in Murcia, was at the end of February, and a month later England began their quest for glory. The event was organised with eight groups of three teams, and England found the opening clash with Poland a tough one. They trailed to an early goal but conjured up an equaliser through Alf Wood, the Manchester City centre-half who never quite made the grade at Maine Road but gave stalwart service to Shrewsbury as both a defender and striker before ending his career at Walsall.

England needed to beat the Irish Republic in their final group game by at least two goals in order to qualify for the quarter-finals. They made no mistake, as goals from John Sissons (three), David Sadler (two) and Don Rogers saw them triumph 6–0. Sadler, of Manchester United, who began life as a centre-forward but later switched to centre-half with great success, scored both goals in the 2–1 quarter-final win over Austria in Rotterdam. Knowles had not exactly sparkled, but he kept his place for the semi-final against Portugal in The Hague, where goals from Sadler (two), Rogers and a certain West Ham youngster called Harry Redknapp enabled England to cruise home 4–0. The Final against Spain in Amsterdam on Sunday 5 April 1964 saw England triumph 4–0, and Knowles found his true form after firing in the first goal from long range. Rogers (two) and Sissons were also on target, and the trophy was duly collected by Howard Kendall, the skipper. Kendall was then with Preston, and he and Sissons also figured in the FA Cup Final at Wembley a month later. Former Leyton Orient goalkeeper Pat Welton was the youth-team manager, and his right-hand man was Wilf McGuinness, the former Manchester United and England wing-half, whose career had been cut short by injury.

Knowles's goal was one of the big moments of his career. In his 1994 Radio Five interview with Rogan Taylor, he recalled it fondly. 'All the way through the tournament I hadn't scored, and they were thinking of dropping me, but they stuck with us. I always remember in the Final, we'd only played 10 minutes, and I was about 35 yards out. I can remember this ball dropping at my feet, and I just hit it and it just flew. I can remember it flying right into the top corner. Then, about five minutes later, I did it again but I hit the post this time and somebody followed up and scored. That made it 2–0 and that was a real experience.'

The Final line up was: Peter Springett (Queen's Park Rangers); Mike Wright (Aston Villa), Bobby Noble (Manchester United), Howard Kendall (Preston), Barrie Wright (Leeds), John Hollins (Chelsea), Harry Redknapp (West Ham), Knowles, David Sadler (Manchester United), John Sissons (West Ham), Don Rogers (Swindon). Everyone of that team went on to have a successful career, apart from Barrie Wright, who moved to the US. Only two of them won full England caps, however; Hollins just one and Sadler four, though as a central-defender. Redknapp, who at the time had still to make his League bow for the Hammers, is now better known for his managerial success with West Ham, Portsmouth and Tottenham but he played around 150 games for the London side before moving to Bournemouth. Kendall also did great things as a manager, bringing the League title and FA Cup to Everton whom, as a player, he had helped win the title in 1970.

Named as Player of the Tournament was Don Rogers, whose lasting claim to fame in a long career with Swindon and Crystal Palace was scoring two of the goals which gave Swindon a shock 3–1 win over Arsenal in the 1969 League Cup Final. Peter Springett was the brother of England 'keeper Ron, and the pair figured in a unique transfer deal in May 1967, which saw Ron leave Sheffield Wednesday for Queen's Park Rangers while Peter moved in the other direction. Mike Wright played nearly 300 games for Villa, while his full-back partner Noble looked an England international in the making after figuring in the Manchester United side who won the First Division title in 1966–67. Alas, injury brought a premature end to his career, and he missed out on United's 1968 European Cup triumph over Benfica at Wembley. Hollins had a long career at Chelsea and also played for Arsenal, while Sissons played over 200 games for West Ham before moving to Sheffield Wednesday.

Redknapp has fond memories of that squad and said, 'Looking back it was no surprise that we did so well because the team was packed with talent. When we played Spain in the Final we absolutely murdered them. We were different class.'

Later to become United's manager in succession to Sir Matt Busby, Wilf McGuinness confirms the high quality of youngsters, recalling it was a privilege to work with them. 'I pushed them hard physically, but I got a positive reaction from them, and it was tremendous to see them all progress so successfully in their subsequent careers. People tend to forget how good England were in the 1960s. We kept producing good players. We won that Youth tournament two years running and then the World Cup in 1966 and should have won it again in 1970.'

McGuinness explained why the youth-team management stood by Knowles during his sluggish start to the tournament: 'The talent was there, you could see it. You knew he would come good – a bit like Berbatov at Manchester United. Peter was not only a class player, he was a good lad. He was a mixer, there was nothing strange about him. He had his fun, and he trained hard. He was just a lovely young man and a talented player. The quality was there, you could see he was going to go places.'

While Knowles was busy helping England's youngsters to glory, Wolves were busy on the transfer front. First, Stan Cullis turned to Swindon to sign wing-half Bobby Woodruff. A useful player as well as having the ability to execute an impressively long throw-in, Woodruff arrived in time to help Wolves to their biggest win of the season, 5–1 at home to Birmingham.

Cullis wielded his cheque book again to sign Liverpool's England inside-forward Jimmy Melia, so there was another obstacle in the way of a return to first-team action for Knowles. However, the seven games after that win over Birmingham saw Wolves fail to register a victory, though five of the matches were drawn. The trouble was that Melia and Peter Broadbent were similar types – scheming inside-forwards, playmakers, not ideal foils for an old-fashioned centre-forward like Ray Crawford. Phil Morgan said as much in his verdict on Wolves' 1–0 defeat at Ipswich. 'Once again the need of a man to go alongside Crawford was made clear,' wrote Morgan. So it was no surprise when Knowles was asked to fill that role.

For the final two fixtures of the season Cullis decided to reshape his forward line. Out went left-wing pair Broadbent and Terry Wharton, Melia moved to inside-left to partner the recalled Dick Le Flem while Knowles, fresh from his heroics in Amsterdam, teamed up with Chris Crowe on the right. It was Melia who dominated the game against Fulham at Molineux on Saturday 18 April 1964, and Knowles was among those who benefited from his promptings. Melia started the scoring on 32 minutes when he chipped home a free-kick after Bobby Woodruff had dummied to take it. After Le Flem had made it 2–0 on 40 minutes, Melia beat Fulham's England Under-23 goalkeeper Tony Macedo with a 20-yard drive before his lobbed pass enabled Knowles to get in on the scoring act with a neat header.

Not surprisingly, it was an unchanged Wolves team who visited Bolton on Friday 24 August and Knowles was again on the scoresheet as they romped to another 4–0 win. Melia again sparkled, but Ray Crawford was the goal hero with three. Bolton were locked in a relegation battle with Birmingham, and a win would have ensured their survival at Blues' expense; however, Blues managed a victory the following day, so it was the Lancashire side who went down. Ron Flowers was the defensive kingpin for Wolves, but it was he who made the opening goal on 25 minutes. He won the ball on the halfway line and, after making ground, hit a cross-shot of such power that former England goalkeeper Eddie Hopkinson could not hold the ball. Crawford was on the spot to turn the ball home. Eight minutes after half-time Crawford struck again. Le Flem crossed to the right, where Chris Crowe found Melia, who set up the chance on a plate for Crawford. Then came Knowles's moment to savour. Bobby Woodruff found Le Flem on the left, and Knowles rushed in at the far post to fire his centre powerfully home. Bobby Thomson's pace set up the final goal as he left the hefty Roy Hartle standing and raced down the left wing before centring for Crawford to collect his third. Hartle was in a long tradition of no-nonsense Bolton defenders, and the *Express & Star's* Phil Morgan noted that two tackles by the full-back made him (Morgan) wince. 'And I was safe in the press box,' added the reporter, who described Knowles as 'another eager performer' for the visitors.

The following day Birmingham beat Sheffield United 3–0 to clinch their survival at Bolton's expense. It was a remarkable recovery by Blues, who had beaten champions Liverpool earlier in the week. Blues could breathe easily, but not manager Gil Merrick, and the former England goalkeeper left the club soon afterwards.

An indication of how Knowles grew in confidence is recalled by Ray Crawford. In his 2008 biography, *Curse of the Jungle Boy*, the centre-forward remembers Cullis at one stage taking Knowles to task for not scoring more goals. The Knowles reply? 'Thanks, Stan, but I'm quite happy just making them for Ray.' Crawford says the remark was made in a laid-back manner which was a hallmark of the Knowles character. Crawford had scored 26 goals in 34 games for Wolves and felt he owed a large proportion of them to the work of Knowles.

So ended Knowles's first season of top-flight football. He could look back on 14 First Division appearances with four goals. The England Youth star was definitely on his way, and fans were already beginning to talk about the bright new prospect. There was not much chance for Knowles to reflect, however, as Wolves set off on a two-week trip to the Caribbean where their schedule included four exhibition matches against Chelsea. The first, in Bridgetown, Barbados, saw Wolves win 3–1, thanks to goals from Ray Crawford (two) and Dick Le Flem, against a strange-looking Londoners side. They were without goalkeeper Peter Bonetti and forward Bobby Tambling, who were on tour with England Under-23s, while Bert Murray had been injured the previous day in a 7–0 win over a Barbados XI. So Chelsea boss Tommy Docherty made a playing comeback, though his place in the second half was taken by trainer Dave Sexton. Le Flem had given Wolves a first-minute lead, which Chelsea centre-forward Barry Bridges cancelled out on 37 minutes. Before the sides met again, Wolves beat the Trinidad national side 4–0 in Port of Spain. Knowles was left out of the team but returned when they played Chelsea in Port of Spain and lost 3–2. He got on the scoresheet, too, making it 2–2 after 70 minutes after David Woodfield, Chris Crowe and Jimmy Melia had inter-passed. All the goals came in the second half. Scottish full-back Eddie McCreadie, playing at centre-forward, gave Chelsea the lead on 47 minutes. Six minutes later Le Flem equalised only for Barry Bridges to gallop away and beat Fred Davies with a cross-shot. After Knowles's leveller, Bridges raced clear again, only to be brought down in the penalty area by full-back Gerry Harris. Up stepped Terry Venables to win it for the Londoners from the penalty spot. Such was the friendly nature of the game that when Chelsea goalkeeper John Dunn sustained an eye injury Wolves let Jim Barron take over. Barron took his chance to keep out several goalbound Wolves shots. Barron was signed by Chelsea in April 1965, but in less than a year at Stamford Bridge he made only one first-team appearance. Subsequently, he played with distinction for Oxford United and Nottingham Forest.

It was Wolves' turn next – they beat Chelsea 4–2 in Jamaica's national stadium in Kingston. It was 1–1 at the break. Wolves' goals came from Crawford (two), Le Flem and an own-goal by Chelsea full-back Frank Upton. The same day brought a momentous occasion for Ron Flowers. With Bobby Moore left out, he captained England for the first time as they hammered the United States 10–0 at Randall's Island, New York. Bobby Thomson was given a game at left-back as partner to George Cohen. The match also saw the

England debut of Charlton half-back Mike Bailey. It would not be too long before Bailey became a Wolves player and set about making himself one of the most highly-rated men in Molineux history.

Knowles next figured in a remarkable 12-goal game as Wolves beat Jamaica 8–4 in Kingston. The tourists led 4–1 at the break only to be pegged back to 4–4 before hitting four goals in the last 15 minutes. In the final meeting with Chelsea in Kingston, Wolves were defeated 3–0. It might have been more had not goalkeeper Fred Davies pulled off a series of saves. He was beaten by Eddie McCreadie, John Hollins and Bobby Tambling. McDonald Sangster, Jamaica's acting prime minister, presented Chelsea skipper Terry Venables with a large silver trophy as the two meetings in Jamaica had seen them get the better of Wolves 5–4 on aggregate. Three days later, Knowles was in the side held 1–1 by Haiti in Port-au-Prince. Not so far away, on the same day, in Sao Paulo, Brazil, Wolves had two men in the team held 1–1 by Portugal in Brazil's four-team tournament. England had lost their opening game 5–1 to the host country, with Pelé at his best, so changes were made, with Bobby Thomson preferred to George Cohen and Flowers in for Liverpool's Gordon Milne.

Wolves had to admit second best to Chelsea again when they met once more, this time in Port-au-Prince, a day after the game against Haiti. Knowles was at inside-right as Chelsea triumphed 2–0 thanks to two goals from Venables. Wolves gave a game to young centre-half Graham Hawkins, then just 18. A day later, Bobby Thomson collected his fourth full cap when he played in the England team beaten 1–0 by Argentina at the Maracana Stadium in Rio de Janeiro. The Argentinians included Antonio Rattin, the man who would gain lasting infamy when he was sent off against England in the 1966 World Cup quarter-final.

New Management

Back home, Knowles was soon able to renew his acquaintance with Les Wilson, the lad he had met in Canada a year earlier. He came to Molineux on trial and would go on to establish himself as a more than useful utility player. Remembers Wilson, 'In the 1963–64 season, I was selected for the BC All Star Team [the youngest player ever selected] to play against the then English League champions Liverpool and also Yugoslavia champions Red Star Belgrade at the famous Empire Stadium in Vancouver. Mr Cullis, being true to his word, sent me a letter inviting me to attend the Wolves pre-season training in early July 1964.' Wilson and Knowles became good pals. As Wilson recalls, 'Peter and I were in digs with Mrs Southwick on the Newhampton Road for well over a year. Peter and I shared a great deal and had an excellent relationship during our time together at the Wolves.'

Knowles's hopes of staking a claim for a regular place were helped by the close-season departure from Molineux of two other experienced inside-forwards. Barry Stobart, a surprise choice in Wolves' 1960 FA Cup Final side, was sold to Manchester City for £20,000 while Chris Crowe joined Nottingham Forest for £30,000. Things were also looking up for Cyril Knowles, Peter's older brother. After making a big impact at Middlesbrough, he was signed by Tottenham for £45,000.

When the 1964–65 season rolled around, Wolves fans had probably accepted that they were no longer one of the First Division's big guns. Their old rivals Manchester United were still up there, but now the challenge was coming from Bill Shankly's Liverpool, Don Revie's Leeds United and Tommy Docherty's Chelsea; however, there was no reason why the Molineux regulars could not expect an improvement on the 1963–64 finish of 16th. How misplaced their optimism would prove!

The writing was on the wall from the opening day of the season when the lively Chelsea youngsters won 3–0 at Molineux. Knowles might have expected to be in the team that day after the previous season's finale of those two 4–0 victories. However, in the pre-season public practice game when traditionally the Colours, the first team, met the Whites, the reserves, Knowles was overshadowed by the old maestro Peter Broadbent, the man on whom he had modelled his style of play. The reserves triumphed 4–3 and Philip Osborn wrote in the *Daily Sketch*, 'Don't start writing Peter Broadbent off yet. This is the decisive message from Wolves' practice match. Manager Stan Cullis chose the men who appeared in the closing two games of last season as the first team, indicating that he is thinking of relegating Broadbent to the reserves. The former England forward replied by producing all his old skills to prove he is still good enough for the First Division.' Osborn also said that Knowles, despite scoring, did not look in the same class, spending too much time waiting, instead of working, for opportunities.

So Jimmy Melia and Peter Broadbent occupied the inside-forward berths for that opening League match, but Knowles was quickly recalled for a return to the scene of his Football League debut – Filbert Street. It was a scoring return, too, but he could not prevent Wolves going down 3–2 to Leicester. Knowles's goal gave Wolves the lead after 20 minutes and was a classy one. He ran on to receive a flighted pass from Broadbent, playing at outside-right, to hook the ball across England 'keeper Gordon Banks and into the net. Knowles also saw a header hit the bar, while left-winger Terry Wharton headed against a post and Bobby Woodruff had two shots graze a post. It was obviously not Wolves' night. Leicester levelled when Howard Riley tapped an indirect free-kick 12 yards out to Frank McLintock, who blasted the ball home. The second goal was a good one as Ken Keyworth headed in a left-wing centre on 42 minutes, but the third came from a Colin Appleton penalty six minutes after half-time when Freddie Goodwin, recalled at right-half, pulled down Mike Stringfellow. Within two minutes, Wharton struck to narrow the lead. The verdict of Phil Morgan in the *Express & Star* was that Wolves were a much improved side after the dismal display against Chelsea. He said Knowles 'did his share splendidly, and Jimmy Melia was able to use his powers of generalship to much greater effect.' Morgan described Knowles's goal as 'a gem.'

After this encouraging display, the same side made the trip to Elland Road to face the emerging football force that was Leeds United. It meant a first game for Knowles in direct opposition to one of football's hard-men, Norman Hunter. Then still not quite 21, Hunter had yet to earn the infamous tag of 'Bites-yer-legs' but was starting to gain a reputation as an uncompromising defender. Yet Knowles had the satisfaction of again giving Wolves an early lead. This time he struck on 13 minutes, being on the spot to tap home a goalmouth rebound. Centre-forward Jimmy Storrie put Leeds level within two minutes, but four minutes from half-time Jimmy Melia set up Ray Crawford to restore the visitors' lead. Leeds, who had been promoted as Second Division champions the previous season, were let off the hook as Wolves became more defensive-minded in the second half. Inspired by their dynamic Scottish midfielder Billy Bremner, the Yorkshiremen levelled with a Jack Charlton header on 63 minutes and won the game eight minutes later when Storrie nipped in to score from close range.

Although it was a three-defeats-from-three-games start to the season, Wolves kept the same side for the midweek home game with Leicester, and it proved a painful one for Knowles as Wolves at last got a point. Just before half-time he was carried off on a stretcher, fearing he may have done damage to his ankle. He had turned it as he ran over the track around the edge of the pitch. Five minutes after the break he was back and completed what Phil Morgan described as 'his most commanding performance in Division One so far.' The *Express & Star* man added, 'It would have been a dramatic touch indeed if he could have turned the game, as he went near to doing several times.' Skipper Ron Flowers was not so lucky in the injury stakes. He and Fred Davies collided and, though the goalkeeper recovered, Flowers was slightly concussed and had to play the rest of the game on the right wing. That meant Peter Broadbent switching to right-half, with Bobby Woodruff at centre-half. It took 35 minutes before Ray Crawford finally broke the deadlock. The 'passenger' Flowers made the chance with a right-wing cross that Crawford headed powerfully home. City equalised within seven minutes as Frank McLintock scored from an indirect free-kick, just as he had done at Filbert Street a week earlier. The ball was tapped to him, and even though Wolves defenders moved out quickly his powerful shot still found its way through. In the second half, Wolves went close several times. Gordon Banks had to palm away a Woodruff drive, and both Knowles and Terry Wharton had a couple of screaming shots just off target. Not that it was all Wolves, as McLintock almost snatched an undeserved win when his rising drive rebounded from the underside of the bar.

If Wolves thought they had turned the corner, they were wrong. Arsenal came to Molineux and won by the only goal of the game, from right-winger Alan Skirton seven minutes from time. Knowles's ankle injury meant he missed this latest addition to Wolves' wretched start to the campaign. He was also absent as things went from bad to worst when Wolves crashed 5–0 at West Ham, half-back Johnny Kirkham being tried in the inside-right position. Geoff Hurst scored twice, and England skipper Bobby Moore also got on the scoresheet as the Hammers proved just too good.

Knowles was fit to return for the trip to Blackburn on Saturday 12 September, but much-changed Wolves went down 4–1 to stay anchored to the bottom of the table. John Galley deputised for the injured Ray Crawford, as did goalkeeper Jim Barron for Fred Davies. George Showell was drafted in at his old position of centre-half while young David Thompson was given his chance on the right wing. Andy McEvoy had put Rovers ahead a minute from the break, and Knowles had a chance to level. Jimmy Melia laid it on for him, but Knowles's shot rebounded from the legs of a defender on the line. Earlier, Galley had seen a header bounce on the bar. With former England winger Bryan Douglas, playing at inside-left, calling the tune, Rovers got well on top, and John Byrom (two) and McEvoy sealed the win before Thompson scored from a corner which Knowles had won. It was overall not the best of days for Wolves or Knowles. Phil Morgan wrote of his display, 'Knowles could not immediately recapture the form he was beginning to show when injury put him out.'

Seven games and only one point – Stan Cullis had never known such a woeful start to a campaign during his 16 success-strewn years as the demanding king of Molineux. Perhaps Wolves could at last find a win when they played the return game with West Ham at Molineux on Monday 14 September? Ron Flowers was absent injured and Jimmy Melia was dropped in favour of Peter Broadbent. Hopes for that elusive win rose when Ray Crawford headed Wolves in front after just three minutes, and Knowles drove home an impressive shot to make it 2–0 on 34 minutes. The match then changed dramatically in the space of 22 minutes, starting with Peter Brabrook's hooked goal in the 39th. Six minutes after the break Gerry Harris raced back in an effort to clear from Brabrook but could only put the ball into his own net and on 61 minutes Harris was penalised for a challenge which enabled Johnny Byrne to give the Hammers the lead from the resultant penalty. Harris did not let his mishaps get him down. In fact it was quite the reverse as he set about retrieving the situation. With 13 minutes left he galloped down the left wing and sent in a drive so powerful that the Londoners' goalkeeper Jim Standen, also a useful cricketer for Worcestershire, could not hang on to the ball. Crawford was on hand to put home the rebound. Harris, the man from the Shropshire village of Claverley, was still not finished. With four minutes to go he slammed a long-range ball into the visitors' goalmouth where Standen misjudged the flight and was beaten. There had been few more popular goals at Molineux. Harris, a key man in the Championship triumphs a few years earlier but not a first choice in the previous two seasons, was a stalwart servant to Wolves and this, only his second goal for the club, had the crowd of 20,000 making enough noise for an attendance twice that size.

Manager Stan Cullis had not been well. On doctor's orders he had taken a break but had returned in time to see the win over West Ham; however, the following day, in a move that stunned the football world, the Wolves board sacked him. Cullis had been at the club as player, assistant manager and manager for 30 years. Many Wolves fans felt at the time that Cullis had been harshly treated by the board, and many expressed their dissatisfaction. John Ireland bore the brunt of it all and has probably been harshly judged over the years. Those who were at the club during his chairmanship always had the highest regard for Ireland and talk of him with much affection. Derek Dougan was among them, and when 'the Doog' returned to the club nearly 20 years later as chairman and chief executive he was instrumental in having Ireland made club president. As a tribute to him, the Molineux Stand was renamed the John Ireland Stand. It always seemed ironic that when Molineux was rebuilt, thanks to Sir Jack Hayward, the North Bank was replaced by the Stan Cullis Stand – nestling right next to the one which bore the name of the man who had been a key figure in Cullis's departure. Ireland was undoubtedly a great servant to the club, and many were unhappy when, in 2003, some years after his death, the stand was renamed the Steve Bull Stand.

Back in 1964, the directors felt something had to be done after Wolves' dreadful start. In such circumstances there is only one person who carries the can – the manager, even if that manager happens to be one of the greatest names in English football.

Young Knowles and his fellow lodger Les Wilson were interviewed by the local newspaper. Maybe if the senior players were keeping quiet, the paper hoped the younger ones might have something to say or at least give them a 'steer' off the record. Wilson recalls, 'I remember that the *Express and Star* interviewed both Peter and myself at our digs on the sacking of Mr Cullis.' The two youngsters were careful not to reveal any dressing room secrets. Wilson recalls, 'Peter and I had the utmost respect for this fine gentleman, even though, as a 17-year-old, I had not a great deal of interaction with him. He always had time for me, though, and on occasions gave me compliments and, more importantly, encouragement. I must have made an impression on him, as Bobby Thomson told me, when he was transferred from the Wolves to Birmingham City, that Stan Cullis, who was Blues boss by then, had also wanted to sign me.'

It was left to the training staff, in consultation with the directors, to name the team to face Blackpool at Molineux four days after Cullis's dismissal. Only one change was made from the side who had beaten West Ham, with fit-again Ron Flowers replacing Fred Goodwin. Blackpool, who included former Molineux winger Des Horne in their line up, added to Wolves' woes by winning 2–1, but their success owed much to the display of their England goalkeeper Tony Waiters. Knowles was one of those denied by him. With three minutes left he let fly from just inside the penalty area, and the shot had 'goal' written all over it before Waiters flung himself across his goal to save. Waiters had also made spectacular saves to deny Knowles and Peter Broadbent in the first half as well as Flowers and Gerry Harris in the second. The goals all arrived in the first 20 minutes. England international Ray Charnley struck for Blackpool on six minutes, and Ray Crawford levelled from a David Thompson pass on 18, only for Graham Oates to restore the visitors' lead two minutes later.

So, Wolves boasted only three points from nine games. It would get worse before it got better. For the visit to Sheffield Wednesday on Saturday 26 September, Wolves had to make a change in personnel because of an injury to Ray Crawford. While Knowles switched places with Peter Broadbent to partner Terry Wharton on the left wing, winger Clive Ford was tried at centre-forward and could have made a name for himself. After just five minutes, David Thompson, the only visiting forward to have a reasonable match, sent over a perfect centre, but Ford slid the ball wide. Thompson was off target with a running header, and Wharton tried a shot which goalkeeper Ron Springett spilled, with no Wolves forward following up. Knowles also got in the act with a spectacular hook-shot that was headed from under the bar. That opening flurry proved a false omen. Wolves faded steadily as the match wore on. Wednesday took the points with goals in the final minute of each half. A foul by Gerry Harris close to half-time enabled Tom McAnearney to open the scoring from the penalty spot. Colin Dobson made it two when his shot took a slight deflection off the foot of centre-half George Showell.

Three days after the Hillsborough match came news that Watford had released their boss to take the vacant job at Ipswich. The man in question was Bill McGarry, former Huddersfield and England wing-half, who would loom large in the final year of Knowles's career.

Knowles continued to wear the number-10 shirt when Birmingham visited Molineux and plunged Wolves even deeper into the dumps by winning 2–0. The managerless home side were worse than ever. In fact, Phil Morgan's *Express & Star* report said their performance 'represented a post-war rock bottom for the club.' Defensive frailty gave Blues their goals. Wolves conceded an indirect free-kick inside the penalty area after a poor backpass by Bobby Woodruff, and the the kick enabled Stan Lynn to score via the far post, which had been left unguarded. Thirteen minutes later Peter Broadbent tried to bring the ball out of the penalty area rather than clear and was robbed by Welsh international Ken Leek, who pivoted and fired the ball into the far corner of the net. A setback though these goals were, Wolves still had enough of the play to have gained something from the game. Unfortunately, according to Morgan, 'what they did not have were forwards with the know-how, speed or drive to turn attacks into goals.' An exception to that criticism was 18-year-old Scottish left-winger Pat Buckley, who was given his debut. He got in several good crosses, but no one took advantage. The whole affair left an even deeper gloom over Molineux. Not even the dismissal of Blues centre-half Winston Foster, 15 minutes from time, could help Wolves salvage the game. A final comment from Morgan, who was always one to encourage rather than criticise, was that 'At the cost of some offensive correspondence, I have tried to give encouragement and have urged others to do so, but if players are not good enough for the class of soccer in which they play – and that is not their fault – all the encouragement in the world must be unavailing.'

International calls meant Wolves' home game with Liverpool on Saturday 3 October was postponed. Bobby Thomson, after his fine displays in Brazil during the summer, kept his place at left-back in the England side who beat Northern Ireland 4–3 at Windsor Park, Belfast. A week later Wolves fans were even deeper down in the dumps as they were hammered 5–1 by Albion at The Hawthorns, where a certain Jeff Astle made his home debut, after two away games since being signed from Notts County. Astle showed the scoring prowess which would make him one of Albion's all-time greats when he put them two up with goals after 25 and 49 minutes. His strike partner John Kaye added two more before Knowles had the satisfaction of reducing the arrears. A Bobby Cram penalty eight minutes from time completed the rout. Wolves had again made changes as Ray Crawford returned as centre-forward after injury while Jimmy Melia and David Thompson formed the right wing. Graham Hawkins made his debut in defence.

Four defeats in a row became five when Manchester United, on their way to winning the First Division title, came to Molineux and won 4–2; however, there was no place for Knowles in a much-changed Wolves side. He would have loved to be on the same field as new wonder boy George Best but would have to wait until the new year for that privilege. While Best and Co were strutting their stuff at Molineux, Knowles was in the Wolves reserve team in the Central League clash, losing 2–0 to their Bolton counterparts before the empty, echoing stands of Burnden Park.

Before Knowles got back into the first team there was plenty of activity at Molineux. Three days after United's win Wolves swooped to sign Carlisle striker Hugh McIlmoyle on 20 October. The Scot had played in the 1961 FA Cup Final for Leicester but had never really secured a first-team place at Filbert Street and so had moved to Rotherham and then Carlisle. It was a shock signing as there had been reports of a bid for Hibs striker Jim Scott. There had been talks with the Scottish club's boss Jock Stein, but the deal failed to materialise. Wolves also wanted Manchester United's ex-Albion half-back Maurice Setters and agreed terms with the Old Trafford club. This also came to nothing as Setters wanted to be allowed to continue living up north, and Wolves would not agree to that.

Played at inside-left, McIlmoyle could not halt Wolves' slide, which went to a sixth successive defeat, 2–0 at Fulham. Eight days after the McIlmoyle signing Wolves did get a new wing-half as another Scot was bought – George Miller from Dunfermline for £26,000. Like McIlmoyle, he had a losing debut as Nottingham Forest won 2–1 at Molineux. It took another arrival before Wolves at last managed their second win of the season. That came at Stoke on Saturday 7 November, five days after Wolves had appointed Andy Beattie as caretaker team manager. Beattie had helped Nottingham Forest avoid relegation in 1960–61 and did a similar job for Plymouth in 1963–64, but this latest rescue task looked to be the toughest yet for the pre-war Preston and Scotland star. Beattie did not immediately see Knowles as a key to his rescue plans for the struggling team. The period of exile for the ambitious young man would be extended as Beattie looked to the experienced Jimmy Melia and Hugh McIlmoyle to fill the inside-forward berths.

In the Wilderness

If the spotlight had moved away from Knowles, others at Molineux were still in the limelight. Bobby Thomson collected three more England caps and Ron Flowers two before 1964 ended. Thomson was in the side held 2–2 by Belgium at Wembley with Chelsea's Terry Venables winning his first cap. It was not one of England's better displays, though former Wolves left-winger Alan Hinton fired in the shot which was deflected home for an own-goal equaliser 20 minutes from time. Thomson kept his place for the 2–1 win over Wales at Wembley on 28 November when Ron Flowers was recalled at centre-half and captained the side. Two future Wolves men were also in the team – Mike Bailey of Charlton at right-half and Nottingham Forest's Frank Wignall at centre-forward. Wignall scored England's goals, while Bailey looked the team's best player. Amazingly, he never received another cap. Flowers was again captain when England sent a side to play Holland to mark the Dutch FA's 75th anniversary. Bailey's place went to Spurs' Alan Mullery, who was making his international debut. It was left to another Tottenham man, Jimmy Greaves, to save England's faces. He grabbed the equaliser four minutes from time as the sides drew 1–1.

Knowles may have been a forgotten man around this time, but his brother Cyril was making progress a-plenty, having caught the eye of England boss Alf Ramsey. Cyril won his first international honour when he was in the Under-23 side who beat their Welsh counterparts 3–2 at Wrexham in November 1964. Peter, however, was having to bide his time. Jimmy Melia and Hughie McIlmoyle kept the inside-forward spots as Wolves followed up the win at Stoke with a 3–1 home win over Tottenham, a 1–1 draw at Burnley and a 1–0 win over Sheffield United at Molineux. That last game was memorable for centre-half David Woodfield, who scored with eight minutes to go. Four games without defeat seemed too good to last – and it was. There followed five successive defeats, but as the gloom descended once more over Molineux there was still no place for Knowles. He continued in the reserve team, often wearing the number-nine shirt. Melia and McIlmoyle made way for Peter Broadbent and Fred Kemp. Then Bobby Woodruff, Ray Crawford and even wing-half George Miller were called up. Melia had not really settled in the Midlands, and on 16 December, four days after he had figured in Wolves' 2–1 defeat at Chelsea, he was sold to Southampton for £30,000. He would help the Saints gain promotion from the Second Division in 1965–66; however, Melia's departure still did not signal a return for Knowles.

Kemp, who would soon follow Melia to Southampton, was just a few months younger than Knowles and at one stage shared the same digs. He remembered Knowles with fondness on *wolvesheroes.com*: 'He was great fun to share lodgings with, daft as a brush, barmy.' He added, however, 'Peter was a terrific player. I had a decent career, most of it away from Molineux, but he had outstanding ability and could have gone a long, long way if he had stayed with it.'

Wolves' fate looked settled, but the side certainly was not, and there came another addition to their ranks on Boxing Day morning. David Wagstaffe was signed from Manchester City in time to face Aston Villa at Molineux in the afternoon. Still only 21, Wagstaffe had plenty of football under his belt with 161 League and Cup appearances for the Lancashire side. There was no happy ending to his festive fairytale as Villa, who had a few weeks earlier signed Wolves old boy Barry Stobart from Manchester City, won 1–0. While Wagstaffe was playing his first game in gold and black, a Wolves legend was playing his last. Peter Broadbent, the player who had inspired Knowles, was dropped after the Villa game and sold to Shrewsbury on 18 January. A player of infinite skill, adored by the fans in his heyday, he was still only 31. Broadbent and Knowles were two of the most gifted players to wear the gold shirt, yet Beattie did not appear to rate them.

The new year began with the happy news that Stanley Matthews had become the first professional footballer to be knighted. New Year's Day 1965 also saw Wolves make yet another signing, with goalkeeper Dave MacLaren joining them for £8,000 from Plymouth. On the same day Argyle paid a similar fee for a replacement, Swansea's Noel Dwyer, who had been a Molineux player just a few years earlier.

The return game with Villa on 28 December was postponed because of snow and ice, but it was Bobby Woodruff who wore the number-eight shirt when Wolves went into action again, losing 4–1 to Arsenal at Highbury at the start of January 1965. The ex-Swindon man kept his place when the FA Cup came around the following week, Wolves drawing 0–0 at Portsmouth and then winning the replay 3–2, thanks to goals from Hugh McIlmoyle (two) and Ray Crawford. The goals were the first in nine games for McIlmoyle, who had now been given the number-nine shirt. The Cup success would give the team's form a boost. They beat Blackburn 4–2 at Molineux and drew 1–1 at Blackpool, where Wagstaffe scored his first Wolves goal. Even though Rotherham held them 2–2 at Molineux in the fourth round of the Cup, Wolves were on a run now and won the replay 3–0. Sheffield Wednesday were beaten in the League, 3–1 at Molineux on Saturday 6 February, with George Miller hitting two late goals from the inside-left spot. That same day Sir Stanley Matthews was making history when he helped Stoke beat Fulham 3–1. At 50, he was the oldest man ever to play in England's top flight.

Miller and Bobby Woodruff were again the inside-forwards at Anfield where Ken Knighton made his debut at left-half for Wolves. Woodruff's early goal silenced the Kop, but second-half efforts from Roger Hunt and Chris Lawler won the game for Liverpool. McIlmoyle had clearly established himself as leader of the attack, and four days after the Liverpool game Wolves sold Ray Crawford to neighbours Albion for £35,000. Crawford, who had once so relished playing alongside Knowles, had been dropped for the replay with Rotherham and it led to a major bust-up with Andy Beattie so that the striker's exit was inevitable. There was another departure at the end of February 1965 when Dick Le Flem, who had never really made an impact at Molineux, was sold to Second Division Middlesbrough for £18,000. Le Flem would make only 10 League and Cup appearances for Boro before moving on to Leyton Orient.

The same inside-forwards were on duty for the fifth-round FA Cup derby at Villa Park, which ended 1–1, and played in the replay at Molineux which finished goalless four days later. It was in that game that Wolves for the first time wore an all-gold strip. In his *Express & Star* report, Phil Morgan wrote that it was a pity that as well as gold shirts and gold shorts Wolves did not have 'goalden' boots with which to take the many golden chances they created.

After 22 League and Cup games without his services being called upon, Knowles at last got his recall. McIlmoyle picked up a knock in the replay but, with Crawford gone and young John Galley sold to Rotherham just before Christmas, there was no obvious replacement. Manager Andy Beattie decided to play Miller at centre-forward in their next League game and for the first time chose Knowles in the first team. It could hardly have been a more demanding return – against Manchester United at Old Trafford on Saturday 27 February 1965. The home side were also in the middle of a Cup run but had won only one of their previous six League matches. This was the day they rediscovered their form as that awesome forward line of John Connelly, George Best, David Herd, Denis Law and Bobby Charlton called the tune. Connelly struck in the fifth minute, but Wolves held out for another hour and four minutes before Charlton made it two. Charlton sewed the game up with his second goal six minutes from time. A 3–0 defeat was comprehensive enough, but Knowles had made the most of his chance.

Knowles loved playing the best, and he had the chance to earn a quick second tilt at the mighty United, for Wolves would have a home sixth-round FA Cup tie with Matt Busby's side if they could finally beat Villa. There were no penalty shoot-outs in those days, so after failing to get a decision on their own grounds the Midland rivals would now do battle on neutral territory – The Hawthorns. McIlmoyle was fit to play, but Knowles had done enough to keep his place, and George Miller was switched back to left-half to the exclusion of John Kirkham. To add drama to the occasion, Albion's ground was covered with a layer of snow. The match was played on Monday 1 March 1965 and proved a cracker. Wolves won it 3–1, and all their goals came from Hughie McIlmoyle. It was probably about this time that the fans first started singing their praises to the centre-forward. The Scot may well have been the first Molineux hero to be honoured in such a way as the North Bank Choir crooned 'Aye, aye, Hughie McIlmoyle' to the tune of *She'll Be Coming Round the Mountain*. It is difficult to recall other Wolves players, even in the heady days of the '50s, ever having such a tribute paid to them. These were changing times, however, and the cult of personality was upon us. In time the fans would sing 'D-D-D-Dougan, D-D-D-Dougan, he's the best centre-forward in the land' to the old tune of *K-K-K Katie,* while David Wagstaffe was serenaded to the 'intro' to the Rolling Stones' *Satisfaction*. McIlmoyle may have hit the goals in that epic replay victory, but Ron Flowers was the outstanding Wolves player.

There were also plaudits for Knowles, who had brought a spectacular save from Villa 'keeper Colin Withers. Phil Morgan was unstinting in his praise in the *Express & Star:* 'Knowles had his best game yet. It was his insistence linked with the enthusiasm of his attacking colleagues that gave Wolves a front-rank quality Villa never quite matched.' Wolves, in their new all-gold strip, led after four minutes when McIlmoyle back-headed home a Gerry Harris free-kick. Villa's Bobby Park, at 18, the youngest player on the pitch, levelled seven minutes into the second half, heading home an Alan Baker centre. McIlmoyle restored Wolves' lead on 69 minutes, driving the ball home from the edge of the penalty area after George Miller's lob had caused Villa problems. McIlmoyle's third was a superb solo effort. He took a pass from Bobby Woodruff and defied three attempts to stop him before letting fly a shot which left Withers helpless.

The bad weather stopped the fifth-round clash with double-chasing Manchester United being played the Saturday after the Hawthorns game, and so it was Wednesday 10 March 1965 when a packed Molineux staged a dramatic encounter. That man McIlmoyle continued where he had left off against Villa, scoring twice in the first 15 minutes. His opening goal, on three minutes, came when he could not get out of the way of a goalbound Bobby Woodruff shot; however, he quickly turned and fired the ball into the net. Then McIlmoyle lifted the ball over the head of centre-half Bill Foulkes and, despite two challengers, won the race to put the ball into the net. It all looked pretty good against the star-studded Reds until a minute before half-time when Denis Law was allowed a free header from a corner-kick. Starting in the 50th minute, United proceeded to turn the game on its head with four goals in 25 minutes – David Herd, George Best, Pat Crerand and Denis Law doing the damage. Knowles reduced the arrears nine minutes from time with a shot that went in off a post. Alas his display, according to Phil Morgan, was in stark contract to his efforts against Villa. 'Knowles, I felt, sometimes found the occasion a bit too much,' wrote Morgan, 'but he did take that goal extremely well.'

George Best had made a big impression on Knowles, who had played against him twice in the space of 12 days. Knowles told Rogan Taylor in 1994: 'It was teams like Manchester United that I used to like playing against, especially against George Best. I can remember the first time I ever met George Best. I met him at Manchester. I can remember talking to him. We were having a chat before the game, and I was surprised how small he was. That's what came across to me – how small he was. But I can remember going onto the pitch, and I was shocked how tall he was when he put a strip on. And then I watched him, and I've never seen a player like him in my life. He was the best that I've ever seen. I would have loved to have had just one game with him – at Wembley!'

Knowles's next game was a far cry from the frenetic Cup-tie atmosphere that had been Molineux – it was before a crowd of under 19,000 at St Andrew's. Yet the match between Wolves and fellow strugglers Birmingham was of much more importance than the Cup. A goal by Terry Wharton six minutes after half-time was enough to win it for bottom-placed Wolves and so put them within three points of Villa and six of Blues, the latter having played three games more. Wolves kept up the good work two days later when they beat arch-rivals Albion 3–2 at Molineux.

It was another battling display from Wolves, who were a goal down on five minutes when a rare slip by Bobby Thomson let in Ken Foggo. Then, after Hughie McIlmoyle had equalised on 49 minutes after turning quickly when receiving a pass with his back to goal, Albion were gifted the lead by Wolves' other full-back Gerry Harris. Racing across goal in an attempt to cut out a Clive Clark centre, he succeeded only in powering the ball past a helpless Fred Davies in the 57th minute. Knowles had a hand – or rather his head – in putting Wolves on level terms within seven minutes. He nodded a Terry Wharton corner towards goal, but just when Ray Potter seemed to have the effort covered Bobby Woodruff redirected the ball wide of the Albion 'keeper. Just before that goal Flowers nearly marred an otherwise blemish-free display when he underhit a backpass – you could pass back for the 'keeper to handle it in those days – and Jeff Astle was on to the ball in a flash. Luckily for Wolves, Davies spotted the danger even more quickly and smothered the ball at Astle's feet. The 'keeper's clearance led directly to Wolves' equaliser. Just three minutes later the turnaround was complete as the new hero of Molineux, McIlmoyle, leaped high to send a downward header past Potter from Buckley's left-wing corner. There was no Molineux return in Albion colours for Ray Crawford, as he was injured and John Kaye deputised.

It was a busy week at Molineux, for the following day the club announced that former Albion and England striker Ronnie Allen was leaving Crystal Palace to become senior coach with Wolves. Manager Andy Beattie said Allen would coach the senior professionals, enabling Bill Shorthouse to concentrate more on the young talent at Molineux. The same day Beattie signed full-back Joe Wilson from Nottingham Forest. He had signed Wilson from Workington when he was boss at the City Ground.

Wolves then made it a hat-trick of derby victories when they beat Stoke at a muddy Molineux. Knowles was not among the scorers but was now well established in the number-10 shirt. His left-wing partner, Pat Buckley, gave Wolves a seventh-minute lead when he turned the ball home after a George Miller shot had hit a post. Three minutes later Bobby Woodruff followed up to score when Laurie Leslie could not hang on to a Buckley shot. Wolves went close later on when both Hughie McIlmoyle and Woodruff took the ball round the 'keeper but drifted too wide to turn it into goal. Stoke, with two vastly experienced men at inside-forward, Jimmy McIlroy, once of Burnley, and Roy Vernon, once of Everton, pulled a goal back through ex-Villa winger Harry Burrows with 17 minutes to go; however, six minutes later Terry Wharton fired home Wolves' third to steady the nerves.

It was perhaps asking too much for Wolves to make it four derby wins on the trot and lift themselves off the bottom of the table. So it proved when on Monday 22 March they were beaten 3–2 at Villa Park, as the home side gained revenge for their FA Cup reverse. With Villa also close to the relegation places, they were no doubt much happier to have two vital League points rather than fleeting Cup glory. They had Wolves reeling with goals in the fifth and sixth minutes, through Alan Baker and Lew Chatterley, but then Knowles started to weave some magic, and it was his pinpoint centre that enabled Bobby Woodruff to head home on 21 minutes. Nine minutes later the deficit was two goals once more as winger John MacLeod beat Bobby Thomson before pushing the ball inside to Chatterley, whose shot went in off the post. Knowles and Hughie McIlmoyle kept plugging away, and in the second half Knowles's powerful shot was only inches wide. Six minutes from time McIlmoyle at last beat Colin Withers when he headed home Pat Buckley's free-kick. Tom Johnson was very complimentary in his *Express & Star* verdict, saying 'the gangling Peter Knowles' was 'outstanding in the Wolves attack.' It was a vital win for Villa, who moved above Birmingham to 20th in the table with 25 points from 32 games. Blues had 24 from 34 and Wolves 22 from 33.

Knowles was out of the Wolves side when Tottenham visited Molineux earlier in the season, but his return meant all was now set for the first game featuring both him, and his brother Cyril and what a game that proved at White Hart Lane on Saturday 27 March! Spurs had decided to re-jig their forward line, dropping one member of their 1961 double-winning side, Terry Dyson, and recalling another, Les Allen. The latter came in at centre-forward, and Scottish international Alan Gilzean moved to inside-left. Welsh international Cliff Jones, who had been playing inside-left, reverted to the left wing while 18-year-old Keith Weller, who would win England caps with Leicester 10 years later, came in for his debut on the right wing to partner England goal ace Jimmy Greaves. The changes certainly produced goals for the Londoners – they hit seven, but Wolves replied with four after an amazing nine-goal second half. The visitors actually led for 27 minutes after Pat Buckley had opened the scoring in the 10th minute. Allen made it 1–1 by half-time, but then things started to go mad. Gilzean (49 minutes) and Eddie Clayton (53) put Spurs 3–1 up. Hugh McIlmoyle (58) got Wolves to within a goal, as did John Kirkham (63), following Jones's goal (61) and then Terry Wharton (74) after Gilzean's second (69). So it was 5–4 to Spurs and Knowles, who had formed a useful left-wing partnership with Buckley, looked certain to make it 5–5. He hit a full-blooded drive towards the top corner of the net, but Tottenham's Scottish international goalkeeper Bill Brown flung himself across goal and managed to clutch the ball under the bar. That was the closest Wolves got to another goal, and two late strikes from Jones gave Spurs a three-goal margin they hardly deserved. Amazingly, Greaves, at the height of his goalscoring powers, had not got on the score sheet.

After the goal-spree at White Hart Lane, there could not have been a bigger contrast three days later when Wolves, and fellow strugglers Fulham fought out a goalless draw at

Molineux. It was not a good night for Knowles, though he and Pat Buckley had started as if they were going to keep up their good work of the previous Saturday. After Hughie McIlmoyle had seen a shot beat goalkeeper Tony Macedo but rebound from the foot of a post, Knowles unleashed one of his trademark drives only to see the ball strike the bar, with Macedo again helpless. Knowles seemed to lose heart after that, not helped by a brief spat with Fulham's ex-England captain Johnny Haynes. After Terry Wharton had seen yet another shot hit the woodwork, Knowles had a chance to break the deadlock late on but miskicked with the goal at his mercy. Fulham were well served by a 20-year-old inside-right named Rodney Marsh. With Fred Davies injured, Dave MacLaren made his home debut in goal.

David Wagstaffe had been sidelined by injury but was back as Knowles's left-wing partner when Wolves took on Burnley at Molineux and lost 2–1. They were thus staring relegation in the face. With the exception of Ron Flowers, they looked like a relegation side, as well. Flowers, who had striven manfully throughout the season to stave off the inevitable, even dug out one of his classic goals, driving the ball home from fully 35 yards on 38 minutes to cancel out Andy Lochhead's seventh-minute opener for the Lancastrians. Flowers moved up front in the last few minutes in a bid to save the game following winger Les Latcham's goal for the visitors on 73 minutes.

Thanks to Alf Ramsey, the tireless Flowers was again available when Wolves tried to keep alive their faint survival hopes against fellow strugglers Sheffield United. Flowers, captain of his country in England's last game, against Holland in Amsterdam in December, was dropped by Ramsey for what in those days was still the highlight of the season – the game against Scotland. Nobby Stiles, Jack Charlton and Chelsea centre-forward Barry Bridges were given their first caps as England led 2–0 at Wembley but had to settle for a battling 2–2 draw, having lost full-back Ray Wilson through injury just before half-time and seen Johnny Byrne reduced to a passenger. This was in pre-substitute days. At Bramall Lane the same day, Wolves took their chances, with Knowles leading the way, to gain a vital win 2–0. Knowles opened the scoring on the hour, taking the ball past reserve goalkeeper Bob Widdowson after it had eluded the home defenders. There was a hint of off-side about it – in fact it looked more off-side than a situation later in the match when Knowles again rounded the 'keeper to slide the ball home only to be denied by a linesman's raised flag. The second goal had come a minute after Knowles's opener, a centre somehow getting through a crowded penalty area so that Bobby Woodruff needed only to tap the ball home from a couple of yards.

Knowles prolonged the inevitable drop a little longer when he scored a dramatic winner at Roker Park on Good Friday as Sunderland were beaten 2–1. Ron Flowers was again his commanding self, but much credit went to goalkeeper Dave MacLaren and to Joe Wilson. Wolves showed their fighting qualities after the setback of conceding a first-minute goal. MacLaren saved a point-blank shot from Dominic Sharkey, but former Birmingham and England winger Mike Hellawell was on the spot to put home the rebound. Wilson paved the way for the equaliser five minutes into the second half, galloping down the right wing to take Terry Wharton's pass and putting over a centre from which Hughie McIlmoyle scored with a downward header. Sunderland had kept MacLaren busy, but after the equaliser there was an almighty scramble in the home goalmouth. John Kirkham's centre from the right caused panic in the Sunderland rearguard as Wharton and then Knowles had shots blocked before McIlmoyle turned the ball against a post. Knowles was not to be denied. In the 87th minute he latched on to a long pass down the middle from Flowers, beat the last Sunderland defender with one of his typical shuffles and then ran on to beat goalkeeper Sandy McLaughlan. It was a special goal by a youngster who was clearly a special player. On the same day West Ham's Brian Dear hit five goals as West Ham beat Albion 6–1 at Upton Park.

If Wolves' hopes had been raised with their successive away wins, they faded very quickly at Molineux the following day when Everton came from 2–1 down to win 4–2. While Wolves' drop into the Second Division after 33 years would surprise the football world, so would the name of one of the clubs who came up. Northampton Town clinched promotion on the day Wolves were losing to Everton, the same day that news came of Leeds and Scotland midfielder Bobby Collins being chosen Footballer of the Year. Collins had helped his side run Manchester United mighty close for the First Division title and also reach the FA Cup Final for the first time in their history. Losing to Everton meant Wolves' fate was out of their hands and not even the completion of a holiday double over Sunderland could make any difference. Wolves won 3–0 at Molineux on Tuesday 20 April 1965, but later in the day Villa gave them the final push by beating Leicester 1–0 at Villa Park. That was Villa's fourth win in six games as they ensured it was Wolves and their neighbours Blues who would take their leave of the top flight. Yet, Wolves at least made the fateful day one to remember – or rather Bobby Woodruff did. He hit an unusual hat-trick – all three goals were headers. Unlike Wolves, Sunderland escaped the relegation battle, but that did not save their manager George Hardwick. The former Middlesbrough and England skipper lost his job at the end of the season.

Knowles helped Wolves to a third successive away victory when they beat Nottingham Forest 2–0 at the City Ground. It was his hard cross that Hughie McIlmoyle diverted with his head to open the scoring on 27 minutes, and he earned high praise from Phil Morgan in the *Express & Star*: 'Knowles excelled with some of his direction-switching passes.' Pat Buckley drove in Wolves' second goal 18 minutes from time and Forest rarely threatened. When they did, they found Dave MacLaren in top form, while Ken Knighton again looked a useful right-back, keeping his old Wolves colleague Alan Hinton quiet on the Forest left-wing.

If relegation was not bad enough, the final act of an ill-fated season would provide a bizarre ending to Knowles's first full campaign as a first-teamer. He, and the Wolves fans among a crowd of under 14,000 on Monday 26 April 1965, must have hoped the side would make a defiant farewell to the First Division against Liverpool at Molineux. Instead, Wolves bowed out with a whimper to a team of reserves. With his side due to play Leeds in the FA Cup Final the following Saturday, Liverpool boss Bill Shankly rested all of his first-team regulars. One of the reserves, Geoff Strong, did play at Wembley, but only because Gordon Milne was injured. In those days clubs were duty-bound to field their strongest line up or else face punishment by the Football League. Liverpool, however, would escape censure. Shankly could produce evidence that every player left out was injured, and so the authorities were powerless to punish him. Shankly may have fielded a reserve side, but they still won the game 3–1. It was a woeful way for Wolves to leave the top flight.

Liverpool had four Football League debutants and one of them, John Sealey, scored on 35 minutes, Strong having been gifted the first on 14 minutes by a Dave MacLaren error. George Miller's poor clearance had led to Sealey's goal, but the wing-half atoned by getting Wolves back into the game two minutes after half-time. Alf Arrowsmith made it 3–1 20 minutes from the end. Stalwart defender Ronnie Moran, later a key member of Anfield's famous boot room, marshalled his young teammates well, and the Reds had little trouble holding on for the points. Hugh McIlmoyle, Bobby Woodruff and Miller all had shots hit the woodwork, and so did Arrowsmith. Sealey's appearance proved to be his one and only first-team game for Liverpool. He did not make it in League football, moving to Chester where he made just three League appearances. It was also a lone Liverpool appearance for Alan Hignett, Bill Molyneux and Tom Lowry, though the last name did play in over 400 games for Crewe. It's worth looking at the Liverpool line up:

Molyneux, Lowry, Hignett, Chisnall, Moran, Ferns, Graham, Sealey, Arrowsmith, Strong, Wallace. In the Cup Final, their team was: Lawrence, Lawler, Byrne, Strong, Yeats, Stevenson, Callaghan, Hunt, St John, Smith, Thompson.

So ended Knowles's first season as a first-team player. He had figured in 23 of his side's 42 League games, as well as two FA Cup ties. He had scored seven goals. If it had been an awful campaign for his club, it had been one of progress for Knowles. In his end-of-season review in the *Sporting Star*, however, Phil Morgan made no mention of him. Morgan named Ron Flowers as the club's Man of the Season, closely followed by Bobby Thomson. Experienced Midland football writer Tom Duckworth had praise for Knowles in the *Sports Argus* annual, saying he was 'an inside-forward with great possibilities.' In their retained list, Wolves put up for transfer only one man of first-team experience – Fred Kemp. He would join Southampton in the summer and later saw service with Blackpool, Halifax and Hereford. Johnny Kirkham, despite playing in the last 12 games of the season, also left the club in the summer. He joined Third Division Peterborough. While one wing-half left Molineux, another, 19-year-old John Holsgrove, arrived from Crystal Palace. Coach Ronnie Allen knew him from his days at Selhurst Park, where he had made an impact after stints at Arsenal and Tottenham as an amateur.

On Friday 30 April 1965 Wolves provided the skippers in what was then a traditional eve-of-Cup Final, game, England against Young England. Ron Flowers captained the senior side at centre-half while Bobby Thomson led the Under-23 outfit from left-back. The match ended 2–2.

The Goalscorer

The difference in standard between the First Division and the Second Division was not as great in 1965 as would be that between the Premier League and the Championship over 40 years later. Clubs like Liverpool and Leeds United had bridged the gap with ease, so relegation was not a footballing calamity in those days. Life in the second tier might also help Knowles build on the good start he had made and he soon started to sparkle as he laced his burgeoning talent with goals a-plenty to cement his place in the affections of Wolves fans. Significantly, among those fans were a growing band of female admirers. Molineux had never seen anything quite like it.

Wolves had enjoyed 26 successive seasons of top-flight football since the early 1930s so the Second Division was a new experience for the majority of their fans. There was something else new about the 1965–66 season: the Football Association made a momentous decision and by 43 votes to 19 they sanctioned a Football League proposal to allow substitutes. It was only one per team, however, and he could only be used in the event of injury. That proviso was, of course, open to abuse, and so it would prove. Eventually the law would be changed to allow a substitution for any reason.

Among the sides who would be standing in the way of Wolves making a swift return to the First Division were Manchester City, and they made a key appointment during the summer when Malcolm Allison was named assistant manager to Joe Mercer. A flamboyant character he may have been, but Allison was an astute coach and would prove an ideal foil to the more paternal Mercer as City embarked on the most successful period of their history.

After all the upheavals of the previous season, Wolves started 1965–66 with Andy Beattie still caretaker boss and Ronnie Allen the first-team coach. Wolves must have thought the Second Division would be to their liking as they controlled the early proceedings of their opening game at Coventry. They were rewarded eventually with a goal by Hughie McIlmoyle on 58 minutes. It was a classic. Bobby Thomson broke from defence, fed Wagstaffe down the left and his cross was met perfectly by the centre-forward; however, a packed Highfield Road, where the home fans had warmed to the innovative managerial style of Jimmy Hill, saw a late transformation that spoiled Wolves' day. Centre-forward George Hudson struck in the 78th and 84th minutes to turn the game on its head. Typical of Hill's determination to give spectators a full day's entertainment was the staging of a netball game before kick-off.

A quick chance to check out the prowess of Manchester City under Mercer and Allison came four days later when Wolves visited Maine Road and again flattered only to deceive. At least Knowles got his first goal of the season. He was on the spot two minutes from time to hit home the rebound after goalkeeper Harry Dowd had pushed out a Ron Flowers shot. That made it 2–1 to City, and that is how it finished; although it took a fingertip Dowd save to deny Flowers a last-gasp equaliser. Benevolent Wolves had provided City with both their goals. The first came on 29 minutes. Terry Wharton fouled his old Wolves teammate Jimmy Murray, leading the City attack, and left-winger Glyn Pardoe powered in the free-kick from the touchline. George Miller dived full length in a bid to head the ball for a corner but succeeded only in putting it into his own net. Wolves continued to keep Dowd busy and almost levelled on 70 minutes when Wagstaffe, skipper against his old club, was put through by Miller. The winger's shot looked bound to sneak in at the far post but was deflected fractionally wide. City's £30,000 winger Mike Summerbee was given little chance to shine by Bobby Thomson, but the City man had the last laugh. His low cross on 85 minutes was deflected into Thomson's path as he chased back and he could not avoid putting the ball into his own net.

Having got off the mark against City, Knowles was about to embark on his best goalscoring period. It began in Wolves' first home game of the season when he collected his first hat-trick for the club as Carlisle were beaten 3–0. Indeed, three might have been five had he made the most of two chances when put clear by astute passes from Hughie McIlmoyle. His first and last goals were down to a striker's instinct to be in the right place at the right time. He opened the scoring on 29 minutes after a Bobby Woodruff shot rebounded from a post and was also on hand in the final minute when the ball ran to him as the visiting defence got into a tangle. His second goal, on 54 minutes, was a cracker, heading the ball home after Terry Wharton had made a run from the halfway line before centring. Knowles was not given the spot-kick duties when Wolves were awarded their first penalty in over a season. George Miller was handed the ball and promptly blasted it straight at goalkeeper Joe Dean who tipped it over the bar. That was a happier memory for Dean, whose last visit to Molineux was as a 16-year-old debutant, in February 1956, in a Bolton side beaten 4–2.

The spotlight would switch dramatically from Knowles to another Wolves youngster, David Woodfield, when Manchester City came to Molineux on August Bank Holiday Monday to clinch an early seasonal double 4–2. With Wolves 2–1 down, the goals coming in the first eight minutes, Woodfield was sent off after a tussle with Mike Summerbee which ended with the Manchester City man disappearing into the seats in the Molineux Street stand. Summerbee emerged with blood pouring from a wound in his forehead which required four stitches. Ironically, the incident occurred as the two chased the ball not realising the referee had already halted play in the City penalty area. It was the first time a Wolves player had been sent off in a League game for 29 years. That drama came after 23 minutes, and there had already been plenty of incident in a whirlwind opening. Dave Wagstaffe had embarked on a solo run through the City defence to fire Wolves ahead after five minutes, but within a minute old Molineux favourite Jimmy Murray headed home a Summerbee centre. After another two minutes City were ahead. Summerbee featured again, laying the ball back to Johnny Crossan, whose low swerving shot found its way through a crowded penalty area and went into the net via Dave MacLaren's shoulder and the inside of the far post. After Summerbee had been replaced by Roy Cheetham, wearing a numberless shirt, the 10-man Wolves laid siege to the visitors' goal, and Knowles ought to have equalised. He had one shot blocked and was off target from the rebound. It proved an expensive miss as on 36 minutes left-winger Dave Connor put Gerry Harris under such pressure that the full-back put the ball into his own net as he tried to divert it for a corner. Still Wolves created chances, and after Bobby Woodruff had fired over the bar 'keeper Harry Dowd denied Wagstaffe and Harris. Dowd continued to defy Wolves in the second half until finally beaten by a Woodruff header nine minutes from the end. Knowles, Hugh McIlmoyle, Woodruff, Bobby Thomson and Harris were among those thwarted by Dowd. As often happens, the side on the back foot broke away and five minutes after Woodruff's goal, a Crossan pass found Mike Doyle running wide of goal but still able to chip the ball home.

A sequel to Woodfield's dismissal came when an FA inquiry in Birmingham cleared him completely – with, to his credit, the support of Summerbee who said afterwards, 'I have always said I was knocked off the pitch by a perfectly fair charge.'

Knowles went goalless again in Wolves' next game but the team, with Joe Wilson recalled in place of Gerry Harris, still managed four as they beat Cardiff at Ninian Park. The

Welshmen managed only one in reply, and that came from a George Johnston penalty, conceded on 75 minutes by Ron Flowers for a foul on John Charles. The Wolves skipper, though nominally right-half, had taken on the task of marking the Welsh legend Charles. The big man, though 34, was still a useful centre-forward and had hit two goals in City's 5–1 midweek win over Derby County at the Baseball Ground. Flowers, however, kept the former Leeds and Juventus star very quiet, and it was the opposing number nine who took the plaudits. Hughie McIlmoyle struck with a header on 12 minutes and stooped low to grab a second within three minutes. Home skipper Gareth Williams could only head the ball into his own net to make it 3–0 after 38 minutes. After Cardiff's penalty, Dave Wagstaffe restored Wolves' three-goal lead with a shot that went in via both posts.

Knowles, soon to celebrate his 20th birthday, may at this stage have thought he had made enough progress to be first choice for the number-10 shirt; however, before Wolves made the midweek trip to Rotherham, there were reports that they were showing interest in a Scottish inside-left, Charlie Cooke. An Under-23 international, Cooke had been signed by Dundee for £40,000, using some of the £70,000 fee they had received from Spurs for Alan Gilzean. While Wolves were beating Cardiff, director Jim Marshall was seen watching the Dundee-Celtic game. It was thought Wolves would also have scouts running the rule over Cooke the following Wednesday when he helped the Scottish League beat the Irish League 6–2 at Ibrox Park, Glasgow. Despite the reports, nothing came of Wolves' interest and in April 1966 Cooke's inevitable move south took him to Stamford Bridge, where he became one of Chelsea's all-time greats. It may well have been apocryphal, but a story went around at the time that Marshall, a bluff Midland businessman, was asked 'While you were in Scotland did you see Ben Nevis?' To which Marshall allegedly replied, 'No, he wasn't playing.'

On the night Cooke was showing his paces at Ibrox, Tuesday 7 September 1965, Wolves came down to earth again, despite hitting three goals, one of them from Knowles. Rotherham won the game at rain-soaked Millmoor 4–3, but the narrow margin flattered Wolves. Phil Morgan said in his *Express & Star* verdict Wolves were 'unbelievably out of touch.' He added, 'Even now, after time to reflect, I find it well nigh incredible that the business-like, but far from brilliant, Rotherham should be able to cause such havoc in the Wolves ranks that there was hardly a man who came out with high marks.' Rotherham let Wolves off the hook in the first half, apart from Les Chappell's back-heel pass that put Keith Pring in to score after 20 minutes. A minute into the second half it was 2–0. Former Wolves striker John Galley sent Barry Lyons away, and he managed to squeeze a shot in at the near post. Ron Flowers's left-wing centre enabled Dave Wagstaffe to reduce the arrears within three minutes, but a mix-up in Wolves' defence saw Bobby Williams soon make it 3–1. Within a minute Knowles made his only telling contribution when he slid home a centre from Hughie McIlmoyle, one of the few Wolves men to emerge with any credit. As the rain continued to pour steadily, Wolves' defence got in a mess once more in the 75th minute, and Williams collected his second. Six minutes from time Galley handled in the penalty area and Terry Wharton was on target from the spot. So, Wolves had lost four of their first six games in their bid to get back to the First Division at the first attempt. It was a rude awakening to life in the Second Division.

Wolves fans desperately needed a lift. They would get it in the shape of two home wins in the space of three days, hitting four goals each time, helped by Knowles's scoring spree. He hit his second hat-trick in a fortnight as Derby were beaten 4–0 at Molineux on Saturday 11 September 1965. This was a day Knowles reinforced his popularity with the home fans as he struck twice in the first 10 minutes and also made the third goal. Phil Morgan wrote in the *Express & Star* that he was so often in the right place at the right time that he could easily have had five goals, rather than three. Knowles was on target in the third and ninth minutes, and in the 21st his centre was netted by Bobby Woodruff. With centre-forward Hughie McIlmoyle a busy provider, Wolves ought to have had a field day against the experienced former Coventry, Chelsea and England goalkeeper Reg Matthews. They eased off, however, and Dave MacLaren had to make two good saves to deny the Rams before Knowles struck again 15 minutes from time.

Wolves were guilty of easing off again two days later, but Knowles took his goal tally to nine goals in eight games when Rotherham were beaten at Molineux. While the Derby team a couple of days earlier had featured a veteran 'keeper, this time the spotlight was on a 19-year-old, Rodney Jones, signed earlier in the day from non-League Ashton United. Unfortunatley, however, a plan to put the teenager at ease before kick-off backfired. Rotherham skipper Peter Madden twisted a muscle as he gave the debutant some practice and had to be replaced by reserve centre-half John Haselden.

Wolves were again two goals ahead inside 10 minutes. Hughie McIlmoyle had Jones palming over a drive after only two minutes but struck after a further two minutes when he headed in Terry Wharton's right-wing centre. On nine minutes Dave Wagstaffe turned the ball over the line after one of Bobby Woodruff's long throw-ins was miscontrolled by Robin Hardy. Knowles got into the act on 32 minutes when his hard-hit shot beat Jones, and then, five minutes from the break, Knowles pulled the ball back for centre-half Dave Woodfield to drive into the net. Rotherham were allowed back into the game, and left-winger Keith Pring scored on 54 minutes before Wolves reasserted themselves. Jones, after his first-half pounding, showed his worth with a fine save from Wharton and a good interception of a Wagstaffe cross before collecting a well-directed header from Knowles, who also missed a clear opening later.

Wolves fans must have thought their team had turned the corner with 15 goals from four games. They were wrong, very wrong. Knowles may have thought that any ideas of signing another inside-forward had been shelved. He was wrong, too. On Thursday 16 September 1965, Andy Beattie paid £40,000 to buy Swindon Town inside man Ernie Hunt, and he was named as substitute two days later for the trip to The Dell to face Southampton. It proved to be one of the worst days in Wolves' history as the Saints, beaten 5–1 at Coventry in midweek, ran riot to win 9–3. The last time Wolves had conceded more goals was on 27 December 1919, when Hull beat them 10–3. That total at The Dell, on a gloriously sunny day, might easily have been bettered as there were still 30 minutes left when the final goal was scored. Dave MacLaren also made several fine saves to deny the home side. One of the architects of the Southampton win was Molineux old boy Jimmy Melia, who wore the number-nine shirt despite playing in midfield. Martin Chivers, a future England striker, collected four goals.

Wolves had had a dream start. They took the lead after only 35 seconds thanks to an own-goal from former Leicester centre-half Tony Knapp. Chivers levelled on four minutes, and left-winger John Sydenham made it 2–1 seven minutes later only for Bobby Woodruff to equalise within a minute. Then Wolves went to pieces as England right-winger Terry Paine (25 minutes), George O'Brien (30) and Chivers (33) made it 5–2 at the break. Chivers scored twice more in the first five minutes of the second half before Knowles, who was hardly in the game, struck to keep his scoring run going. Sydenham (55) and Paine (60) took the total to nine, and there it ended. With subs allowed only in the event of injury, Hunt was not called upon and must have wondered what sort of team he had joined as he watched the mayhem unfold in front of him.

It was a sad end to Andy Beattie's period as caretaker boss. A few days before the Southampton game he had informed the board he would be leaving because of personal reasons, the most important being the serious illness of his wife. Beattie's reign came to an end two days after the Dell humiliation, and Ronnie Allen and trainer Joe Gardiner chose six of the team to play in the reserves against Liverpool reserves – MacLaren, Wilson, Thomson, Miller, Wharton and Wagstaffe. It did them good to get quickly back into action as they shared six goals at Anfield, coming from three down at half-time to draw thanks to a Terry Wharton hat-trick. When Allen and Gardiner chose the team to face Bury at Molineux on Saturday 25 September 1965, only Bobby Woodruff and George Miller were dropped. As well as new boy Hunt, John Holsgrove was given his Wolves debut.

There was an interesting trio of teenagers in the Bury line up. At number-nine was 19-year-old Colin Bell. He would move to Manchester City before the end of the season and would go on to become a Maine Road legend and win 48 England caps. At inside-left was 17-year-old Alec Lindsay, who would move to Liverpool and make a name for himself at full-back and also be capped for England. At outside-left was Gordon Roberts, a former Wolves youth-team forward, who had been transferred from Molineux the previous week. Unlike the other two, Roberts failed to carve out a Football League career.

Naturally, the eyes of home fans were on the new men. The stocky Hunt impressed with his close control and ability to distribute the ball, while Holsgrove was given the task of closely marking experienced inside-right Billy Griffin and did so to telling effect. But there was no keeping Knowles out of the limelight. After Dave Wagstaffe had turned home a Terry Wharton centre on 14 minutes, Knowles made it 2–0 nine minutes after half-time. His goal was a header to a centre by Joe Wilson, whose displays at full-back had endeared him to the Molineux faithful. What the stocky defender lacked in finesse he more than made up for in commitment. Wharton was not to be denied, and he completed a 3–0 win when he shot home from a narrow angle with 20 minutes to go. On the same day nine-goal Southampton were brought back down to earth when they lost 1–0 at Rotherham.

Speculation was still rife as to what the Molineux board would do about the managerial situation. There was a quick indication as to who was their target. Press reports linked former Huddersfield and England wing-half Bill McGarry with the job. He had impressed in his first two managerial posts, at Watford and Bournemouth, before taking over at Ipswich in October 1964. Wolves chairman John Ireland was in touch with his opposite number at Portman Road, John Cobbold, but the East Anglians' board eventually said 'Nothing doing.' So Ronnie Allen was allowed to continue in charge of the first team at Molineux; however, the desire to get McGarry to Molineux had merely been put on the back burner. Wolves may not have picked up a new boss from East Anglia, but they did pick up a win there when they met Norwich for the first time in the clubs' history.

Peter Knowles the promising teenager became Peter Knowles the 20-year-old on 30 September 1965. Two days later he celebrated by scoring as Wolves won 3–0 against the Canaries at a sun-drenched Carrow Road. Wolves kept an unchanged side against a City team who included another one-time Molineux teenage sensation, Gerry Mannion, on the right wing, as well as prolific Welsh striker Ron Davies at centre-forward. Again Wolves did their scoring in the early part of a game. Their wingers were in sparkling form, Dave Wagstaffe giving them the lead on eight minutes with a jinking run that ended with a cross-shot. Then Terry Wharton ran on to score from a well-judged Ernie Hunt pass on 27 minutes. On 40 minutes, Hunt did it again for Knowles to fire in his 12th goal of the campaign. He had thus scored in six successive games. Dave MacLaren had been called on to make a couple of early saves as Norwich made a bright start, but the Canaries faded as Ron Flowers and Dave Woodfield took control, well-supported by John Holsgrove.

Without doubt, Knowles had now captured the hearts of the Wolves fans, particularly the younger element – a fact reflected in the songs of the North Bank Choir. Though 'He's here, he's there, he's every f***ing where, Peter Knowles, Peter Knowles' was hardly Lennon and McCartney standard, it did confirm the young man's cult status. The North Bank regulars did not always use such coarse language and once managed to finish third in a BBC competition to find the best Kop choir. Favourites Liverpool came second with Rotherham the unlikely winners.

In that splendid book, *We Are Wolves*, produced by the club's fanzine, *A Load of Bull*, Tony Eagle captures the affection in which Knowles was held: 'Hero worship came in the form of Peter Knowles. After a game, you could ask him for his autograph (he once signed my school tie which I still possess) and have a good chat with him. He wasn't that much older than the kids he was talking to and he had a Beatles haircut like most lads of that era (me included). A great bloke and a rich talent (if a little flawed occasionally), it broke my heart when he eventually packed it all in.'

If Knowles was enjoying his best goalscoring run, so too was winger Dave Wagstaffe. When he gave Wolves a sixth-minute lead against Leyton Orient at Brisbane Road it was his seventh goal in nine matches. He had never before scored so regularly and would never do so again, preferring in subsequent years to lay on the openings for others. Knowles had nearly opened the scoring in the second minute when his snap shot hit a post. Then Wagstaffe hit home a Hughie McIlmoyle centre, but it was left to home inside-left Gordon Ferry to provide the other goals in another 3–0 win. He put through his own goal on 21 minutes and repeated the error 11 minutes after the break. Orient staged a token revival, but Dave MacLaren made a fine save to keep out a header from Orient's teenage full-back Dave Webb. Later in the season, Webb would score against Wolves in spectacular fashion, but for Southampton, not Orient.

Knowles renewed his scoring streak when the revival after the Southampton debacle brought a fourth successive 3–0 win. This time the victims, at Molineux, were Middlesbrough. Knowles struck after only eight minutes, driving the ball home after seeming to have lost his chance. On 29 minutes Ernie Hunt fired home his first goal for the club, but he later injured a foot and limped off just after half-time. That enabled Fred Goodwin to make a little bit of club history as Wolves' first substitute. He came on to see Boro have their best spell, but Dave MacLaren made flying saves to deny Bill Gates and Jim Horner. Then it was the turn of visiting 'keeper Eddie Connachan to show his worth, denying Hughie McIlmoyle, Goodwin and Dave Woodfield. However, Woodfield had the final word, driving home Terry Wharton's cross in the last minute.

Hunt's injury led indirectly to Knowles having a change of partner on the left wing when Wolves visited Huddersfield, who were then top of the table. Pat Buckley came in for his first game of the season so that Dave Wagstaffe could switch to the right wing with Hughie McIlmoyle in the number-eight shirt and Terry Wharton tried at centre-forward. It was Wharton's goal that gave Wolves their 1–1 draw at Leeds Road. Tony Leighton had put Town in front on 52 minutes, but the lead lasted only two minutes. Wharton moved out to the left and was found by a precision pass from Knowles and had only to beat the goalkeeper.

With Ernie Hunt fit again, Wolves' attack returned to a familiar look when Crystal Palace visited Molineux. Yet they had a frustrating afternoon as goalkeeper John Jackson played the game of his life to make save after save. Knowles had the final say, lobbing the ball over the 'keeper as he advanced for the match's only goal on 51 minutes. Knowles's strike had an added distinction as it made him the League's top marksman with 14 goals, while the win meant Wolves had risen from 14th to fourth in the Second Division since their Southampton mauling. It had not been a good day for Palace. Engine failure meant their train was late arriving in Wolverhampton, and so it was 3.30 by the time the game kicked-off.

Wolves' revival meant all was set for them to push on and make a genuine impact in the race for promotion. Instead they proceeded to draw their next three matches, and Knowles learned how quickly fortunes could change in football. He was dropped. Yet first he kept up his goalscoring momentum as he took his seasonal total to 15 from 16 games when he struck after 12 minutes against Preston at Deepdale. His was a solo effort, and seven minutes later Terry Wharton made it 2–0 with a vicious cross-shot. Dave Wagstaffe went close twice after that as a third goal eluded the visitors. So Preston were able to mount a second-half fightback, and it brought them a point despite the solid defensive work of John Holsgrove and Joe Wilson. Burly home centre-forward Alex Dawson, a one-time Busby Babe, caused plenty of problems, but it was left-winger Frank Lee who began the recovery with a goal on 62 minutes. Wolves still looked like holding out for a win but were denied late on when Howard Kendall's shot took a deflection off Holsgrove's boot to earn Preston a share of the spoils.

A week later it was Wolves' turn to come from behind and grab a point when Charlton visited Molineux. The game also provided the chance for home fans to run the rule over Athletic's England half-back Mike Bailey. This barrel-chested bundle of energy did not disappoint. He had an impressive game, showing all the qualities that Molineux regulars admired in a half-back. The Londoners also had another man who caught the eye, goalkeeper Mike Rose. His best of several first-half saves was when he fingertipped over a Terry Wharton drive, but the 'keeper could not prevent Hughie McIlmoyle breaking the deadlock after 33 minutes. Wolves had made their first goalkeeping change of the season, Fred Davies coming in for Dave MacLaren, who had broken a bone in his foot. Davies had a quiet first half but was much busier in the second and brought the house down when he saved a penalty by centre-forward Ron Saunders on 63 minutes. That came six minutes after Bailey had put Charlton level, but Saunders was not to be denied and gave Charlton the lead after 71 minutes. A neat header from Ernie Hunt cancelled it out within two minutes. Rose then kept Wolves at bay, but the spotlight fell on Knowles when he was presented with a great chance to win the match but slammed the ball wide. Before that, both Ron Flowers and McIlmoyle had seen efforts hit a post.

With John Holsgrove impressing at left-half and Bobby Woodruff still among the reserves, Scotsman George Miller was well down the pecking order. So it was no surprise when he was sold to Hearts for £20,000 two days before Wolves took their unbeaten sequence to nine games with a 2–2 draw against Plymouth at Home Park. Knowles did not have the best of days, however, in a match that had no shortage of drama. It was credit to Wolves that they shared the spoils as they had to play with only 10 men for the last 32 minutes after Dave Wagstaffe had been sent off. Waggy had established himself as a potential matchwinner, and it was inevitable that opponents would do their best to curb his talents. On this occasion the close attention handed out to him saw the left-winger for once not walk away after being fouled. Right-half John Williams brought him down, and Wagstaffe promptly aimed a kick at the Plymouth man. Wagstaffe afterwards apologised to Williams and to the referee. Yet, when one recalls some of the rough treatment Waggy used to suffer it is a wonder he did not snap more often.

At the time of Wagstaffe's dismissal, Wolves were already trailing, youngster Richard Reynolds having headed Plymouth in front on 48 minutes. Wolves also had the handicap of a less-than-fit Terry Wharton, who had pulled a muscle after 15 minutes. On the hour Hugh McIlmoyle headed Wolves level, but they looked to have handed Plymouth victory with a comical goal four minutes from time. David Woodfield squared the ball to Joe Wilson, who nonchalantly glided it back to where he thought goalkeeper Fred Davies was, but Wilson had not checked on Davies's position. The ball rolled gently into the net. That should have been that, but there was still more drama and another unusual goal to come. With two minutes left goalkeeper John Leiper caught a high centre from McIlmoyle just beneath his bar and was promptly barged into the net by Ernie Hunt. The referee signalled a goal and afterwards stifled all arguments when he said the fairness of the charge was irrelevant as he had given the goal to McIlmoyle because Leiper had caught the ball behind his line. Plymouth had not made the most of their one-man advantage; although Davies was severely tested by a volley from inside-left Mike Trebilcock. The 'keeper's downward dive kept the ball out.

Trebilcock was beginning to make a name for himself but could little have imagined that he would write his name into English football history before the season was over. He would join Everton for a Plymouth record of £23,000 just before the turn of the year and in May would be a surprise choice in the Merseysiders' FA Cup Final side against Sheffield Wednesday. To complete the fairytale story of his selection ahead of England centre-forward Fred Pickering, Trebilcock would score twice at Wembley to cancel out Wednesday's 2–0 lead. That set the scene for Derek Temple to hit Everton's winner.

Dropped Again

If big things were happening for Plymouth youngster Mike Trebilcock, the same was not true for Knowles. After his wonderful start to the season he was looking a little jaded. Yet it was still a surprise when it was announced before kick-off that he had been left out of the side to face Portsmouth at Molineux towards the end of November 1965. Into his place came Bobby Woodruff, who only the day before had asked to come off the club's transfer list. Woodruff promptly opened the scoring after two minutes, and the goals just would not stop, as Wolves led 6–0 at half-time. The second half, which also featured a brief snow storm, saw the sides share four goals as Wolves ran out 8–2 winners. Woodruff, Hughie McIlmoyle and John Holsgrove ended with two goals each, the others coming from Ron Flowers and Dave Wagstaffe. Joe Wilson put through his own goal for the second game running to get Pompey on the scoresheet and lanky centre-forward Ray Hiron hit their other consolation. Wolves' win was not the biggest of the day, however, as Brighton beat Southend 9–1 at home in Division Three.

Not surprisingly, Wolves kept their eight-goal formation for the trip to Bolton. Burnden Park had often been an unlucky ground for Wolves and not only did they lose 2–1 but they also had three men injured – John Holsgrove, who had to go off at half-time, David Woodfield and Hughie McIlmoyle. While the last named recovered from his knock the ankle injuries to the other two meant Knowles's exile would prove a brief one. Before he got his recall, however, there came news that the man who had given him his Football League debut, Stan Cullis, was back in management just over a year after his shock dismissal from Molineux. Cullis was made boss of Birmingham City with a five-year contract.

On the same day, Saturday 11 December 1965, Wolves, with Knowles restored to the number-10 shirt, beat Ipswich 4–1 despite trailing to a goal in the first minute by Danny

Hegan. To make up for the absence of Woodfield and Holsgrove, Bobby Woodruff, the man who had displaced Knowles, was switched to left-half with Graham Hawkins making his second League appearance at centre-half. While Knowles did not get on the score sheet, Woodruff did. He did what Ernie Hunt had done in the fourth minute and headed home a Terry Wharton cross. The other goals were also headers, McIlmoyle nodding in a Hunt lob on 38 minutes and Wharton putting home a cross from McIlmoyle on 66 minutes. There was more disruption for Wolves, however, Ron Flowers having to go off with a back injury.

Although Knighton had been substituted for the injured Flowers, it was young Les Wilson who came into the team when the skipper had to miss the game against Middlesbrough at Ayresome Park. Born in Manchester but raised in Canada, Wilson was Knowles's pal, and Knowles would have taken great pleasure in his progress. The new boy found most of those around him below their best as Boro won 3–1. Terry Wharton had gone close twice in the opening minutes before Wolves were sent reeling by goals from centre-half Dickie Rooks and inside-right Ian Gibson in the eighth and ninth minutes. Knowles made virtually his only contribution with a goal 10 minutes later, but on 22 minutes teenage centre-forward Arthur Horsfield completed the scoring. Dave Wagstaffe was one of the few Wolves men to emerge with credit as he said his farewells before starting the 14-day suspension brought about by his Plymouth dismissal.

Wilson was allowed to continue his planned Christmas return to Canada as John Holsgrove was fit to face Bristol City at Molineux on Monday 27 December 1965. That game, as so often happens at Christmas time, attracted a bumper gate of 32,526, some 10,000 more than the previous best that season. The home contingent must have been hoping to see Wolves get their promotion momentum going once more. Instead, they saw them held 1–1, mainly thanks to the heroics of former Shrewsbury goalkeeper Mike Gibson. The match saw the good and bad side of Knowles. He was the first to test Gibson with a point-blank shot in the opening minutes, but the City equaliser 13 minutes from time could be traced back to an error by Knowles on the frozen surface. One of the faults displayed early in Knowles's career was the tendency to overdo the clever stuff. It was just such a piece of trickery that saw the visitors gain possession and go to the other end of the pitch to force a succession of corners. From the last of these, veteran former England man John Atyeo headed home at the near post. City's uncompromising centre-half John Connor gave Hughie McIlmoyle little chance to shine and Knowles, too, had little impact. Phil Morgan, in his *Express & Star* report, reckoned 'Knowles obviously disliked the uncomfortable conditions so that, in effect, Wolves were functioning on three cylinders up front instead of the usual five.' Gibson was eventually beaten in the 59th minute by Wagstaffe's deputy, Pat Buckley. Even then, the 'keeper saved Buckley's original shot before being beaten from the rebound. Buckley ought to have won the match three minutes from time but hooked a great chance wide.

A quick chance for Knowles to atone for his largely anonymous showing came when the sides met again the following day at Ashton Gate. He made ample amends, crowning a fine display by scoring the game's only goal 12 minutes from time. It came when one of Bobby Woodruff's long throw-ins was flicked on by Hughie McIlmoyle for Knowles to round a defender and hook the ball home. Remarkably, the gate at Bristol was bigger than that at Molineux the previous day. It topped 36,000 – 16,000 better than any previous Ashton Gate attendance that season – as the club used their new floodlights for the first time.

New Year's Day brought news of an MBE for Swansea's Welsh international stalwart Ivor Allchurch, but there were few honours for Wolves even though they beat Leyton Orient 2–1 at Molineux. It took a last-minute save by fit-again 'keeper Dave MacLaren to prevent Tony Nicholas grabbing an equaliser for the struggling Londoners. MacLaren had also helped Wolves take the lead in the ninth minute. His long kick was flicked on by Hughie McIlmoyle and, as Orient defenders hesitated thinking the ball would reach their last line Vic Rouse, Terry Wharton nipped in to score. After that, former Spurs and West Ham wing-half John Smith began to dictate the pattern of play, and Orient did not look like a side destined to finish bottom of the table. In the 76th minute Wolves clinched the two points when Ernie Hunt controlled the ball from a Bobby Woodruff long throw-in and drove home a cross-shot. Joe Wilson then spoiled an otherwise impressive display by misplacing a pass to Dave Metchick who promptly drove the ball home to ensure an edgy final few minutes.

With Ron Flowers fit again after missing a few games through injury, Knowles was dropped for the trip to The Valley to face Charlton on Saturday 8 January 1966. He was struggling to recapture his early-season form, and Bobby Woodruff moved up from half-back to partner Dave Wagstaffe, who had completed his suspension. It was Waggy who created Wolves' goal on 67 minutes. He fought to regain possession, and his centre was headed into his own net by left-half Peter Burridge. A foul by Joe Wilson on left-winger Len Glover enabled Mike Kenning to net from the penalty spot to give the Londoners a point. So began another period of exile for Knowles as Wolves went into two vital home games against fellow promotion hopefuls. He was named as sub but was not called upon as goals from Ernie Hunt and Bobby Woodruff helped see off Huddersfield 2–1. A week later Wolves made short work of Cheshire League side Altrincham in the third round of the FA Cup, winning 5–0, with Knowles's replacement Woodruff a scorer.

Just before the Cup tie had come the sad news from Molineux that injury-hit centre-forward Ted Farmer had finally decided to retire. Farmer had made an historic top-flight debut by scoring 28 goals in 27 League games in 1960–61. Fast and fearless, Farmer won England Under-23 caps and had the ability to become one of the club's all-time great strikers. Alas, it was not to be.

Again Knowles was an unused substitute when the same team were named for the crunch game with Coventry at Molineux. The win over Huddersfield had put Wolves level with the Sky Blues and just a point behind leaders Manchester City, so the significance of the meeting of the Midland rivals was clear. It attracted 44,718 fans, Wolves' best League gate since September 1962, but it proved a bad day for those sporting gold-and-black scarves. A goal from former England and Burnley striker Ray Pointer gave Jimmy Hill's team a 1–0 win they thoroughly deserved. But the defeat did not signal a recall for Knowles. Wolves kept the same side for the trip to Carlisle when Hughie McIlmoyle was made captain for the day against his old club. It proved an unhappy return for the striker who, along with the rest of his team, missed a host of chances as Wolves were beaten 2–1.

A decision on whether to recall the unhappy Knowles was taken out of the hands of coach Ronnie Allen because Bobby Woodruff was ruled out by a boil on the leg for the FA Cup fourth-round visit of First Division Sheffield United on Saturday 12 February 1966. So Knowles was able to face the side from his home county, and he made the most of his chance with two goals in two minutes as the Blades were ushered out 3–0. Wolves had gone ahead on 31 minutes when Hughie McIlmoyle headed home Terry Wharton's centre, but a lively Sheffield side made them wait until the 65th minute for their second. It was a fine goal, too. Knowles, who had earlier gone close with a couple of solo runs, swung the ball wide to Wharton and ran full pelt for the goalmouth to meet the winger's low cross. When the ball duly arrived, Knowles hit it with some considerable ferocity into the net. If that was a special goal, his second, two minutes later, had some luck about it. Dave Wagstaffe, at his best on the left wing, created the opening for Knowles, but his shot struck the foot of the near post. Unfortunately for United, their former England 'keeper Alan Hodgkinson had dived to try to save and was still grounded when the ball rebounded on to the back of his head and into the net.

It should have been a day of triumph for Knowles, but the ill-discipline that was always lurking below the surface of his character marred his display and brought a rare rebuke in print from the *Express & Star's* Phil Morgan. The veteran football writer added a footnote to his report, 'Peter Knowles had his name taken by referee A.E. Dimond (Harlow), which seems a good opportunity for a word of advice to this young man whose potential is so high. Enthusiasm is one thing, but petulance, which he has shown far too often, is something quite different. It is better curbed now, since it adds nothing to his undoubted football efficiency and could even land him, and the club, in trouble.' Tough words indeed, but they reflected the personality of Knowles in those early days. All great players have a touch of arrogance, but at this stage in his career Knowles was displaying a touch of cockiness which threatened to hamper his progress. Maybe it was a reflection of his general discontent at being in and out of the team.

A sequel to the game saw Knowles make public that discontent. Ron Wills quoted Knowles in the *Daily Mirror* as saying, 'I want to go to London. I want to be where the bright lights and everything are. If you don't go to Italy, you go to London – that's where the money is.' According to Wills, Knowles had twice asked for transfers during that season and, despite being refused both times, was still determined to move. Knowles added, 'I don't care if I'm in the team next week, the week after that and the week after that. I still want to leave.'

In his interview with Rogan Taylor many years later, Knowles reckoned he made no fewer than 19 transfer requests during his time at Molineux. He told Taylor, 'Well, when I played, Wolves weren't going anywhere. I always wanted to play for a big club. Like some of the players today, they want to go abroad because they want to see what it's like, and I was the same, I just wanted to play for a big club. I always wanted to play for somebody like Manchester United or Liverpool and just see what it would be like to play with really outstanding flair players.'

Getting away from a club was not easy in the 1960s, however, and clearly Wolves were unlikely to release a player of such potential. It could also have been the case that big clubs would think twice about buying him at that stage of his career. He had been getting a reputation, and maybe the Manchester Uniteds, Liverpools and Tottenhams would bide their time until he had settled down. Little could they have guessed that the influences that eventually made him a better-adjusted person would also lead him to turn his back on football fame and fortune.

For the visit to Molineux of relegation-haunted Cardiff, Knowles stayed in the team and was the centre of some bewildering tactics. Wolves seemed to give the Welsh side far too much respect and often had only Knowles and wingers Terry Wharton and David Wagstaffe left upfield. Such were the strange tactics that Phil Morgan asked Ronnie Allen if he was trying something new. He got short shrift, Allen replying that if the players were trying something different it was down to their own initiative and not at the request of the coach.

Yet Wolves still managed a 2–1 win thanks to Wharton's goals in the space of three minutes either side of half-time. Former Lower Gornal Athletic player George Andrews replied for Cardiff.

Knowles was in an unchanged Wolves team against Derby County on their infamously muddy Baseball Ground pitch, and he had the ball in the net after only 20 seconds. Alas, Knowles had clearly handled. Apart from the four corner areas, the pitch was a sea of mud, not an unfamiliar sight at the famous old stadium. Wolves led twice but had to settle for a 2–2 draw. Ernie Hunt opened the score after 17 minutes, and when he was brought down in the penalty area soon afterwards the referee turned down appeals for a penalty but awarded Wolves an indirect free-kick. The visitors were out of luck again when the Rams levelled on 24 minutes. David Woodfield and County inside-left Alan Durban fell in the mud as they tangled, but a free-kick was given, from which Eddie Thomas scored. Wolves went ahead 17 minutes into the second half when Dave Wagstaffe fired in a shot from Ron Flowers's centre and Hughie McIlmoyle diverted it home. Derby levelled again 13 minutes from time. Thomas netted from a cross by former Newcastle outside-right Gordon Hughes.

While the spoils were being shared in Derby, Mike Bailey was helping Charlton win 2–1 at Leyton Orient. It would prove to be his last game for the Addicks as two days later (Monday 28 February) the England international was at Molineux and liked what he saw, agreeing to join Wolves for a fee of £40,000. Bailey, who a day earlier had celebrated his 24th birthday, would prove an inspirational figure during his Molineux career, but he could easily have been parading his talents at Tottenham, rather than Wolverhampton. Spurs, in March 1964, had been looking for a successor to their captain Danny Blanchflower and also had granite-hard half-back Dave Mackay out with a broken leg. Though they signed Alan Mullery from Fulham, it seems Bailey was the man they wanted for the midfield role. In his autobiography, *In Defence of Spurs,* Mullery recalls the meeting with Spurs boss Bill Nicholson to finalise his transfer. The man who had guided Spurs to the double in 1961 asked Mullery if he would join Spurs as a full-back. Mullery was adamant that he wanted to play half-back or he would not sign. The player got his way. Wrote Mullery, 'Looking back on the conversation, I feel that if I had agreed to play full-back, Bill would certainly have signed Mike Bailey.' Ironically, when Bailey was at his peak with Wolves it was Mullery who kept him out of the England team. Bailey had become only the seventh Charlton player to be capped for England, but he would never add to his two caps – a scandal in the eyes of all Wolves fans.

Bailey did not have an immediate chance to meet his new colleagues, as straight after the Derby game they had been whisked off for a few days at Lytham St Anne's, near Blackpool, to prepare for the fifth-round FA Cup visit of mighty Manchester United on Saturday 5 March 1966. Matt Busby's team came to Molineux four days before they were due to travel to Portugal to meet Benfica in the European Cup and, as they had done almost exactly a year earlier, beat Wolves after trailing 2–0. Sadly for Knowles, home fans would forever recall the game because of his moment of madness that proved the turning point. The drama had begun early on when referee Kevin Howley awarded Wolves two penalties in the first nine minutes, first when Pat Crerand brought down Ernie Hunt and then when Bill Foulkes handled. Each time Terry Wharton made no mistake from the spot. On 23 minutes Crerand's centre was headed home by his fellow Scottish international Denis Law, but Wolves kept their lead until half-time. They were still looking lively when Knowles's slip turned the match on 62 minutes. After another intense spell of Wolves pressure a United clearance was collected by Ron Flowers who slipped the ball to Knowles. Everyone in the ground must have seen the lurking John Connelly, but Knowles did not as he tried to turn the ball back to goalkeeper Dave MacLaren. Connelly intercepted and centred for the lethal Law to head home the equaliser.

Knowles immediately doubled his efforts to try to make amends, but another unlucky slip let United in again. This time it was Flowers who made a rare error. His attempted clearance struck George Best who pushed the ball out to David Herd and raced into the penalty area to meet the inside-forward's cross. Just seconds earlier Hughie McIlmoyle had seen a downward header pushed against a post by United's veteran Irish goalkeeper Harry Gregg. To complete the comeback, Best laid on a final goal for Herd in the last minute. Confirmation, if it were needed, that Wolves had been beaten by a fine side came the following Wednesday when United beat Benfica 5–1 in the second leg of their European Cup quarter-final in the Stadium of Light. As at Molineux, Best was the star, and such was the superb display of the long-haired Irishman that the tabloids dubbed him 'El Beatle.' Amazingly, United were subsequently beaten in the semi-final by Partizan Belgrade.

Amid all the fuss about the Cup defeat, Wolves made a low-key signing when they paid out £5,000 to sign 22-year-old goalkeeper Evan Williams from Third Lanark. Despite his Welsh-sounding name, he was a Scot, born in Dumbarton. On the day of Manchester United's epic win in Lisbon, high-riding Southampton were doing some useful transfer business in time for their visit to Molineux on Saturday 12 March. The Saints signed full-back Dave Webb, still only 19, from Leyton Orient. The man destined to become a Cup Final hero for Chelsea, would steal the limelight from the other debutant, Mike Bailey. After a goalless first half, Webb turned up in the home penalty area to score with a spectacular scissors-kick. That goal on 51 minutes was wiped out 11 minutes later when Ernie Hunt ran in to head home at full pelt a short centre from Terry Wharton. David Woodfield was the man who had to make way for Bailey, Ron Flowers switching to centre-half, but Woodfield still made a telling contribution. He was substituted for the injured Bobby Thomson 13 minutes from time, and his cameo role was highlighted by a 25-yard shot which deserved to win the game. Unfortunately for Woodfield, Saints 'keeper Campbell Forsyth was equal to the moment, making a flying save to deny him.

The strike partnership of Knowles and Hugh McIlmoyle was clearly going through a bad patch, and for the trip to Bury Woodfield was the surprise choice for the number-nine shirt. He made a pretty good go of it but Bury, struggling to avoid relegation, won the game thanks to its only goal, scored by Paul Aimson, newly signed from York City. The Lancashire side also gave a debut to George Kerr, signed from Barnsley, the latter filling the gap left by the sale of highly-rated youngster Colin Bell to Manchester City. While Bell was impressing in his new club's 2–1 win at Derby, Wolves were well out of sorts, with Knowles and Ernie Hunt having little effect on the proceedings. Phil Morgan made no bones about it in the *Express & Star*, saying Woodfield had 'no support from inside-men who were below par and wingers who chose the complicated rather than the simple way.' Knowles was clearly struggling, and the goal-laden start to his season was now just a memory.

The need to rest Knowles was obvious to Ronnie Allen. Hughie McIlmoyle was recalled to the number-10 shirt for the visit of Norwich City, but when tonsillitis laid low Ernie Hunt there was no reprieve for Knowles. Mike Bailey was given the number-eight shirt. Knowles had to be content with sitting on the bench as the unused sub as David Woodfield justified his run at centre-forward by scoring both goals, the second five minutes from time, in a 2–1 win. As it turned out, Bailey looked far from happy up front, and for the home game against Preston a week later he wore yet another shirt – number-six. Well-again Hunt, McIlmoyle and Woodfield scored the goals in a 3–0 win, all the scoring being in the first half on a rainy day when conditions were far from easy. It was even muddier at Selhurst Park a week later when an unchanged Wolves side won 1–0, thanks to yet another Woodfield goal.

Knowles was among the 14 players Wolves took to St Andrew's on Easter Monday for the derby clash with Stan Cullis's Birmingham City; however, the only change to the starting line up was the switching of Ron Flowers and Mike Bailey, so the latter was in his more accustomed right-half role. Holsgrove, not Knowles, was given the sub's shirt but was not needed in the 2–2 draw.

As often happened over Easter in those days, the sides played a quick return fixture, meeting the following evening at Molineux, where Knowles made a return to action in an unexpected position. Terry Wharton was left out and Knowles was asked to play on the right wing and did so to some effect. What looked a blatant case of hands in the penalty area by Blues half-back Ron Wylie was ignored a few minutes before Wolves went ahead, Hughie McIlmoyle beating goalkeeper Jim Herriot with a looping header on the half-hour mark after a short corner routine by Dave Wagstaffe and Bobby Thomson. The second goal did not arrive until the 67th minute, and Knowles played a big part in it. The move was begun by one of the crusading runs from full-back Joe Wilson that had helped make him a cult figure with Wolves fans. He slipped the ball inside to Knowles, whose precision pass put Ernie Hunt through for a run which ended with a scorching shot past Herriot.

Goalkeeper Herriot's name would eventually become famous world wide and even lend itself to an area of Britain. When James Alfred Wight found a publisher for his first book about his experiences as a vet in Yorkshire he wanted to remain anonymous, so needed to come up with a pen name. While still trying to make up his mind he happened to be watching TV highlights of a Blues match in which Herriot was outstanding. Wight decided that 'James Herriot' would be just right for his *nom de plume*. Who knows, if he had begun his writing earlier, what we now call Herriot Country might have been Merrick Country!

Wolves' five-point Easter meant they were on 47 points, behind leaders Manchester City and second-placed Huddersfield, who were both on 48. Wolves had played 38 games, one more than Huddersfield but three more than Southampton who were staging a late assault and were on 43 points. City had, like the Saints, played 35 games, so Wolves' chance of promotion was an outside one – but not if they could win their last four games. That hope quickly vanished in a frustrating match when Plymouth, struggling to avoid relegation, held Wolves 0–0 at Molineux, with Knowles, still on the right wing, out of touch like the rest of the forwards. It said much that many of Wolves' best attacks were due to raids by full-backs Joe Wilson and Bobby Thomson. Wolves would have gone second had they won because Huddersfield lost 4–1 at Derby on the same day. Ominously, Southampton edged closer with a 1–0 home win over Crystal Palace while Manchester City swept Bolton aside 4–1 at Maine Road.

Knowles's brief flirtation with the art of wing play now came to an end. For the vital trip to Portsmouth, Pat Buckley was preferred in the number-seven shirt though he and left-winger Dave Wagstaffe swapped places soon after kick-off. Bobby Kellard (13 minutes) and centre-forward Ray Hiron (83) hit the goals that gave Pompey a 2–0 win on a day Wolves could have stolen a march on their promotion rivals. Manchester City, Huddersfield, Coventry and Southampton were all involved in 1–1 draws – with Ipswich, Cardiff, Leyton

Orient and Preston respectively. Five days after the Portsmouth game, Wolves said farewell to full-back Gerry Harris, who signed for Walsall. He had been at Molineux for 12 years, making his debut in the epic 5–4 win over Luton in 1956. He had won two First Division Championship medals and an FA Cup-winners' medal with Wolves, as well as four England Under-23 caps.

The outside chance of promotion was as good as gone when Wolves entertained Bolton in their final home game of the season. That view was obviously shared by the casual fans as fewer than 16,000 were at Molineux to see Knowles celebrate his recall to the side with a fine display in a 3–1 win. He was restored to the number-10 shirt, and the experiment of playing David Woodfield as a striker was abandoned, Hughie McIlmoyle returning to his centre-forward role. Woodfield still got a piece of the action, coming on as substitute for Joe Wilson, who limped off after 65 minutes. It was indicative of the place Wilson had gained in the affections of the diehards that he was cheered all the way to the dressing room. By that time, after a goalless first half, winger Gordon Taylor had broken clear to give Bolton a shock lead. That was on 57 minutes, and a minute later Knowles marked his comeback with the equaliser. Phil Morgan said in his *Express & Star* report: 'Knowles capped a busy display with a fine header that seemed to please him as much as it did the crowd. Earlier, Knowles had been prominent with some excellent ball control and some lively shooting.' It was Knowles's first goal in the League since December. McIlmoyle put Wolves in front 10 minutes from time with a header, having earlier had one cleared off the line. The best goal of the game came two minutes from the end. Terry Wharton, restored to the right wing, cut inside and unleashed a 25-yard drive that was past former England 'keeper Eddie Hopkinson almost before he realised what was happening.

Four days later Manchester City won 1–0 at Rotherham, thanks to a Colin Bell goal, to make certain they would be promoted to the First Division. Southampton would join them as runners-up.

The Prankster

Knowles would collect his 19th League goal of the 1965–66 season on Saturday 7 May 1966, and it put Wolves into a 2–1 lead over Ipswich at Portman Road. It was a false omen. Ipswich were 4–2 up at the break and ran out 5–2 winners. It was a happy debut for Town's 17-year-old full-back Mick Mills, who was taking the first step in a distinguished career which would in time see him become England's captain. Knowles had an unexpected partner on the left wing as Ronnie Allen sprung a shock by dropping Dave Wagstaffe and playing Pat Buckley. The chunky Scottish winger justified his selection with a goal on 10 minutes to cancel out the shock second-minute strike by former Wolves man Ray Crawford. Graham Hawkins, who had done so well the previous weekend, and had generally impressed in his spell at centre-half, found Crawford and his strike partner Gerry Baker, brother of Forest's Joe, quite a handful. Hawkins was not alone in having an off day, but it was his own-goal that put Ipswich 3–2 ahead on 30 minutes following Baker's equaliser 11 minutes earlier. Five minutes from the break, Hawkins saw his backpass intercepted by Baker, who put Crawford in for his second goal. Hawkins's nightmare continued six minutes after half-time when Crawford dispossessed him and set up future Wolves man Danny Hegan for the fifth.

The reason behind Wagstaffe's surprise omission, which was hushed up at the time, was, according to Wagstaffe, a piece of typical Knowles mischief for which Waggy carried the can.

It all happened at the hotel in Bury St Edmund's, where Wolves always stayed the night before a game against either Ipswich or Norwich. The players had to be in their bedrooms by 10.30, but Wagstaffe had gone to the room being shared by Dave Woodfield and Ernie Hunt for a chat before finally turning in. They then heard the sound of doors being knocked and the raised voices of chairman John Ireland and director Jim Marshall. As the room

Wagstaffe was sharing with Dave MacLaren was first along the corridor, the winger realised the two directors would have found out he was missing. So Wagstaffe hid under a bed in the Woodfield-Hunt room until the chairman and Mr Marshall had called and then left. Recalled Wagstaffe, 'I was in the most farcical situation I had ever been in. A professional footballer under the bed with the chairman's slippers 3in from my nose.'

When Wagstaffe sneaked back to his own room and was eventually confronted by the directorial duo he found out what all the fuss was about. A couple strolling along the pavement in front of the town centre hotel had been drenched by some water thrown from an upstairs window. It came from a floor whose bedrooms were occupied only by the Wolves party. The hotel manager passed on the complaints from the angry passers-by to the Wolves officials and that sparked off the door-to-door inquiries. Despite his protests of innocence, Wagstaffe was next morning told to leave by Ronnie Allen, who gave him some cash to pay for his train journey home. Pat Buckley had already been summoned from Wolverhampton to take his place.

Wagstaffe spent some weeks of the early close season wondering if he had a future at Molineux or whether he would be on the transfer list. He eventually got a letter telling him to attend a board meeting. He did not get an apology but was told that the Ipswich incident was now closed. At the meeting chairman John Ireland was seated looking down at some papers in front of him and the rest of the directors silently flanked the table. Wagstaffe recalled, 'He rose from his chair and without even looking at me, the papers still in his hand. Still looking down at the papers he began, "A serious incident occurred at the hotel during our stay at Bury St Edmunds. No action will be taken about this incident, it will never be mentioned again; indeed, it is forgotten. Thank you, gentlemen." He sat down, apparently still looking at the papers in his hand, and never even glanced my way. Jack Howley [Wolves' secretary] held the door open and showed me out. As we walked along the corridor he whispered, "That's the nearest thing to an apology anyone will ever get from a board meeting."'

Wagstaffe said he later learned that the water had been thrown from the window by Knowles. It was the sort of silly prank which amused the youngster in those days. Wagstaffe was not angry with Knowles, apart from wishing Knowles had owned up, but he was upset that Ireland and Marshall had presumed him guilty without a proper hearing. Wagstaffe said, 'Peter was prone to doing silly things on a whim, but I did not bear him any malice. The people I was really annoyed with were John Ireland and Jim Marshall for jumping to conclusions without investigating the matter thoroughly.'

That Knowles was the culprit had been known to all the players at Bury St Edmund's, and the word eventually got back to the Molineux powers that be. That was why they summoned Wagstaffe to the board meeting. As far as Wagstaffe knows, Knowles never got punished for the incident.

Perhaps that stupid prank at Bury St Edmund's was indicative of Knowles's immaturity, a thing often reflected in his football. Even though Wolves' season had ended in disappointment Knowles could certainly look back on a campaign of satisfactory progress, tempered by that tendency to cockiness which would raise doubts about his temperament. That view of his progress was confirmed by that doyen among Midland football writers Tom Duckworth. In the *Sports Argus* annual for 1966–67 he wrote, 'Peter Knowles could have a great future with a little more self discipline.' Phil Morgan, in the *Sporting Star*, said Knowles had finished the season in brilliant form, but he awarded his Player of the Year accolade to full-back Joe Wilson. Knowles had played 33 League and FA Cup games and scored 21 goals to make him the club's leading scorer, three ahead of Hughie McIlmoyle. At that stage of his career he was far from content, however, as evidenced by his transfer requests which would continue each time he found himself out of favour.

Clive Corbett, then just a young fan, sums up the impact Knowles had made: 'I saw my first match in March 1965 (Stoke at home), and Peter was the rising star and one of the few bright spots in Andy Beattie's fast-falling team. In the 1965–66 season he was the mainstay of the team in many ways. He was certainly my early hero and my first yellow star badge purchase – these were little plastic stars in the style of Wild West sheriff badges with black-and-white pictures behind Perspex that adorned my hand-knitted bobble hat. Much to my dismay, I can't find a single one!'

Another with fond memories is John Lalley, who used to write a lively fan's column each week in the *Sporting Star*, the rapport Knowles had with youngsters being a thing that stays with him. 'I remember as a kid collecting autographs outside the old players' entrance in Waterloo Road. Occasionally, the small yellow gate allowing a way into the old enclosure was left open, and we would nip in to watch the players training. Most times, a groundstaff member, or club secretary Jack Howley, would send us on our way before locking the gate behind us. But one sunny morning, during pre-season, a group of us got in and were allowed to watch unhindered. With our scrapbooks at the ready we were amazed when Peter Knowles called us to him before lying sprawled out on the beautiful early August Molineux grass just outside the tiny players' tunnel. He signed all of our photographs and asked us kids our Christian names before autographing them all with a personal dedication. The groundsman asked us to move off the pitch and go to the shale perimeter which was a feature of Molineux in those days. Peter said to us, "Do as he says" but he joined us and finished signing all our pictures. Even as kids, we knew he could be unpredictable and a bit flash, but I never saw him refuse to sign an autograph for a youngster. And the signature was always properly done, 100 per cent legible, not a rapid squiggle that today's superstars give to admirers on the rare occasions they allow fans anywhere near them. On another occasion, Peter asked three or four of us to go on to the deserted old South Bank terrace and retrieve the footballs as he and a couple of apprentices had some shooting practice. We were delighted to involve ourselves, and he thanked us when the drill was completed. We left the ground chuffed to bits.'

In the summer of 1966 the nation's eyes turned towards the World Cup Finals, but there was only one Wolves player close to the action – Ron Flowers. Some Wolves reference books wrongly state that Flowers made the preliminary party of 40 for the Finals but not the final 22. That is wrong. Flowers was certainly in the squad and might easily have been at centre-half in the Final itself as a cold made Jackie Charlton a doubt on the eve of the match. Charlton recovered to figure in England's 4–2 extra-time win over West Germany and Flowers, who had made his debut for England in 1955, thus ended his international career with 49 caps.

There were no additions to the Wolves squad during the summer but Bobby Woodruff left the club, signing for Crystal Palace for £35,000. If Knowles thought that Woodruff's exit would mean his place was secure, he would soon be proved wrong. Ronnie Allen, whose good work was recognised by the board making him team manager, would soon be bringing in a new rival for the number-10 shirt.

After the drama of the World Cup Final on Saturday 30 July 1966, there was just a three-week gap before the football season got under way once more. There was time for Wolves to make a two-match pre-season trip to Switzerland, where their first match, in the Letzigiund Stadium, was against FC Zurich who had won both the League title and the national Cup. The home side were managed by Ladislao Kubala, a member of the Barcelona side who had humbled Wolves in the European Cup in 1960. Zurich ran out 3–1 winners, despite substitute Ken Knighton giving Wolves the lead in the 54th minute. Allen chose the game to try out a few moves and to encourage an early version of 'total football', with defenders often attacking and attackers sometimes defending. Knowles, Ernie Hunt and Mike Bailey all tested the home 'keeper with some smart shots, and Knowles received praise from the *Express & Star's* Phil Morgan for his 'preparatory work in midfield'. Goals from Leimgruber, Martinelli and Kunzli in the last half-hour gave Zurich victory.

In his match report, Morgan had listed Wolves in the traditional 2-3-5 formation, but it is interesting to note that for the match against Servette the team were in a 4-2-4 formation, the one which had proved so successful for Brazil in their 1958 World Cup triumph and for Walter Winterbottom's England side who did so well in the 1960–61 season. Allen used Graham Hawkins and Ron Flowers as centre-backs, with Mike Bailey and Hughie McIlmoyle as the two in midfield. McIlmoyle, however, did not look at ease in his linkman role and was replaced by Les Wilson at half-time. The match, which ended 1–1, began with temperatures in the 80s (Fahrenheit) and ended with the floodlights on. Mike Bailey was the star Wolves man, driving his side on despite the heat and managing three times to get clear through for one-on-ones with the 'keeper without finding the net. Knowles also failed to score when clean through, but Wolves deservedly took a 22nd-minute lead when Bailey's pass found Ernie Hunt, who lobbed the ball home via the crossbar. Servette, who had been runners-up to Zurich in both League and Cup, levelled from the penalty spot through Nemeth after Joe Wilson had handled on 38 minutes.

Just as they had done the season before, Wolves started their Second Division campaign with two defeats, the first coming at Molineux against Stan Cullis's Birmingham City. Cullis had signed two Chelsea forwards during the summer – former England centre-forward Barry Bridges and winger Bert Murray. Another Wolves legend, Billy Wright, was also in the news during the summer. His four-year reign as Arsenal boss had not been a success, in the eyes of the Highbury board, and he was sacked. Little did the board and fans know, but Wright had brought to Highbury many of the men who would win the double for the Gunners five years later. The close season also saw the Football League Cup receive a double boost. Only champions Liverpool and FA Cup-winners Everton declined to enter it, so there were a record 90 clubs in contention, including, for the first time, Wolves. The other shot in the arm for a tournament that had limped along since its introduction in 1960–61 was the decision to have the Final at Wembley. Previously, the Final had been played on a home and away basis. While Wolves had shunned it, neighbours Albion, Birmingham and Villa had not and each had won it.

The opening match against Blues saw the visitors win 2–1, thanks to two goals from debutant Murray. There was also a new face in the Wolves line up, manager Ronnie Allen giving a debut to 19-year-old John Farrington on the right wing. Farrington made a promising start, twice going close in the first 10 minutes. He fired his first chance wide, but Jim Herriot parried the second only for Knowles to fail to put home the rebound. It was an eventful debut for Farrington as his misdirected clearance led to Murray's first goal on 52 minutes, and his cross brought a scoring header from Hughie McIlmoyle 13 minutes from time to give Wolves hope. By that stage, however, Blues were two up thanks to Murray's goal in the 67th minute.

Changes were forced on Ronnie Allen for the trip to Ipswich a week later. Centre-half Ron Flowers was injured so David Woodfield earned a recall and on the morning of the game goalkeeper Dave MacLaren was taken ill, which meant Fred Davies had to be rushed by car from Wolverhampton. Knowles kept his place but was switched to his old spot at inside-left to partner Dave Wagstaffe, while Ernie Hunt was given the number-eight shirt. Wolves had scorned chances against Blues, and the story was the same at Portman Road. All the goals came in the first 20 minutes. Danny Hegan struck in the second and eighth, only for Hughie McIlmoyle to reduce the lead immediately by heading home a Wagstaffe centre. Hegan's first came despite appeals from Wolves that he had handled the ball, while his second was a stunning volley. Although Frank Brogan made it 3–1 on 20 minutes, Wolves, according to Phil Morgan in the *Express & Star*, had enough of the play to have turned the match. Morgan also said Knowles lacked his usual shooting accuracy.

After their poor start, things would soon improve, helped by the camaraderie which Ronnie Allen encouraged among the players. Dave Wagstaffe recalled that team spirit was fostered by Allen, and one of the things that the players enjoyed was an impromptu game of mini cricket. Said Waggy, 'I don't know where it came from, but a miniature cricket set appeared in the dressing room. The stumps were about 15ins high and the bat was about the same. There was a small rubber ball about the size of a squash ball. We made up our own game, the idea being that every time whoever was batting put bat to ball it was counted as a run. Sounds easy but with a pitch only 5m long and at least 15 fielders crowding round the bat you were lucky to last more than half a dozen balls.

'Peter, being a Yorkshireman, was not too bad at cricket but he would get bored just playing a defensive game and sometimes have a lash at the ball, making us all dive for cover as it ricocheted round the room off the walls. On at least a couple of occasions Peter managed to smash the ball straight through the frosted windows. Jack Dowen [one of the training staff] came dashing into the dressing room, having heard the sound of breaking glass. "Oh no!" he shouted disappointedly, knowing that he would have to spend the morning sitting there waiting for the glaziers to come and repair the window.'

Knowles may have respected Stan Cullis, the man who signed him, but he enjoyed training better when Allen took over. 'I liked training with the ball,' Knowles recalled, 'and when Ronnie became our manager he allowed me to express myself, especially in the big games. Manchester United was the game I always looked forward to. Best, Law, Charlton – to be able to match your skills with theirs was always a challenge to me, especially in front of a full house.'

For their third game of the season, against Cardiff at Ninian Park, Knowles formed a new right wing with Pat Buckley, who was preferred to John Farrington; however, for most of the match Wagstaffe played on the right and Buckley on the left. The team also had the inspirational Joe Wilson back, but the match seemed to be heading for a goalless draw until Knowles helped break the deadlock 15 minutes from the end. From the left wing he sent the ball way across field where Mike Bailey, who had had a storming game, headed it into the goalmouth where Hughie McIlmoyle eventually scored after some jostling for possession. Fred Davies then stopped Cardiff's attempt at a quick equaliser by tipping over the bar a header from George Andrews. Although Cardiff had done their best, often with some rough tactics, to curb the dangerous Wagstaffe, they could not stop the tricky winger fashioning two goals in the last five minutes. First he saw a typical pinpoint centre converted with a running header from McIlmoyle, then Waggy set off on a mazy run down the left before laying a goal on a plate for Buckley.

If Wolves fans thought their side had at last turned the corner, they were brought quickly down to earth when Bristol City came to Molineux and thoroughly deserved the 1–1 draw which brought them their first point of the season. The forward set-up of Cardiff was confirmed, but it was a punchless display by Wolves despite having the lion's share of possession. Knowles was the first home player to get a shot on target – after 34 minutes. Four minutes into the second half City took the lead through right-winger Roger Peters. His shot was deflected and hit one post, then the other, before finally going into the net. Knowles had the satisfaction of getting his first goal of the season when he equalised on 68 minutes, and one of Wolves' rare direct moves saw Wagstaffe put Ernie Hunt through for a shot which rebounded off goalkeeper Mike Gibson's legs.

A Rival

If Knowles, boosted by his goal against Bristol City, thought his season was about to take off, he got a rude awakening. Not only was he dropped, but his place was taken by a newcomer, brought to the club in dramatic circumstances. In the programme for the match at Molineux on Wednesday 7 September 1966, the name of David Burnside appeared in the Crystal Palace line up. Burnside duly played – not for the Londoners but for Wolves! Manager Ronnie Allen swooped to sign his former Palace teammate on the morning of the game. Allen and he had also played together at Albion, where the young Burnside had first caught national attention with his ball-juggling skills to entertain fans, and the TV audience, before kick-off and at half-time at big games. He had proved he was more than just a showbiz act, however, and served Albion and Southampton well before joining Palace. Burnside said after his signing, 'There was a time when I wanted to be a great individual player, but I have grown in experience since then and have learned that football is a team game.' Allen explained the move with, 'I think he is the man I need to do a particular job in the Wolves set-up.' So Knowles was suddenly out of favour, though the Palace game brought a recall for Terry Wharton on the right wing. Burnside crowned his debut by giving Wolves the lead, only for Steve Kember to equalise. In time, the rivalry for a first-team place between Knowles and Burnside would be reflected by the fans on the terraces. You were either a Knowles fan or a Burnside fan, it seemed, and there would often be sustained chants of one name quickly countered by the other. Thus you would hear 'Peter Knowles, Burnside, Peter Knowles, Burnside' echoing around Molineux.

The 1–1 draw with Palace meant Wolves had only four points from their opening five games, but the same line up were on duty for the visit three days later to Carlisle when Ernie Hunt scored twice in a 3–1 win. On Tuesday 13 September came confirmation Knowles was still out of favour when Wolves played their first-ever Football League Cup tie, beating Third Division Mansfield 2–1 at Molineux. The number-10 shirt was given to 19-year-old Bob Hatton. Wolves trailed to a Bill Curry goal which was wiped out by a Terry Wharton volley. Wharton thus became Wolves' first-ever scorer in the competition, contrary to at least one Wolves record book which wrongly gives that honour to Hatton. The debutant did score, but his goal was the winner. Knowles was not even on the bench when Blackburn Rovers visited Molineux four days later. Seventeen-year-old Ian Wallace, who had signed professional forms earlier in the week, was sub and came on for the injured Ernie Hunt five minutes from time. Hunt had scored twice early in the match. David Burnside, restored to the inside-left spot, and Terry Wharton completed a 4–0 victory on a brilliantly sunny afternoon. As for Wallace, that proved to be the only five minutes of Football League action in his career. He later went into non-League soccer.

While the goals were flowing in at Molineux, it was a bad day for Southampton goalkeeper Campbell Forsyth, who broke his leg in the match with Liverpool. That led to the Saints' quick search for an experienced replacement, and they turned to Dave MacLaren, who had lost the number-one spot at Molineux to Fred Davies. MacLaren went to The Dell for about £4,000, Wolves knowing that if anything happened to Davies, they had young Phil Parkes and Evan Williams waiting in the wings.

Wolves continued to do fine without Knowles, and the new-look forward line really went to town – or rather to City – when Cardiff were the midweek visitors. Wolves were two up after five minutes and ran out 7–1 winners, with Terry Wharton hitting three goals, including two penalties. Other goals came from Ernie Hunt, Bobby Thomson, Hughie McIlmoyle and Dave Wagstaffe. Ken Knighton was Wolves' unused sub, but Knowles's exile ended unexpectedly when a stomach muscle injury ruled Hunt out of the trip to Bolton. It looked a tough time to return to action, too, as Bolton were top of the table with 13 points from eight games, compared with fifth-placed Wolves' 10 from eight. However, Wolves rose to the occasion to earn a 0–0 draw, the stars of the display being Fred Davies and centre-half David Woodfield, the latter completely subduing Bolton's Welsh international centre-forward Wyn Davies. Hughie McIlmoyle and Burnside had also been doubtful but played despite carrying knocks. Burnside had to come off after nearly an hour, but McIlmoyle battled on and nearly silenced Burnden Park when his header to a Dave Wagstaffe centre looked a certain goal, only for 'keeper Eddie Hopkinson to palm the ball against a post. Just before that Knowles had headed home a Terry Wharton cross only to be ruled offside. It was nevertheless a useful return for Knowles, whom Phil Morgan described as an 'eager stand-in for Hunt.'

star of the future, Knowles is third from the left on the front row in this picture of the Wolves
〕uth team, who in 1962 reached the Final of the FA Youth Cup. David Woodfield is the man with
〕e ball at his feet. Coach Bill Shorthouse, who died in September 2008, is on the back row. Next
〕 him is full-back Bobby Thomson.

uch! Knowles is grounded during one of his early games for Wolves.

Youngster with his eye on the ball and the future – an early picture
Molineux.

Glory with the England Youth squad after winning the 196
Amsterdam tournament. Knowles (right) has his arm around
youthful Harry Redknapp, while skipper Howard Kendall holds the
trophy aloft as he is chaired by Alf Wood and Mick Wright. Also
the picture are John Hollins and (in front) David Sadler, while on the
left is Wilf McGuinness, part of the squad's management team.

The Wolves squad eagerly anticipating the 1964–65 season. Little did they know that ahead of them lay relegation and the end of Stan Cullis's reign as manager. Back row (left to right): John Kirkham, Chris Crowe, Dick Le Flem, Peter Broadbent, Fred Davies, Gerry Harris, David Woodfield, George Showell, Bobby Woodruff. Front row: Cullis, Fred Goodwin, Terry Wharton, Ron Flowers, Bobby Thomson, Ray Crawford, Peter Knowles, Joe Gardiner (trainer). On ground: Jimmy Melia and Ted Farmer.

All steamed up…enjoying a sauna with Knowles at Heath Town Baths are Pat Buckley, Terry Wharton, Dave Wagstaffe and Ron Flowers.

Posing in the all-gold strip which Wolves first wore for the replayed FA Cup-tie with Aston Villa in February 1965.

Back home with the Cup. Ronnie Allen holds the trophy won dramatically in the 1967 USA tournament. With Knowles are David Wagstaffe, Ernie Hunt (in hat), Terry Wharton and general manager Jack Howley.

Is this a record? The Wolves players hope so as they record a club song. Knowles is at the back next to Dave Wagstaffe, while in front are Joe Wilson and David Woodfield.

A thoroughly modern 1960s football idol – smartly-dressed Knowles with his beloved sports car.

nowles looks on as Wolves receive a pecial piece of memorabilia before ie FA Cup tie with Everton in ebruary 1967. John Addenbrooke fficially hands over the ball used vhen Wolves famously beat Everton i the 1893 Cup Final when .ddenbrooke's father was the club ecretary. Wolves chairman John reland holds the match ball likely to e used in the 1967 clash at Molineux which ended 1–1.

Having a break from a Cannock Chase training run, Knowles enjoys a welcome cup of tea. With him on the left is Fred Davies, while on the right are David Wagstaffe and John Holsgrove.

ime for a glass of Champagne in the Molineux boardroom after a 4–1 win over ury in April 1967 had clinched promotion. Vith Knowles are Phil Parkes, John iolsgrove and David Wagstaffe.

ubstitute Knowles looks on as Derek Dougan leads an attack on the Crystal Palace goal in the nal game of the 1966–7 season. Wolves lost 4–1 and so missed out on going up from the econd Division as champions.,

Left: A winning smile — Knowles at the banquet to celebrate Wolves' promotion to the First Division in 1967.

Showing the result of hi excursions...Knowles on Wolve successful 1967 USA tour.

Still smiling — Knowles can pose even when doing an action shot for the camera.

Three steps to a goal...Top: Derek Dougan fires in shot on goal against Burnley at Molineux in Septembe 1967. Centre: Burnley full-back Fred Smith clears o the line, but Knowles is lurking to put home the loos ball. Bottom: Knowles yells his delight as he makes th score 2–1 to Wolves who eventually won 3–2.

Chairman John Ireland presents Knowles with a benefit cheque to mark five years as a professional with the club in October 1967.

Shadowing England World Cup hero Geoff Hurst as Wolves take on West Ham.

The way it was…Knowles at the wheel of his sports car.

Pre-season picture with Terry Wharton, Alun Evans and manager Ronnie Allen.

The joy of a goal…scorer Knowles yells his delight.

Mr and Mrs Peter Knowles after their wedding in Wolverhampton on 4 July 1968.

A happy couple. Knowles carries his wife on the steps of the register office.

One of his best...Knowles scores with an overhead kick against Newcastle in November 1969. It was his second goal in a 5–0 win, the side's first game after the sacking of Ronnie Allen.

A family gathering before the Spurs-Wolves FA Cup tie at White Hart Lane in January 1969 as Jane Knowles talks to her footballing sons Peter and Cyril before the game. With her is younger son Richard.

With two girl fans after the 1968 Cup-tie at Tottenham and his younger brother Richard in the background.

In action at White Heart Lane in February 1969, as Spurs's recent signing Roger Morgan tries to dispossess Knowles during the 1–1 draw.

Beatles haircut – the 1960s football idol.

With the ball, and the football world, at his feet but Knowles would soon give it all up.

One of Knowles's last League appearances in action against Southampton at the Dell.

An ear-bashing for the ref. Knowles is clearly upset by a decision during the FA Cup tie against Tottenham at White Hart Lane in January 1969, but match official Norman Burtenshaw seems in no mood to hang around and listen.

News has broken that Knowles has become a Jehovah's Witness and may quit football, and he is greeted by a posse of reporters at Molineux, among them freelance Ron Warrilow (far right).

As he talks to the Press a paper carries the front-page story that Wolves fans hoped was untrue.

The cover of the programme for the League Cup clash between Wolves and Tottenham in September 1969 features the Knowles brothers, but Peter would play only one more high-profile match.

A last formal photo. Lining up for the pre-season team picture in August 1969.

Knowles arrives at Molineux for training after the news had broken that he was going to give up football after the game against Nottingham Forest in September 1969.

Long-serving *Express & Star* Wolves reporter Phil Morgan does his best to dissuade Knowles from turning his back on football.

Knowles's name appears in the a Wolves League line-up for the last time – in the programme for his final match, against Nottingham Forest at Molineux on 6 September 1969.

MLINEWS Match-day Magazine Volume 2 Number 5 1/-

'Club of the Year'
(See Pages 2, 12, 13)

Saturday,
September 6th, 1969
Kick-off. 3.0 pm

WOLVES 3
(Gold shirts, black shorts)
1—PHIL PARKES
2—LES WILSON
3—DEREK PARKIN
4—MIKE BAILEY
5—JOHN HOLSGROVE
6—FRANK MUNRO
7—JIM McCALLIOG
8—PETER KNOWLES
9—DEREK DOUGAN
10—HUGH CURRAN
11—DAVE WAGSTAFFE
Sub.—JOHN McALLE

NOTTINGHAM FOREST 3
(Red shirts, white shorts)
1—ALAN HILL
2—PETER HINDLEY
3—JOHN WINFIELD
4—BOB CHAPMAN
5—TERRY HENNESSEY
6—HENRY NEWTON
7—RONNIE REES
8—BARRY LYONS
9—DAVE HILLEY
10—JOHN BARNWELL
11—IAN MOORE
Sub.—BILL O'KANE

Referee: R. Darlington (Runcorn, Cheshire).
Linesmen: Red Flag—P. T. Beaumont (Fish-gate).
Yellow flag—J. R. Davies (Gower, Glam.)

WOLVERHAMPTON WANDERERS FOOTBALL CLUB

Knowles (extreme left) may have been in his last days at Molineux, but he was there to welcome a newcomer, full-back Bernard Shaw from Sheffield United, who is greeted by Sammy Chung, Bill McGarry's second in command.

The posters which greeted Knowles outside Molineux as he arrived for his final game — against Nottingham Forest on 6 September 1969.

Before the kick-off against Forest Knowles has time to give fans a wave before signing a few autographs.

He may be turning his back o[n] football, but Knowles cann[ot] hide his joy as he celebrate[s] Derek Dougan's goal again[st] Forest.

It's all over. Knowles races to the dressing room a[t] the end of the game against Nottingham Forest.

With *Express & Star* sports writer John Dee alongside, Knowles walks around the Molineux pitch so he can leave via the Molineux Street stand rather than the main entrance after his final match.

Clutching a farewell present, a Bible, Knowles leaves Molineux after his final game in September 1969 as a girl fan wipes away a tear.

Follow my leader, coaching youngsters in a Wolverhampton Council scheme not long after giving up football.

What a difference a few years can make: Knowles in his early years at Molineux...

...and Knowles at the height of his career, making sure he looks good for the front cover of a football magazine.

Some 38 years after he called a halt to his playing days, Knowles is still in demand to sign for autograph hunters. With him for the 2007 launch of a book by Wolves goalkeeping legend Bert Williams, are (left) popular comedian and Wolves fan supreme Ian 'Sludge' Lees and 1950s centre-forward Roy Swinbourne.

He may be in his 60s and the hair may be grey, but he retains the looks that once set female pulses racing.

The verdict on Knowles was not so good from the *Express & Star's* Morgan when next Wolves struggled to beat Charlton. He and David Burnside were below their usual standard, said Morgan, which made centre-forward Hughie McIlmoyle and wingers Terry Wharton and Dave Wagstaffe have to work that little bit harder. Wolves still created plenty of chances but were denied by some inspired goalkeeping from Charlie Wright. An unfortunate error by Charlton's young full-back Billy Bonds, when he slipped trying to clear, let in McIlmoyle to win the game on 61 minutes. Bonds, then 20, later moved to West Ham where he became a cult figure and played in well over 650 League games. There was an even younger man in the Londoners' line up, however, right-half Peter Reeves, who was 17. Knowles showed his petulance once more and was booked by referee Wallace, as was Charlton's rugged former Leicester centre-half John King. The referee also managed to get himself knocked out when he collided with a player and needed some on-field attention.

If Knowles's plan was still to move to London, or a big club elsewhere, he had a chance to show the London football writers what he could do when Wolves took on First Division Fulham in the third round of the League Cup at Craven Cottage. Alas, Knowles blew his chance to impress, but he was not alone in having a bad night. Wolves lost the game 5–0 as Fulham's former England men Bobby Robson and Johnny Haynes called the tune. Phil Morgan pulled no punches in his *Express & Star* report: 'Fulham had a plan and made it work, to the confusion of Wolves, who looked to have none; Fulham had mobility, on and off the ball, but Wolves had a leaden-footed look; Fulham had lots of lively ideas and an ability to indulge in some fancy passing which, when Wolves tried to copy it, merely emphasised their shortcomings.' The Londoners did not progress past the fourth round. Blackpool, destined to finish bottom of the First Division, beat them 4–2 at Bloomfield Road.

Heads had to roll after such a dismal display, and Knowles was among them. Graham Hawkins, who had enjoyed a good run at left-half, made way for John Holsgrove. David Burnside was also dropped, but Ronnie Allen stressed it was because he felt the former Palace man was not fully fit. The surprise change was at left-back, where Bobby Thomson was dropped in favour of transfer-listed Ken Knighton. Thomson had just been named as skipper of England Under-23s for the game against Wales Under-23s at Molineux the following week. So when Wolves beat Portsmouth Knowles had to play in the reserves at Newcastle, along with Thomson and another England international Ron Flowers, getting a try-out after his lengthy injury. Knowles played at centre-forward for the reserves who earned a 2–2 draw. Fit-again Ernie Hunt took over from Knowles, while Bob Hatton was given his League debut against Pompey and made the most of it with a goal after just 30 seconds to set Wolves up for a 3–1 win.

While Knowles was a long way off getting an international call, he must have enjoyed seeing his brother Cyril, the Spurs left-back, score in England's 8–0 defeat of Wales in the Under-23 clash at Molineux. One of Wolves' Fulham tormentors, Allan Clarke, scored four times, other goals coming from Chelsea wing-half John Hollins (two) and Burnley winger Ralph Coates, who was in sparkling form.

Nine League games without defeat had put Wolves among the promotion contenders but their push came to a halt at Boothferry Park, three days after the Under-23 game, when Hull beat them 3–1. The home goals all came before half-time, before Mike Bailey grabbed a late consolation, his first goal for Wolves. That win put Hull top of the table as the night before Bolton had lost 2–1 at Bury. The Bolton scorer was Wyn Davies in what proved his final game for the Burnden Park club before being bought by Newcastle for £80,000. Before Wolves could pick up the pieces there was speculation that Villa were interested in signing Ron Flowers; however, the rumour was quickly denied by both camps. Flowers was back in the first team a week after the Hull setback and Bobby Thomson and David Burnside also got recalls as Plymouth were beaten 2–1. This was followed by Wolves' first-ever game against Northampton, and they won it 4–0 at the County Ground, Ernie Hunt collecting a hat-trick. Two goals from Hughie McIlmoyle then saw off Millwall 2–0 at Molineux before a 2–2 draw at Rotherham on Saturday 12 November 1966 was enough to put Ronnie Allen's men on top of the table. They led on goal average, but it could have been by a point had not former Molineux man John Galley equalised 11 minutes from time. Wolves, Ipswich and Crystal Palace each had 22 points at that stage.

No doubt this was a period when Knowles renewed his transfer requests. He was restless, desperate not just for a taste of first-team action but for a taste of it with a top club in the First Division. He was given the sub's shirt for the visit of Preston but was not used as the Lancashire side were beaten 3–2, only thanks to a last-minute penalty from Terry Wharton. Wolves had let slip a 2–0 half-time lead before a linesman signalled that North End skipper Nobby Lawton had handled to give the home side a reprieve. The match saw a competent debut for 19-year-old goalkeeper Phil Parkes, deputising for the injured Fred Davies. Knowles was not among the 12 players who went to Bury the following week and lost 2–1, but he was given the number-12 shirt again for the visit to Molineux of promotion rivals Coventry on the first day of December. Once again, Knowles failed to get into the action as the Sky Blues triumphed 3–1. It was a vital win for Coventry, who thus trailed Wolves by only a point.

After successive defeats it was time for change and back came Knowles but not in one of the inside spots. For the visit to Norwich City he was given the number-nine shirt that had been Hughie McIlmoyle's exclusive property in the previous 19 League games. Graham Hawkins was given the number-two shirt instead of Joe Wilson but operated at left-half with Ron Flowers taking on the full-back role and doing so to great effect. Wolves won 2–1, despite going a goal down in 90 seconds. Gordon Bolland had struck first, but Knowles silenced the home fans at Carrow Road with an equaliser on 15 minutes. He hit a vicious cross-shot that went in off goalkeeper Kevin Keelan's knees. The winner 12 minutes from the end was made by Flowers, who made a right-wing overlap and exchanged passes with Terry Wharton before putting over a centre which Wagstaffe headed home. The winger reckoned it was the first time he had ever scored with a header in first-team football. *Express & Star* man Phil Morgan described Knowles as a 'busy worker' and said he had been unlucky with two more efforts, despite not getting much support from his inside-forwards until the latter part of the match. The Canaries included 23-year-old Scot Hugh Curran in their attack. Within a couple of seasons he would be a Wolves player.

Knowles had done enough to keep his place and Wolves named the same side for the game with Birmingham at St Andrew's, where they had not been beaten since 1939. Wolves fans must have thought their wonderful record there would continue when they took the lead after just 57 seconds and were two up in the 35th minute. Dave Wagstaffe scored Wolves' first-minute goal, and Mike Bailey drove in their second but Blues, fired by former Wolves striker Bobby Thomson, playing at right-half, scored three goals in the final 22 minutes to run out 3–2 winners. Barry Bridges raced on to a Geoff Vowden through pass to begin the revival on 68 minutes, and nine minutes later Mike Bullock fired home the equaliser. Knowles went down in the penalty area but Wolves were refused a penalty, and then Ernie Hunt had a fine shot blocked by goalkeeper Jim Herriot. Four minutes from time, a Bridges cross from the left went right across goal to Vowden, who fired the ball home via the inside of a post. David Burnside was limping for much of the game, but Wolves had no excuse for failing to give plenty of the ball to Wagstaffe in the second half, who had looked to be a real source of danger to the home defence. Coventry were held 2–2 at Hull but drew level with third-placed Wolves on 26 points from 21 games. Ipswich led the table on goal average from Carlisle, both having 27 points from 22 matches..

Both Knowles and Burnside were dropped for the Christmas double header with Derby which saw Wolves go back to the top of the table. Hughie McIlmoyle was restored to the centre-forward role, and Bob Hatton given another chance as his strike partner. The reshuffle certainly worked as, on Saturday 24 December 1966, Wolves won 5–3 at Molineux despite going behind to an Alan Durban goal in 40 seconds. The home side roared back to lead 3–1 through McIlmoyle, Terry Wharton (penalty) and Hatton, only for County to make it 3–3 by half-time thanks to Durban and a John Richardson penalty. Wharton restored the lead soon after half-time, and Hatton collected his second 13 minutes from the end.

The return, two days later, was far less frenetic as Wolves strolled home 3–0 thanks to goals from McIlmoyle, Hatton and Wharton. Not surprisingly, the same forward line were named for the visit of Ipswich on the last day of 1966; however, a change had to be made in defence as Graham Hawkins had been taken off with damaged ligaments at Derby. John Holsgrove had substituted for him, but a new face now came into his side to make up for Hawkins's absence. Ron Flowers's full-back career was shelved, and he moved back to left-half enabling Gerry Taylor, a 19-year-old from Hull, to make his debut at right-back. Alas, a crowd of 28,425, the best of the season so far at Molineux, saw Wolves held 0–0 with Hatton wasting a hat-trick of good openings. Nevertheless, he kept his place for the trip to Ashton Gate on Saturday 7 January 1967, where Bristol City included Wolves old boy Chris Crowe, newly signed from Nottingham Forest. It was another former Forest man, John Quigley, who scored the game's only goal on 62 minutes.

Fans like John Lalley recall how Knowles appeared frustrated at seeing Ronnie Allen so often give preference to David Burnside. Lalley's view that Knowles should have been in the side was confirmed in that match at Ashton Gate. He remembers, 'I was on the terraces at Bristol City in the days before strict segregation of opposing fans, and a couple of mouthy Bristol fans turned to me and belligerently demanded to know, "Why isn't Peter Knowles playing?" They, even as opposition fans, admired his individuality, and the rebel streak he loved to radiate.'

Hatton again missed some good chances, as did McIlmoyle, so it was no surprise when Knowles got a recall for the home game against Carlisle a week later. It was another frustrating result as Wolves were held 1–1, Knowles going close to marking his return with a goal only to see a shot thud against the bar. Dave Wagstaffe finally created the opening that enabled Ernie Hunt to put Wolves ahead on 61 minutes. Wolves were made to pay for their misses when winger George McVitie fired home a screamer to give Carlisle a share of the spoils six minutes from the end. Hughie McIlmoyle chose to wander rather than stay in the middle, and Hunt and Knowles found themselves without a target man. When McIlmoyle did make an orthodox run through the middle he ended it by blazing the ball high into the crowd.

While Wolves were drawing with Carlisle, Coventry were beating Norwich at home to go two points clear at the top. McIlmoyle was dropped for the trip to Blackburn, and Bob Hatton was given a chance at centre-forward; however, the spotlight fell not upon Hatton or Knowles but on left-winger Dave Wagstaffe. As a true matchwinner with the ability to beat players at will and put over tantalising crosses, Waggy had become a marked man. Most of the time he kept his head when some questionable tactics were used to try to halt him, but at Ewood Park he finally lost his composure. Wagstaffe looked on his game in the first half when Mike Bailey had a shot deflected against the post while Knowles lifted a shot just over the bar; however, Wagstaffe was getting quite a buffeting from home right-back Mike Ferguson, a former winger. He was reprimanded by Barnsley referee Keith Styles for his first tackle on Wagstaffe, catching him with a flailing arm, and his next put the Wolves winger over the touchline, where he stayed for three minutes as he received treatment. Wagstaffe managed to stay cool as the rough stuff continued, but when he did retaliate in the 42nd minute up trotted referee Styles, book in hand. The result was Wagstaffe's dismissal, but it was learned afterwards he had been sent off because he steadfastly refused to give the referee his name. The 10 men rose to the occasion as the heavy Lancashire rain reduced the pitch to a mud heap. They withstood all Blackburn could throw at them with David Woodfield the kingpin of a rugged defence.

The aftermath of Wagstaffe's sending off saw Wolves chairman John Ireland condemn the treatment being handed out to the winger week-in, week-out. While he did not condone the winger's refusal to give his name to the referee, leaving the official with no option, Ireland took the opportunity to offer some mitigation. 'I think he is entitled to expect some protection from the official against some of the treatment he is getting from opposing players,' said Ireland. 'Provocation may not be an excuse – in this game he was blatantly kicked, tripped and hit in the face – but he was certainly provoked. This "Stop Wagstaffe by any means" is not fair to the player, and I feel both he and the club are entitled to more protection from referees than we have been getting. If this sort of thing continues I am afraid one of these days Wagstaffe may be seriously hurt.' The chairman revealed that at the end of the game he had taken Wagstaffe to the referee to apologise. The upshot of the incident came at Derby, when an FA inquiry did not ban Wagstaffe but severely censured him and fined him £25.

Wolves kept the same line up when League action was put on hold for a week in favour of the FA Cup. Their trip to Third Division Oldham proved to be one of those occasions that Wolves diehards love to recall. Above all it provided vindication for those of us who cannot understand why some fans insist on leaving a game a few minutes before the final whistle. This one at Boundary Park showed why it pays never to depart early. Trailing 2–0 with two minutes to go, Wolves snatched a draw thanks to goals from two unlikely scorers. Mike Bailey powered through to hit home a left-foot shot on 88 minutes, and then a shot from another defender, John Holsgrove, was turned for a corner in the last few seconds. The flag-kick brought the equaliser, the ball coming out to left-back Bobby Thomson who hit it instinctively and saw his shot fly into the net via the underside of the crossbar. It was quite a finish, and it had been quite a start for former Wolves man Ken Knighton, who had joined the Lancashire club in November. He collided with teammate Reg Blore in the opening seconds and eventually had to be replaced on 17 minutes. Two minutes after that former Stoke winger Keith Bebbington put Oldham ahead, and it looked all over when he struck again 13 minutes from time. Then came the face-saving goals which, though welcome, could not mask an off-key Wolves display. Phil Morgan wrote in the *Express & Star*, 'Good work by Dave Wagstaffe and Terry Wharton did not get the response it deserved from the three inside-men, of whom only Peter Knowles tended to look the part with any promise of authority.' The match was watched by a crowd of nearly 25,000 which highlights the magic the Cup still had in those days. Oldham's average League gate for the season was just under 10,000.

More evidence of the FA Cup's pulling power came four days later, Wednesday 1 February 1967, when the replay attracted nearly 40,000 to Molineux where Wolves made the most of their reprieve by winning 4–1. This was one of those occasions when Knowles tried some of his fancy stuff. He did not do so until the match was sewn up but still earned a rebuke from Phil Morgan. The reporter described Knowles's 'one or two juggling efforts' as 'completely pointless' but obviously felt he had otherwise had a good match – 'Not that Knowles did not play his part when it was urgently necessary. He did all he had to do busily and once pulled off a splendid penalty-area tackle to save a most awkward situation.' Morgan also praised the half-back line of Mike Bailey, David Woodfield and John Holsgrove and noted that goalkeeper Fred Davies was back to his dominant best. It took Wolves 25 minutes to get in front, and the goal by Ernie Hunt was greeted almost in silence as most thought he was offside when he turned a Bailey pass around Oldham 'keeper David Best. However, to the surprise of everyone, referee Peter Rhodes signalled a goal. Five minutes later the cheers were spontaneous as Woodfield rose to power home a header from Terry Wharton's corner. A defensive mix-up nine minutes into the second half let in Bebbington to put Oldham back in contention only for Wharton to restore the two-goal lead within five minutes with a left-foot drive. Hughie McIlmoyle, whose header to a Bailey free-kick early in the game had brought a spectacular save from Best, sealed the win 20 minutes from time when he volleyed the ball home from a headed Bailey pass. This would prove to be McIlmoyle's last goal for the club.

Wolves knew victory over Oldham would bring them a money-spinning home tie with Cup holders Everton, but more important was to keep the promotion push on track. They did so in fine style in a 5–2 home win over Bolton. Knowles again played a key role, his passes enabling Bob Hatton, given his chance in the number-nine shirt, to score two goals. Brian Bromley had silenced the home fans with a first-minute goal, but Ernie Hunt wiped it out on 10 minutes. Hunt had been one of several injury doubts and had to play with his right thigh strapped. It did not seem to affect his agility, however, as he took the ball with his back to goal and turned it wide of Eddie Hopkinson. Hatton's first on the half hour made it 2–1, but it was not until 20 minutes from time that Hunt's header made it 3–1. Bromley struck again within four minutes only for Hatton to widen the gap once more on 79 minutes and Dave Wagstaffe to complete the win.

It was in this game that Knowles's outrageous showmanship was seen when he decided to sit down on the ball to rub salt into the wounds of the beaten visitors. It might have had the home crowd roaring with laughter at the sheer cheek of it, but it was guaranteed to annoy the opposition. Franny Lee certainly boiled over and aimed a kick at Knowles. That incident, sparked by Knowles's showboating, would have repercussions when Lee's talent began to blossom and made him a target for a Wolves transfer bid.

Knowles's good form continued at The Valley where Charlton were beaten 3–1 despite taking a 17th-minute lead through their recent signing from Grimsby, Matt Tees. Knowles completed the revival with the final goal, 12 minutes from time, when he diverted a lob into the goalmouth over goalkeeper Charlie Wright's hands. He had earlier been denied a spectacular goal from an Ernie Hunt pass – Knowles fired home a screamer, but Bob Hatton was in an offside position. Hatton had in the 27th minute cancelled out Tees's goal, but the goal of the game came on 61 minutes from centre-half Dave Woodfield. From a Dave Wagstaffe corner, he headed the ball forward but not powerfully enough to reach goal. However, he was first to the ball as it dropped to volley it into the net.

The visit of Everton to Molineux for the FA Cup fourth-round clash gave Knowles what he relished – the chance to parade his skills against one of the country's top sides in front of a packed house and in the spotlight of the national media. He loved such opportunities and seemed to be making the most of this one until he had to go off with a knee injury in the 50th minute. Phil Morgan wrote of Knowles in the *Express & Star*, 'He had obviously chosen this day to prove how good he can be in top company and was succeeding up to the time he got into a sandwich and received his injury. He stayed long enough to make one clearance off the goalline and then gave way to Hugh McIlmoyle. But he had done really splendidly and played a big part in helping Wolves out of their initial nervousness to a position in which it was they and not the holders who were the more menacing.' Knowles made a point of bringing potential matchwinner Dave Wagstaffe into the action, and it was Waggy who paved the way to Wolves taking the lead. He beat Tommy Wright and Colin Harvey before putting over a centre which Bob Hatton headed against a post. Terry Wharton was on the spot to score from the rebound with 29 minutes gone. Everton goalkeeper Gordon West, a future England international, then kept Wolves at bay, keeping out goalbound efforts from Ernie Hunt, Mike Bailey and Hatton. Yet one goal looked like proving enough until a controversial incident 12 minutes from time. World Cup hero Alan Ball was making a swerving run across the penalty area when he made the slightest of contacts with Dave Woodfield. The England man made the most of it, a 'skill' at which he was adept, and went sprawling. Referee George McCabe said 'yes' to the penalty appeals, and Ball brushed himself down to score from the spot. So it ended 1–1 and McIlmoyle's 40 minutes would prove to be his last of first-team action. The attendance of 53,439 brought receipts £17,130 19s 6d which was then a club record.

Knowles had the chance to play on the big stage he relished when three days later over 60,000 were at Goodison Park for the replay. He was much in evidence, even though the Merseyside giants won 3–1. He had a shot blocked in an opening assault on the home goal, as did Terry Wharton, while a volley from David Woodfield was held just under the bar by Everton's first-game hero Gordon West. That save led almost directly to the first goal on 11 minutes. West's clearance found Alex Young who fed Jimmy Husband for a shot from 25 yards out which caught Fred Davies by surprise. Soon afterwards, Knowles might have equalised but West dived to turn his volley for a corner. Another costly error saw Everton go two up on 35 minutes. Davies threw the ball out to Gerry Taylor, but he lost it to Colin Harvey. He found Derek Temple who scored from the edge of the penalty area. Six minutes later Wharton's volley brought Wolves back into the game, but five minutes into the second half Husband struck again. That finished matters, and even though Knowles continued to feature prominently with some neat touches and skipper Mike Bailey kept driving his men forward, Wolves could not reduce the arrears. The way was now clear, as is traditionally said in such circumstances, to concentrate on the League.

At this stage of his career, Knowles was still prone to let the desire to 'showboat' get in the way of his continued progress, a fact well-respected writer Alan Hoby highlighted in a feature article on Wolves in the *Sunday Express*. Wrote Hoby, 'Another Wolves sparkler when he cuts out the occasional ridiculous antic is inside-forward Peter Knowles.' Hoby put this to manager Ronnie Allen whose response was, 'It's only youthful exuberance. Peter is a bit of an exhibitionist, but he is also a born footballer.'

Bob Hatton had not got much change out of Everton's England centre-half Brian Labone and he and Fred Davies were dropped for the visit to Portsmouth on Saturday 25 February. Phil Parkes was given another chance in goal but the surprise choice for the number-nine shirt was David Burnside. Clearly, Hugh McIlmoyle, so recently a crowd favourite, no longer figured in Ronnie Allen's plans. He would be sold to Bristol City the following week. Knowles was a scorer at Fratton Park where an incident-packed game saw Wolves come from 2–0 down to win 3–2, with three goals in the final 20 minutes. Inspiration for the fightback was Mike Bailey, who took Dave Wagstaffe's through pass to reduce the arrears on 71 minutes. Portsmouth had been given a flying start with two goals from right-winger Trevor Portwood (15 and 27 minutes). After his goal, Bailey set up the equaliser eight minutes later with a pass that Knowles headed past goalkeeper John Milkins. Eight minutes from time Milkins made a painful exit. He and David Woodfield went up for the ball and with both still grounded, Wagstaffe's centre was headed into an empty net by Ernie Hunt. Milkins had broken his arm, and his place in goal was taken by Ron Tindall, a one time Chelsea forward converted to a defender. Tindall made the most of his emergency role with a flying save to deny Knowles a second goal. BBC *Match of the Day* cameras were there that day and, without today's sophisticated technology, missed the winning goal. Their camera was too busy focusing on the grounded Milkins!

The camera did, however, capture that Knowles gesture which helped cement his place in Wolves folklore. After his goal he deliberately belted the ball high out of the ground, not exactly a difficult job at Fratton Park. The ball was not returned, and the story goes that Pompey later sent Knowles a bill for replacing it. The ebullient forward was clearly not thinking straight amid all the excitement, and when the third goal went in he dashed into the net to retrieve the ball, which is what teams usually do when they are still trailing and want to ensure a quick restart. As well as collecting the ball he did a quick piece of juggling with it on his head as he trotted through the ranks of despondent Pompey defenders.

Life-long Wolves fan Clive Corbett well remembers the sitting-on-the-ball incident against Bolton and the booting of the ball out of the ground at Portsmouth. 'It was outrageous things like this that so endeared Peter to me.' he says. 'I was brought up in a loving home but one where I was taught respect and restraint, so to see such behaviour as a 10-year-old secretly thrilled me since I knew that I would never have the guts to do it myself.'

The antics at Fratton Park were typical of Knowles at that time, and he was clearly enjoying a run of good form, but it came to an abrupt halt when relegation-candidates Northampton came to Molineux a week later and made Wolves struggle for their 1–0 win. Their tough-tackling Scottish half-backs John Macken and John Kurila kept Knowles and Ernie Hunt in check. Fortunately for Wolves, the defence were at their best and 19 minutes from time Dave Wagstaffe settled the issue, firing home a Terry Wharton centre via the underside of the bar. The win kept Wolves in second place and a week later, when Wolves were without a game, bottom-placed Northampton did them a favour by holding table-topping Coventry 0–0. So Wolves trailed the Sky Blues by three points but had a game in hand.

Bob Hatton, with Hugh McIlmoyle departed, may have been forgiven for thinking that his recall against Northampton indicated the centre-forward spot was up for grabs. If that was the case he soon received a reality check as Molineux was about to see the arrival of a legend. Much-travelled Derek Dougan was signed from Leicester City for £50,000 which equalled the club-record fee paid for Jimmy Melia. The Doog, who had hit 16 goals in 31 League games for Leicester that season, was 29 and had proved a colourful character during his years with Distillery, Portsmouth, Blackburn, Villa and Peterborough. His natural football skills were never in doubt, however, and if the signing by Ronnie Allen was a gamble it proved to be one that paid off handsomely. At Molineux, Dougan found his spiritual football home and showed the most consistent form of his career.

Stateside Jaunt

If the spotlight was on the lanky new number-nine at Home Park, Plymouth, on Saturday 18 March 1967, it was Knowles who stole the show by hitting the only goal of a game dominated by a high wind which made good football nigh impossible. Knowles's strike came on 55 minutes when Pat Dunne, goalkeeper in Manchester United's Championship side of 1964–65, could only palm into the air a Terry Wharton hot shot. The inside-left was on the spot to nod the ball into the net. On other occasions the wind would play tricks with the ball so that sometimes it soared in an arc and on other occasions it dropped abruptly or was blown off course. Young Phil Parkes again shone in goal and good news for Wolves came after the match – leaders Coventry had been held 1–1 at home by Bolton and so the gap at the top was down to two points.

Knowles was on target again when Wolves met Hull at Molineux a week later, but there was no stealing the limelight from Dougan this time. The Irishman made a memorable home debut, hitting a hat-trick in Wolves' 4–0 win. The Easter weekend and Doog's bow meant the gate was over 5,000 more than the previous Molineux match, and the extra fans must have been impressed with what they saw. Dougan's first goal on 37 minutes came after goalkeeper Ian McKechnie had failed to hold on to a Bobby Thomson shot. On the hour Dougan glided the ball home to complete a Mike Bailey-Terry Wharton move; however, his third topped both those efforts and is a goal that Wolves fans who saw it still talk about today. It began when Wagstaffe turned up on the right wing. He beat one defender before centring to the far side of the six-yard box where Wharton headed the ball back across goal. The ball was dropping behind Dougan, but the centre-forward deliberately flicked it up over his head with his left foot and, with the same foot, volleyed the ball home when it dropped in front of him. One had expected before the game that the Irishman might eventually establish a special rapport with the Molineux fans – little could one predict that the love affair would have begun so quickly. Clearly, Doog was the sort of larger-than-life character to whom Knowles would warm. The *Express & Star's* Phil Morgan confirmed in his match report that Dougan 'brought the best out of his fellow forwards and seemed particularly to inspire Peter Knowles.' Knowles's goal was a header six minutes from time.

While the abiding memory of that game is Dougan's hat-trick, a little Knowles cameo also stuck with Clive Corbett and no doubt many other Molineux regulars. 'Peter's celebratory swing on the North Bank crossbar after Doog's second goal was a great moment,' recalled Corbett. There was an almost child-like enthusiasm about Knowles and that is why youngsters of Corbett's age warmed to him.

Coventry, by winning 1–0 at Blackburn, stretched their unbeaten League run to 14 games but they did not have a match on Easter Monday, 27 March 1967. So Wolves would play the game in hand they had on the Sky Blues when they visited Huddersfield for the first of a traditional home-and-away Bank Holiday duel. One goal was enough to give Wolves victory at a sunny but blustery Leeds Road and take them back to the top of the table on goal average. Knowles figured in the move which enabled Terry Wharton to score on seven minutes but also got himself booked. The goal came when Knowles and Mike Bailey took the ball down the right wing. Knowles found Derek Dougan, who flicked the ball on to Dave Wagstaffe. He cut in, then rolled the ball to Terry Wharton to flick home. Wagstaffe was one of several players to be booked by referee Kevin Howley and Knowles – typically – collected his caution for thumping the dead ball into the crowd. Wolves had to play without the injured Ernie Hunt, and his right-wing partner Wharton limped off on the hour. Huddersfield, who lost centre-half John Coddington with a broken jaw on 40 minutes, were parading a couple of highly promising young full-backs. One of them, Derek Parkin, would soon join Wolves and go on to set a club record number of appearances, while the other, Chris Cattlin, would join Coventry. Former Manchester United man Jimmy Nicholson and one-time Birmingham and England winger Mike Hellawell were the home men booked.

The stage was thus set for the return meeting the following night in front of the biggest Molineux League gate of the season, 40,929, and Knowles took centre stage to score the game's only goal to maintain his side's position at the top. Knowles had been in the limelight even before the game as a knock at Huddersfield threatened to keep him out and allow promising teenager Alun Evans a first-team debut. Terry Wharton and Ernie Hunt were already sidelined, so Knowles's presence was needed. He recovered in time for the match, however, and was always in the thick of the action, missing several chances, most of them made by in-form Derek Dougan. Knowles got the ball into the net on 19 minutes but was adjudged to have given a Huddersfield defender a nudge. Dave Wagstaffe was a constant menace on the left with the sort of old-style wing display which helped win him a special place in the fans' affections. Yet the goal owed nothing much to subtlety. A big kick from goalkeeper Phil Parkes on 44 minutes was headed on by Dougan and left Knowles in the clear to run on and beat goalkeeper John Oldfield. Knowles could easily have collected a hat-trick, but it was not to be. With Coventry winning 2–0 at home to Northampton both they and Wolves were on 49 points. Significantly, third-placed Blackburn were six points adrift. All three had played 35 games.

The spotlight fell on Derek Dougan on Saturday 1 April 1967 when his last-gasp goal earned Wolves a draw against Millwall at the so-often hostile Den. As his teammates rushed to congratulate Doog a fan ran onto the pitch as if to join in the celebrations. In fact, his intent was far from friendly, and he aimed a kick at the centre-forward before being restrained. A few days later the 20-year-old fan appeared before magistrates at Greenwich and was fined £5 after admitting using insulting behaviour. The lad, Albert Yates, told the court, 'I am sorry for what happened. I'm afraid I got too enthusiastic.' Magistrate Mr Alan Stevenson told him, 'This is not the work of a sportsman. It never used to happen in the old days.'

The match had seen Phil Parkes several times deny veteran striker Len Julians. The former Arsenal and Nottingham Forest man finally beat him on 57 minutes. It was the first time Wolves had conceded a goal in over 500 minutes but their defence, with David Woodfield and John Holsgrove always in the thick of the action, ensured there were no more. Knowles, switched to inside-right to partner John Farrington, had a subdued match and was injured with 15 minutes left. His departure came just after Dave Wagstaffe had missed a great chance to put Wolves level. The winger was brought down by full-back John Gilchrist and, with regular spot-kick expert Terry Wharton not playing, volunteered to take the resultant penalty. His kick was saved by Lawrie Leslie, the former Scottish international 'keeper. Leslie was at fault in the final minute when a raid by Mike Bailey ended with Bryan Snowdon trying to get the ball back to the 'keeper. Leslie could not hold on to the ball, and Dougan was on the spot to earn the vital point. It was enough to keep Wolves top as Coventry were held at home 2–2 by Derby. If the attack on Dougan bordered on the comical, the after-match scenes were anything but. Several scuffles were reported with one Wolves fan needing hospital treatment after being set upon by Millwall supporters.

With Ernie Hunt fit once more, Knowles was relegated to substitute as Wolves beat Rotherham 2–0 on Saturday 8 April 1967, a match played in the evening as the Grand National had been televised during the afternoon. It was a remarkable race in that a host of horses fell to leave outsider Foinavon clear to grab an unlikely win. There was no stumble by Wolves, however, and Hunt struck after only 30 seconds when Derek Dougan back-headed a Mike Bailey long throw and then Dougan made it two on 10 minutes, heading home a Dave Wagstaffe free-kick. With Coventry held at Crystal Palace – their fourth draw in six games – Wolves moved a point clear.

Knowles's absence from the side was brief. Right-winger Terry Wharton was not 100 per cent fit for the trip to Preston the following Saturday, so Knowles was recalled to wear the number-seven shirt. A win would virtually clinch promotion if Blackburn lost at Plymouth. It took just two minutes for Wolves to give their large contingent of followers something to cheer about at Deepdale. Mike Bailey set David Burnside up to slide a pass through for Ernie Hunt, who raced clear, drew goalkeeper Alan Kelly and then slotted the ball home. Both Knowles and Derek Dougan went close as Wolves stayed on top until three minutes before half-time when Hunt struck again. The goal came from a corner by Knowles. David Woodfield headed the ball forward, and Hunt scored with an overhead kick. It could have been three a minute later, but Bailey's volley hit the bar. That kept Preston in the match, and they set nerves jangling when Ernie Hannigan pulled a goal back 11 minutes after the break.

Blackburn crashed spectacularly, 4–0 at Plymouth, so, to all intents and purposes, Wolves were back in the First Division. To equal Wolves' 54-point total, Blackburn and Ipswich would have to win their last four games and Wolves lose their final four. Even in that unlikely event it would still need something spectacular as the goal averages were: Wolves 2.00, Ipswich 1.34 and Blackburn 1.16. Not that Wolves' revival made much impact nationally, for on the same day hundreds of Scottish fans were jigging across the Wembley turf after their country had become the first side to beat England since the World Cup triumph the previous year.

Ipswich's hopes of catching Wolves ended in midweek when they lost at home 2–0 to arch rivals Norwich, so all was set for a party atmosphere when Bury visited Molineux on Saturday 22 April. With Terry Wharton fully fit, Knowles's role in the proceedings was limited to the last half hour. He was named as substitute and came on when full-back Gerry Taylor was injured. By that stage Wolves were 3–1 up thanks to Wharton's 12th-minute penalty and goals by Derek Dougan (18 minutes) and David Burnside (54), with George Jones (39) replying for bottom-of-the-table Bury. Knowles, sporting a new haircut, did his best to get into the scoring act. He had a header saved by goalkeeper Neil Ramsbottom and then put the ball into the net, only to be ruled offside. Dougan made it 4–1 on 67 minutes to complete a move of old-style Wolves simplicity. Phil Parkes caught the ball, threw it to David Wagstaffe, and his telling pass put Dougan clear to thump the ball home off the underside of the bar. A crowd invasion of the pitch at the final whistle resulted in boss Ronnie Allen and his players making an appearance in the directors' box to acknowledge the cheers. Afterwards they toasted their success with champagne in the boardroom. To complete a memorable afternoon, Coventry were held 1–1 at Cardiff so Wolves looked title favourites with a two-point lead at the top and three games to play. The first of those was against title rivals Coventry at Highfield Road.

The showdown on Saturday 29 April 1967 has gained a special place in Sky Blues history. It attracted a record crowd of 51,455, bettering the previous best of 44,930 against Villa in 1938. Ignoring announcements over the public address, fans scaled the floodlight pylons, the roof of a tea bar and the enclosure roof to try to get a better view. Many youngsters were ushered to the front of the crowd and allowed to sit on the track around the pitch. Motorcyclists from the Royal Corps of Signals had to cut short their pre-match display as they eventually could not lap the pitch in safety. The fans sitting around the edges of the pitch were also warned to keep as far back as possible or the game would not start. It was the sort of special atmosphere that Knowles relished, and the injury to Gerry Taylor meant he could have a full taste of it. Ronnie Allen fielded a strange-looking line up, with Mike Bailey at right-back and Ernie Hunt taking over the number-four shirt so Knowles could slot into the attack. For the second game running, Graham Hawkins had to deputise for David Woodfield at centre-half. Despite the makeshift line up, Wolves had the better of the first half, and three minutes from the break Knowles put them ahead after being sent clear on the left by a Derek Dougan pass. It all went wrong on the hour, however, when Coventry scored twice in the space of four minutes, each time aided by unlucky deflections. Ernie Machin's equalising shot was diverted by John Holsgrove, and then Ian Gibson's effort looked to be well covered by Phil Parkes, only for the ball to strike Hawkins's boot and loop over the Wolves 'keeper. The visitors did not lie down, though, and it was Knowles who almost put them level, his lob hitting the bar. Welsh winger Ronnie Rees hit the Sky Blues's third with five minutes left. So Coventry had collected a fourth successive win over Wolves, and the clubs were level on 56 points.

A week later the title race swung back in Wolves' favour when they beat Norwich 4–1 at Molineux and Coventry were held 1–1 at Ipswich. Knowles took no part in the proceedings, despite his useful contribution at Coventry. The experiment of playing Mike Bailey at full-back was scrapped. The skipper was restored to the number-four shirt, and Joe Wilson was given the task of deputising for Gerry Taylor. The changes meant Ernie Hunt resumed his front role, to Knowles's exclusion. The substitute's task went to Graham Hawkins, and he was needed after only 40 minutes when Mike Bailey was injured. Goals from Derek Dougan (two), Terry Wharton and Hunt saw Wolves home. On the same day Villa lost 4–2 at home to Everton to seal their relegation from the First Division along with Blackpool. The repercussions were speedy. Within three days Villa's manager Dick Taylor, chief scout Jimmy Easson and assistant trainer Johnny Dixon were fired.

Bailey's injury paved the way for Knowles to return to the squad when Wolves ended the season against Crystal Palace at Selhurst Park. Hawkins took the skipper's place, with Knowles given the number-12 jersey. But by the time Knowles was called into action at the start of the second half, as substitute for Terry Wharton, the game was virtually over. Palace led 3–0 with goals from Danny Light, after only three minutes, Wolves old boy Bobby Woodruff and Jack Bannister. Hunt pulled one back, but Barry Dyson completed an emphatic 4–1 win. Coventry took full advantage of Wolves' slip, beating Millwall 3–1 at home to become Second Division champions.

Although there was ample reason for Wolves to celebrate, Knowles's season had not seen him build on his excellent progress of the previous campaign. He had started only half of Wolves' 42 League games and made two substitute appearances but totalled only eight goals. He was no longer a first choice, with Ernie Hunt and David Burnside established in the inside-forwards spots. Ronnie Allen must have felt at the time he signed Burnside that Knowles was too much of a loose cannon, something confirmed by Phil Morgan when he looked back on the season. Referring to the early part of the campaign, he wrote, 'Peter Knowles, the irrepressible young blood with so much ability, but not enough stability, was not hitting the high spots.' Morgan did admit that Knowles had eventually made a useful contribution to the promotion campaign: 'Knowles, too, had his moments and scored some vital goals to prove once again what a player he can become when he finally sheds his somewhat extended boyishness.'

He may have been in and out of the team, but there was no doubt Knowles was first choice with the younger fans, his pop star looks making him especially attractive to a growing band of female fans. Evidence of this came with the suggestion that he might even cut a record. John Ogden, that superb *Express & Star* feature writer, used to cover a vibrant Wolverhampton music scene in those days and recalls an approach being made by one of the town's leading lights, Roger Allen: 'Roger managed quite a few bands and put on gigs and was, I suppose, Wolverhampton's Brian Epstein,' said Ogden. 'I remember writing in my column that he wanted Peter to make a record, and a week later he was given permission by Wolves. For some reason it never happened, though the team did bring one out.'

Roger Allen, who now lives in Spain, cannot recall exactly why Knowles the pop star never came about but certainly remembered approaching him: 'Peter and I got on well, even though I was a few years older,' recalled Allen. 'I don't think I ever heard him sing, not that it would have been a problem. I could have made even me sound good! If he had stayed in football I'm sure it would have happened. I think it may have been overtaken by events when Peter became a Jehovah's Witness. I tried hard to get him into playing football and still having his religion. We had long talks and Bill McGarry asked me to see if I could get him to change his mind, but I couldn't. It was such a shame. He was a great talent, two great feet, great balance, great awareness, he had the lot.'

Wolverhampton Council marked Wolves' promotion with a banquet at the Civic Hall, and Knowles and his teammates were presented with silver salvers. There would be no time for the young Knowles to reflect on his League season, however, as two weeks after it ended Wolves were off to the US. They had been invited to represent Los Angeles in the United Soccer Association League, which would run for virtually two months. Skipper Mike Bailey, who had been named Midland Footballer of the Year to collect the *Birmingham Evening Mail* trophy, was not in the squad who started what proved an incident-packed adventure. Bailey was with an FA party, virtually an England squad, to take part in the Expo International Tournament in Montreal. Sadly for Bailey, he was injured and did not play in any of the three matches. With Bailey elsewhere it meant a chance for Knowles as David Burnside was switched to the half-back line.

Wolves began their American adventure by drawing 1–1 with Brazilian side Bangu in the famous Houston Astrodome before a 35,000 crowd. Playing on artificial turf, Bangu, who included seven of Brazil's World Cup squad in England the year before, led against the run of play through Borjeas. Centre-half David Woodfield earned Wolves a draw when late on he came up for a corner and headed the ball home.

Apart from Graham Hawkins, deputising for Woodfield who had been injured in training, Wolves were unchanged for their home debut in the competition and again trailed early on. Uruguayan side Cerro, playing as 'New York Skyliners', took a first-minute lead in Los Angeles, but 15 minutes later Ernie Hunt drew the opposing 'keeper and lobbed home an equaliser. Burnside volleyed what proved to be the winner from 25 yards just before half-time.

Next up were Stoke, the sides meeting at Stoke's base in Cleveland, Ohio. Torrential rain nearly brought a postponement as the Americans were worried about possible damage to the outfield at the baseball park. Officials of both clubs won the argument to play, but the match ended 0–0. Knowles set up what looked like a winner for Wolves, when he pulled the ball back from the left for Dave Wagstaffe to volley home, but the referee disallowed it for off-side. Stoke included some notable veterans, among them former Arsenal and England forward George Eastham, Welsh international Roy Vernon, once of Everton, and Allen's one-time Albion teammate Maurice Setters. Knowles and Ernie Hunt both picked up injuries and had to be replaced.

Knowles was fit enough for the next match, against Hibernian in Toronto, but injuries were piling up. So much so, that when David Burnside needed replacing it was goalkeeper Fred Davies who came on, while an injury to teenager Alun Evans saw Ronnie Allen pressed into service. Wolves won the match 2–1, Bobby Thomson crashing home a 25-yard shot to put them ahead. Derek Dougan tripped one of the Scots to concede a penalty from which Hibs equalised, but the Irishman made amends by hitting the winner 15 minutes from time.

When Mike Bailey linked up with the team, he too was carrying an injury and so was not in the side who returned to sunny Los Angeles on Wednesday 14 June and hammered Sunderland 5–1, Knowles scoring the final goal. Others came from Hunt, Pat Buckley (2) and Dougan, the sides being level 1–1 at the break. It was after this match that an American journalist, Ed Fitkin, wrote a glowing tribute to Knowles, and it illustrates the impact Knowles had made both at home and in the States, as well as confirming the extrovert nature of the young man.

Fitkin wrote, 'Peter Knowles scored his first goal in North America last Wednesday night and promptly did a cartwheel. To those who have watched this 21-year-old's meteoric rise to soccer prominence, such an antic was not unexpected. Peter is so full of life that even though he is maturing into a standout soccer player, he still can't resist the impish impulses that have caused Americans to liken him to baseball's [Jimmy] Piersall in his heyday. With his Beatle haircut, his youthful good looks and his infectious grin, Peter has the teenage girls chanting his name in Wolverhampton – and now Los Angeles. Earlier in the game last Wednesday, before his goal and his cartwheel, he had been knocked down near the corner flag. He lay motionless, flat on his back, then folded his hands on his chest as if ready for burial. Moments later, after the crowd had laughingly applauded, he got up and went about his breezy and brisk way of tantalising the opposition with his speed and his variety of clever manoeuvres.'

The Fitkin views appeared in the programme for the game against Glentoran, and Knowles lived up to his star billing, having his best game of the tour as Wolves beat the Irish side, representing Detroit, 4–1. Again he scored the final goal, after Thomson, Hunt and

Dougan had struck to put Wolves in control. 'Peter had one of those days when he was able to try everything and succeed,' Ronnie Allen reported back via phone to the *Express & Star*.

It was off to Washington next for the Los Angeles Wolves, where they met Aberdeen and met up with a man who would become one of Molineux's greatest servants – Frank Munro. What a first meeting it proved to be! Munro and David Burnside were sent off after a clash 16 minutes from time. The Wolves man was trying to take a throw-in, but the Scot stood in close to impede him. Burnside finally lost his patience and threw the ball at Munro, who promptly flattened him. A year earlier the International Board had ruled that a player dancing up and down in front of an opponent trying to take a throw-in would be guilty of ungentlemanly conduct (unsporting behaviour, as it is now known) and should be booked. So Ronnie Allen felt the referee had made the wrong decision and generally lost control of what proved a tough encounter. Burnside had notched Wolves' equaliser in a 1–1 draw. Injuries saw Wolves use three substitutes, little knowing that it was against the rules of the tournament – a fact that would have consequences later on and would lead to Wolves and Aberdeen locking horns twice more.

Film star Maureen O'Hara was given the honour of kicking-off after being introduced to Wolves and Shamrock Rovers when the sides met at the Los Angeles Coliseum on Sunday 25 June. Wolves were odds-on favourites to beat the Irishmen but were held 1–1. It took a Terry Wharton penalty to level the score, after Dave Wagstaffe, in tip-top form, had been upended. Knowles, keeping up his record of playing in all the games so far, nearly won the match but saw his shot rattle the bar.

If the game against Aberdeen was incident-packed it was nothing compared with Wolves' meeting with Dutch side ADO in San Francisco. It brought a first defeat for Ronnie Allen's men as two of his players went off injured and two more were sent off, as well as one from ADO. A tough-tackling Dutch right-back roughed up Dave Wagstaffe, who had to go to hospital with a cracked rib, and his replacement, Pat Buckley, went off soon afterwards with a damaged ankle. The referee then sent off ADO's right-winger, his only offence seeming to be that he remonstrated with his colleague who was dishing out the rough stuff. Ernie Hunt followed when he retaliated after being fouled. It was then that the only goal of the game arrived as Dutch skipper Piet Dezotete saw his long-range shot deflected past Fred Davies by David Woodfield. Then Derek Dougan got his marching orders. He put his hand on the referee's shoulder when questioning his decision not to give Wolves a penalty after Terry Wharton had been brought down. 'Just plain ridiculous' was Ronnie Allen's verdict. He added 'We could do with some English officials out here. This man lost control completely, and the game was spoiled.'

Fortunately, there was a better referee when the sides met in Los Angeles two days later and Wolves gained revenge 2–0. Mike Bailey, though not fully fit, was pressed into service as the injury crisis continued, and Fred Davies was again used as an outfield sub. To the goalkeeper's delight, he got down low to head Wolves' second goal from a Terry Wharton centre after coming on to replace Bailey. Wharton, in sparkling form, had headed Wolves in front from a Bobby Thomson centre after a goalless first half. Wolves attracted their biggest home crowd so far, 11,572, and among them was English entertainer Tommy Steele. He was making a film in LA and hosted the tourists on a tour of Warner Brothers Studios a few days later.

When Wolves were held 2–2 by Cagliari of Italy in Los Angeles, Knowles was in the wars. Tedda took a kick at him and got himself sent off, and Knowles had to be taken off 20 minutes from time. Derek Dougan headed the ball back for Ernie Hunt to put Wolves ahead but Boninsegna levelled. When Mike Bailey was upended inside the box, Terry Wharton restored the lead from the penalty spot, only for Longoni to make it 2–2.

Although fit enough to play in Wolves' next match, Knowles did not finish it. He became the latest victim of some weird refereeing as Wolves were held 2–2 by Dundee in Dallas. Wolves had just gone 2–1 up after 30 minutes when Knowles was felled by a really tough tackle. Wolves were awarded a free-kick, but Knowles obviously felt the perpetrator should have at least been booked. Instead, Knowles was sent off, presumably for arguing. 'A ridiculous decision,' said Ronnie Allen. 'They send players off for the slightest thing over here.' In a match played in 100 degrees Fahrenheit, things had begun well for Knowles. He chipped home an equaliser after a Mike Bailey shot had been blocked. On a pitch a mere 60 yards wide, Bailey had a hand in the second goal. His throw-in to the near post saw Bobby Thomson race in to fire the ball home. With Phil Parkes defiant in goal, Wolves' 10 men held out until three minutes from time.

That should have been Wolves' final group game, but their use of three substitutes against Aberdeen meant the match had to be replayed. Whatever the outcome, Wolves would be in the Final as top of the Western group, but an Aberdeen win would put them above Stoke to top the Eastern section. The Scots made the most of their second chance and won the match at Washington 3–0. After a goalless first half, Frank Munro was again prominent, making a goal for former Leeds man Jim Storrie. Future Manchester United stalwart Martin Buchan made it two and then set up Storrie for the third.

So Wolves and Aberdeen would meet yet again, this time in the Final at Wolves' 'home' ground in Los Angeles – and what a storming game it proved to be on Bastille Day, Friday

14 July! Knowles got Wolves off to a flying start, firing them ahead in the first minute. Goals from Jim Smith and Frank Munro, with a penalty, put Aberdeen 2–1 ahead by half-time. The Scots were down to 10 men, however, Smith having been sent off for a foul on Dave Wagstaffe. There was a hectic bout of scoring starting in the 63rd minute. Knowles's centre was nodded across goal by Ernie Hunt for David Burnside to make it 2–2. Jim Storrie promptly put Aberdeen 3–2 up before Burnside quickly completed his hat-trick to see Wolves 4–3 in front, first heading home from fully 18 yards and then turning in a Dougan centre from the left. Aberdeen would not lie down, however, and Munro headed home a long through ball two minutes from time to take the game into extra-time.

Derek Dougan put Wolves 5–4 up with just seven minutes of the extra half-hour to go, and Terry Wharton ought to have made it 6–4 in the final minute, but Bobby Clark saved his penalty. Indication of the fatigue that had set in was that Knowles audaciously lay full length, relaxing on the 18-yard line as Wharton took the kick. It was a unique moment – the only occasion the winger ever missed from the spot. Still the drama was not finished, and Aberdeen had just enough time to go back upfield and themselves win a penalty. Munro made no mistake, so it was 5–5 and into more extra-time, only now it was sudden death – the first to score would be winners. Bobby Thomson paved the way for the decider when he overlapped down the left wing and saw his shot-cum-centre turned into his own net by Ally Shewan.

As the players walked up to collect their winners' trophies, there was more clowning from Knowles. To emphasise how exhausted he was he crawled on his knees when it came to his turn to receive his memento.

So Wolves were champions, and there were plenty of celebrations back at their Sheridan-Wiltshire Hotel afterwards, an occasion Knowles and the rest enjoyed to the full. The Final line up was:

Wolves: Parkes, Taylor, Thomson, Holsgrove, Woodfield, Burnside, Wharton, Hunt, Dougan, Knowles, Wagstaffe.

Aberdeen: Clark, Whyte, Shewan, Munro, McMillan, Petersen, Storrie, Smith, Johnston, Buchan, Wilson.

Attendance: 17,824.

Still thought of by most of his teammates as a bit of a 'Jack the Lad' who did not miss a trick, Knowles enjoyed the taste of luxury in America. The Wolves players were given a meal allowance and, though he at first used the cash to dine out with the others, he realised it was a waste of money. A regular sunbather, he noticed that the wealthy visitors to the hotel always left most of the huge salads and side dishes which accompanied their food when they ate at the chalets around the hotel pool. So Knowles would help himself to the leftovers. As Dave Wagstaffe noted, 'It was very enterprising, so much so that he was able to save most of his food allowance money. After nine weeks away he returned home to buy himself a brand new Triumph Spitfire with the help of the cash he had saved.'

That car would fit in perfectly with the Knowles persona of that time. His talent, personality and good looks made him a hero to female fans, and he enjoyed it. Jane Davenport, a pupil at Wolverhampton Girls' High School, recalls her innocent admiration for the player. 'He used to park his car in Queen Square or Dudley Street in the centre of town, and we would go there after school on a Friday afternoon and loiter near the car in the hope we might see him. We were barely in our teens and I suppose it was a sort of schoolgirl crush. We would afterwards often go to the Golden Egg café, which was the McDonald's of its time, and have a burger. When he met his future wife and she became his girlfriend we were all jealous of her.

'A lot of the players lived on the Fordhouses estate, and there was a girl at school who lived on that estate, and I'm sure I became friends with her so I could go over to her house. When there I would suddenly remember something I needed from the shops so we could walk to the local shops past the footballers' houses on the off chance we would see one of the players. I don't think we saw many, but it was just the excitement of it.'

In Full Flower

It was no surprise that Ronnie Allen began the 1967–68 season by giving a vote of confidence to the men who clinched promotion, and that meant no place for Knowles. Early in the season the club said goodbye to one of their greatest servants, Ron Flowers joining Northampton Town, where he would eventually become player-manager. He had made his debut for Wolves in 1952. The manager's faith was justified as the team began with a 2–1 win at Fulham, a 3–3 home draw with Albion and then a 2–0 defeat of Leeds at Molineux. The Albion match saw Phil Parkes sent off after angrily confronting the referee because Tony Brown had clearly fisted the ball in for the equaliser.

At last Knowles got some first-team action in the return game with Albion at The Hawthorns on Wednesday 30 August 1967, though he again did not make the starting line up. Wolves trailed 2–1 at half-time, but Ernie Hunt was handicapped by a knee injury so Knowles was given the whole of the second half as substitute. He made little impact as Albion scored twice more to win 4–1. For the trip to Everton Les Wilson, not Knowles, was given the number-12 shirt. Wilson came on at half-time for Dave Wagstaffe, who had been unwell with a throat infection before the game, and became the first Wolves sub to score. Wilson's goal was quickly followed by a Terry Wharton penalty, but Everton had already scored four times.

Knowles's absence from the first team did see him figure in an unusual reserve-team game against Bury at Molineux. An injury crisis meant young 'keeper Phil Weir, son of the fondly-remembered *Express & Star* journalist Alan Weir, was named as substitute, and when Brian Thompson was injured he was pressed into service. Weir came on to replace Fred Davies in goal, however, the latter moving into attack. To complete a rare night, Weir made several fine saves and Davies, as he had done in the US, headed a goal to complete Wolves'

2–0 win. Phil Morgan reported in the *Express & Star* that Knowles 'had a lot to do with organising Wolves' good second-half show.'

With Wagstaffe now sidelined by his illness, Knowles got an unexpected first start of the season, with the added bonus of facing his brother as Wolves took on Tottenham at White Hart Lane on Wednesday 6 September. Left-back Cyril earned the Knowles family bragging rights as Spurs won 2–1, but it was a much better display by Ronnie Allen's team. Jimmy Greaves sliced through the visitors' defence to open the scoring on seven minutes, but on the half hour Terry Wharton's crossfield run paved the way for Ernie Hunt to put Wolves level with a cross-shot. Knowles could then have transformed the game when Wharton went between two defenders and crossed, but Knowles's first-time volley hit the side netting. It was a costly miss as Jimmy Robertson curled a shot past Fred Davies on 40 minutes, and that proved to be the winning goal despite a late rally by Wolves.

Just when it seemed Knowles's only chance of first-team football was if one of the regular forwards was injured, the way unexpectedly opened up for him. Manager Allen decided to sell Ernie Hunt, accepting an £80,000 bid from Everton. The transfer did not go down well with Wolves fans, however, who liked the all-action, goal-getting inside-man. Allen tried to pacify them by saying he hoped quickly to sign a replacement. Whoever his target was, no signing materialised, and Knowles was given his second full game of the season for the visit of Leicester City. This was the chance he had been waiting for after playing second fiddle to Hunt and Burnside for so long – and the maturing young man would make the most of it as the season unfolded.

Although Knowles scored against Leicester, Wolves were beaten again, this time 3–1. David Nish and Jackie Sinclair scored first-half goals for the Foxes before Knowles reduced the arrears on 57 minutes. Mike Stringfellow sealed the defeat with a goal nine minutes from time. Phil Morgan wrote that Knowles, whose goal was a volleyed effort, had 'done a good day's work'.

Four successive defeats became five when Wolves visited Huddersfield in the League Cup and were ushered out of the competition 1–0. It was little consolation to Knowles that he and Derek Dougan were rated two of the few who emerged with any credit in the visiting side – goalkeeper Phil Parkes and John Holsgrove were others – as again the team struggled. Dave Wagstaffe spent much of the evening back in defence, so much were Wolves under pressure. Waggy had been switched back to the left with John Farrington partnering Knowles. Despite the efforts of Knowles and Dougan, Wolves failed to cancel out the goal from Colin Dobson on 13 minutes.

He may have been back in the first team, but Knowles was still restless to be with a bigger club. One national paper reported that Nottingham Forest and Leicester were keen to sign him but had been told by Wolves that there was no chance until they had signed players themselves. One suspects that, though Knowles would have jumped at a move to a big club, Forest and Leicester would not have fallen into that category in his eyes. He would have been interested if it had been Manchester United, Liverpool or Tottenham calling. If anything would make him more settled it would be a role of greater responsibility – and that was what he was given.

The defeat at Leeds Road represented a low point in the season. Something had to be done. Full-back Bobby Thomson and right-winger Terry Wharton were fit again, but there was a change by manager Ronnie Allen which would be a turning point in Knowles's career. David Burnside was dropped, and Knowles given the task of orchestrating things in midfield, allied to the drive of skipper Mike Bailey. It was a role in which Knowles revelled. His talent, of which there had been plenty of glimpses, was about to blossom into full flower. He was even given Burnside's number-10 shirt, allowing 17-year-old Alun Evans to make his debut at inside-right for the trip to West Ham on Saturday 16 September 1967.

Wolves beat the Hammers 2–1 and Knowles, with a rejuvenated Bailey, played a key role. With the score at 1–1, he even found time to help out in defence and won unstinting praise from Phil Morgan who wrote, after praising Wolves' defence 'Talking of defenders, who should show up among them but Peter Knowles who put everything into his midfield role. His calm goalline dribble out of danger was something to remember for a long time.'

Anyone who thought Knowles was merely a goalscorer, saw in all its glory the potential of the young man in that fine win at Upton Park against a home side parading their famous World Cup-winning trio Bobby Moore, Martin Peters and Geoff Hurst. Young Evans also rose to the occasion and sidestepped Moore neatly almost to score on his debut. It was Evans's run and shot after 35 minutes that brought a rebound for Derek Dougan to give Wolves the lead. Hurst levelled with a header within a minute. Dougan, at his flamboyant best, got plenty of stick from the home crowd but had the last laugh when Wagstaffe put him through to score the winner with a cross-shot three minutes from time.

Now Knowles could set about establishing himself in the side and take on more authority in midfield along with Mike Bailey. It was these two, along with Derek Dougan, who nursed Evans through an impressive home debut against Burnley a week later, the youngster crowning his day by scoring two minutes from time to give Wolves a 3–2 win. While adapting to his more constructive role, Knowles had clearly not lost his goal touch and twice gave Wolves the lead, his goals being cancelled out each time by penalties from Burnley inside-left Gordon Harris. Knowles struck first on 17 minutes after one of Bailey's long throw-ins and was on hand to score eight minutes after the break after goalkeeper Harry Thomson had parried a Dougan shot. Knowles was also using his passing ability to make the best use of wingers Terry Wharton and Dave Wagstaffe. In short, a fine all-round player was emerging.

On-field tantrums were less in evidence with Knowles's growing football maturity. After all, he was no longer a youngster, and Saturday 30 September would bring his 22nd birthday. By coincidence, he shared the birthday with Alun Evans, who was four years his junior. Fittingly, both marked their special day with a goal against Sheffield Wednesday at Hillsborough. Knowles's came with a shot from outside the penalty area in the fifth minute to finish off a move he had himself begun. His well-timed pass put Wagstaffe away on the left, and the winger's cross was turned back to Knowles by Evans. By the time Evans found the back of the net, Wolves were 2–1 down courtesy of goals from Vic Mobley on 18 minutes and centre-forward John Ritchie on 64. Evans struck even later than in the Burnley match, a run by Bailey paving the way for his equaliser in injury time. Again Knowles had begun the move with a raking pass out to Bailey on the right wing. Phil Morgan's verdict was that Knowles had enjoyed one of his best games. He wrote, 'It was he who splayed the ball about to the wingers when he sensed the close attention being paid to Derek Dougan by the uncompromising Sam Ellis.'

On the way home after the game the players paused to drink a birthday toast to Evans, who made a brief speech in response – 'Thanks, lads, for making my first three games in the First Division so happy.' Knowles was not there to join in the party, however, as he had been given permission to stay in Yorkshire to visit his family and spend his birthday evening with them. Evidence that Knowles was more settled came a few days later when chairman John Ireland presented him with a benefit cheque, something players received after five years with a club. For good measure, Knowles signed a new contract and afterwards remarked, 'It looks as though I'm here for life.'

Was Knowles at last reaching a maturity which would help his football progress? He certainly felt so and confirmed it in an article in the *Sporting Star*. He wrote, 'Wolves have been good to me. They have treated me well – better than I have deserved sometimes. Now we are playing well and in the First Division with a young team and a good manager I know this is the place for me. In the past I have done things of which I have been ashamed. But then I was young and wanted to make a name for myself. I thought the best way to do it was to be controversial and push myself forward. People might say I am still young but I have grown up a lot in the last year. Football is everything to me. I couldn't do any other job because I am a lazy person. I used to lie awake at night wondering how I could become a big name. Now I know the best way – by playing as well as I can and by earning respect as a good sporting player. Gone are the days when I would pick the ball out of the net and kick it out of the ground. My mum wrote me a letter when I did it at Portsmouth and it made me think. Now I want to be Peter Knowles the footballer. I wanted to leave Wolves last year because I always seemed to be the scapegoat for our defeats and I thought I was indispensable. Now I know I wasn't.'

Football has a habit of bringing you quickly down to earth, and if a 2–2 draw at Hillsborough was a useful result, a similar score against Newcastle at Molineux on the first Saturday in October was not so good. Wolves, in general, and Knowles, in particular, had recovered well enough after the shock of a Tommy Robson goal for the Geordies after seven minutes. John Holsgrove had headed Wolves level 10 minutes later, and it was Knowles's cheeky back-heel which created the opening for Terry Wharton to fire Wolves in front on 26 minutes. That should have opened the floodgates, but Knowles, Dougan and Evans all missed good opportunities as Dave Wagstaffe sparkled and created chance after chance. Although David Woodfield had kept Newcastle's much-vaunted Welsh centre forward Wyn Davies quiet, the visitors still had the final say with an equaliser from right-winger Bryan Robson 17 minutes from time.

It was about this time that skipper Mike Bailey, such a force for Wolves in the late 1960s and early 1970s, was going through a rare bad patch which meant greater responsibility falling upon Knowles. Yet Bailey still had moments of influence on the match at Maine Road when Wolves went down 2–0 to Manchester City thanks to early goals from Mike Doyle and Neil Young. Bailey laid on a neat centre for Derek Dougan to net, only for referee Pat Partridge to rule offside, and then Bailey rode a tough tackle and ran through to put the ball in the home net again only for the official to pull him back for the original foul.

Such was Wolves' fortune but they soon got a welcome first win in four games when Arsenal visited Molineux on Monday 23 October 1967. The game was delayed a couple of days because of international calls, Dougan playing for Northern Ireland on the Saturday, as did Terry Neill of the Gunners who also had Ian Ure in the Scotland team. A crowd of 36,664 were given a glimpse of a new goalkeeper thanks to Phil Parkes's suspension following his dismissal in the Albion match. Scotsman Evan Williams made his bow and did well enough to have the North Bank choir chanting 'We've got a goalie!' The team also had a midfield that night, as Bailey found his touch once more and, with Knowles, drove the side on to a rousing 3–2 win. Derek Dougan headed them in front after only four minutes, and Knowles saw a long-range drive flash just wide. There were other early misses, and Wolves paid for them when George Graham strolled through the home defence to equalise. While Knowles and Bailey were on song, the star of the show was Dave Wagstaffe who led Arsenal a merry dance on the left wing. Waggy's corner had laid on the opener for Dougan, and then he skipped through the Arsenal defence on the hour to tee up a goal for Alun Evans. Waggy's pass brought Dougan his second goal before winger George Armstrong struck for the visitors 13 minutes from time.

It was yet another sound display from Knowles. He was oozing confidence and got his reward with an international honour to add to those he had won at Youth level. He was named in the England Under-23 side to face Wales Under-23 at Swansea, with manager Ronnie Allen commenting, 'His selection is well deserved. He has disciplined himself to do the job I want him to do, and it has been good both for him and the team.' Before his international bow, Knowles had a somewhat low-key build-up when Wolves drew 1–1 with Sheffield United at Bramall Lane. Alan Woodward gave the Blades the lead just after half-time, and Dougan equalised within 10 minutes, but Wolves had new 'keeper Williams to thank for a point, his last-minute full-length dive keeping out a goalbound Willie Carlin header.

Blades full-back Len Badger would team up with Knowles for the Under-23 game at Vetch Field on Wednesday 1 November 1967 in an England side who included several future internationals: Liverpool 'keeper Ray Clemence, his clubmate Emlyn Hughes and Chelsea centre-forward Peter Osgood being the most notable. On paper the England team looked far stronger than the Welsh, but the rain which fell throughout the game proved a great leveller. Most of the crowd of 14,928 got a soaking along with the players and the *FA Yearbook's* report of the 2–1 win by England said, 'The game was a credit to both teams and spectators alike.' Osgood, like Knowles making his Under-23 debut, gave England the lead after only eight minutes, volleying the ball home from a free-kick taken by his Chelsea colleague John Hollins. The *FA Yearbook* report added, 'By half-time the pitch was a morass. Good football was out of the question, and it would have been no surprise if the referee had abandoned the game.' The teams played on and Geoff Thomas fired in an equaliser on the hour. The winner came 13 minutes from time when Don Rogers, who had starred with Knowles in the England Youth team, powered home a shot after Osgood's header had put him clear. One report said, 'Knowles was in superb form in the early stages but later when the heavy rain made the pitch a veritable mudbath he, like all the rest, found himself largely bogged down.' It was still a satisfactory debut for Knowles who would have enjoyed playing alongside players from Liverpool, Chelsea and Manchester United. The line up at Swansea was:

Wales: Walker (York), Coldrick (Cardiff), Collins (Tottenham), Powell (Wrexham), Mielczarek (Huddersfield), Thomas (Swansea), Lewis (Cardiff), Hawkins (Leeds), Roberts (Swansea), Jones (Bristol Rovers), Walley (Watford).

England: Clemence (Liverpool), Badger (Sheffield United), Hughes (Liverpool), Kendall (Everton), Sadler (Manchester United), Hollins (Chelsea), Rogers (Swindon), Knowles (Wolves), Osgood (Chelsea), Birchenall (Sheffield United), sub Payne (Crystal Palace), Kidd (Manchester United).

While Knowles was teaming up with new players at Swansea, one of his clubmates at Molineux was unexpectedly on the move. Terry Wharton was sold to his home-town club Bolton for £70,000, a record buy for the Lancastrians who earlier in the season had sold Francis Lee to Manchester City. With well over 200 appearances for Wolves and still only 25, Wharton was taking a step down as the other Wanderers were then in the second tier of English football, the Second Division.

As for Lee, he could have been a Wolves player, according to Dave Wagstaffe, had it not been for that incident involving Knowles. 'We were playing Bolton, and Peter sat on the ball,' recalled Wagstaffe, 'It was the sort of thing Peter would do in those days, and Francis Lee was really incensed and took a kick at him. Well, some time afterwards Ronnie Allen was all set to sign Franny Lee, but John Ireland got to hear about it and said there was no way a player who had done what Lee had done to Peter would be joining Wolves. If it wasn't for that we could well have had Franny Lee, and that would have been really something.'

Wolves' loss was undoubtedly Manchester City's gain as Lee played a major part in the team who won the First Division title, the FA Cup, European Cup-winners' Cup and League Cup in a glorious era under the Mercer-Allison managerial regime. He also collected 27 England caps.

So, with Wharton departed, for the visit of Coventry to Molineux, Knowles had John Farrington as his right-wing partner, and it was the winger who created the first of two goals by Knowles which brought a 2–0 victory. Farrington beat full-back Mick Kearns and pulled the ball back sweetly for Knowles to head in at the far post. That was on 36 minutes, and six minutes later an overlapping run by Bobby Thomson and a through pass by Mike Bailey led to a goalmouth scramble which Knowles resolved by slipping the ball home. Both goals were scored while Wolves were down to 10 men after Dave Wagstaffe had limped off. He came back but was replaced in the second half.

If Knowles was in top form so, once again, was Bailey, still figuring in Sir Alf Ramsey's England set-up though unable to gain preference over Alan Mullery, who seemed to have made the number-four shirt his property in succession to Nobby Stiles. Bailey was given an outing in the Football League XI early in November 1967 for the game against the League of Ireland in Dublin, which the visitors won comfortably 7–2, Southampton's Martin Chivers hitting three goals.

Wolves had brought on centre-half Graham Hawkins for the injured Wagstaffe against Coventry and kept him in the number-11 shirt for the trip to Nottingham Forest, and the defence-minded line up went down 3–1 despite Bobby Thomson hitting a rare goal to wipe out Henry Newton's early strike for the home team. Two men who would serve Wolves in the not-too-distant future scored Forest's other goals – Frank Wignall and John Barnwell.

Knowles did not figure too prominently in that one, but he did his best to inspire a Wolves comeback in a seven-goal thriller with Stoke at Molineux. Wolves were two down after 10 minutes when John Mahoney and Calvin Palmer struck for the Potters who went three up on 33 minutes through Harry Burrows. Then came a Wolves revival begun by John Holsgrove's headed goal, followed by a trip on left-winger Pat Buckley which gave Knowles the chance to show his ability as a penalty taker. He chose the subtle method and stroked the ball past England 'keeper Gordon Banks. The comeback was complete when Buckley, playing as Wagstaffe's deputy, levelled 20 minutes from time. Stoke had the last word with a Bloor header in the final minute.

A winger was still a top priority for Wolves and the *Express & Star* reported in late November 1967 that Swindon's Don Rogers, who had partnered Knowles in the Under-23 international, had turned down a Molineux move which, the paper claimed, would have made him the highest-paid winger in the game. So Pat Buckley was still on the wing when Wolves lost 2–1 at Liverpool, but Knowles missed the game through a damaged shin. That let in David Burnside, and he kept the number-10 shirt for the home game against Southampton, Knowles coming back into the team in place of Buckley. Knowles would not attempt to emulate the wing play of Waggy but still had a decisive impact on the game. Wolves won 2–0 thanks to scoring twice in the last six minutes. Let Phil Morgan explain. He wrote in the *Express & Star*, 'Because Peter Knowles, deputising for the still sorely missed David Wagstaffe, remained essentially Knowles instead of trying to imitate his absent colleague, Wolves were able to snatch this imperative home victory just when it looked as though the Saints would defy them. The pass that put the ball through for Derek Dougan for the first goal was typical Knowles and so was the corkscrew shot with which he scored himself.'

Even though playing in the number-11 shirt, Knowles was happy with his form. There was even more reason for happiness in the Knowles family. An injury to World Cup hero George Cohen meant that Peter's brother Cyril was given his England debut at right-back against the USSR at Wembley on Wednesday 6 December 1967. No doubt Peter was pleased for his brother but would have loved it to be him playing alongside Bobby Moore, Bobby Charlton, Geoff Hurst and Martin Peters. Unfortunately it was not a winning debut for Cyril, as the talented Soviet side held the world champions 2–2.

Cyril Knowles was not the first lad from Fitzwlliam to play for England, nor, indeed, the first from his street. Albert Webster, a lifelong Fitzwilliam resident, furnished me with the information that Tom Smalley was born in Kinsley and lived in the same street as the Knowles family. Smalley, one of the stars in Major Frank Buckley's fine 1930s Wolves side, was capped by England against Wales at Cardiff in 1936.

Peter still figured in England manager Sir Alf Ramsey's plans and was named in the Under-23 side to face Italy Under-23s. He gained his selection even though Ramsey did not have a chance to run the rule over him against Chelsea at Stamford Bridge. Snow caused the game to be postponed so that Knowles was next in action four days before the Under-23 game, helping Wolves beat Fulham 3–2 at Molineux and scoring two goals into the bargain. With Dave Wagstaffe fit again, someone had to drop out and as the experienced Dave Burnside had made the most of his chance, it was young Alun Evans who was omitted. This meant Knowles's midfield role was forsaken for a more forward one, and he duly obliged. Joey Gilroy had given the Londoners a 27th-minute lead which Knowles cancelled out nine minutes later. David Woodfield headed Wolves in front from a right-wing corner just on half-time. With veteran former England skipper Johnny Haynes pulling the strings, it was no surprise when Fulham levelled on the hour through Bobby Moss. Knowles then won the game, blasting the ball home from close range three minutes from time. Phil Morgan wrote in the *Express & Star*, 'It was appropriate Knowles should be the scorer. He and Dave Wagstaffe, returning after his five-week injury lay-off, were the only home forwards carrying any real threat.'

Continued Progress

For the Under-23 game at the City Ground on Wednesday 20 December 1967, Knowles would figure in a 4–4–2 formation playing alongside Howard Kendall, Jon Sammels and John Hollins in midfield. The two strikers were Martin Chivers and Brian Kidd. If the pitch at the Vetch Field had been bad, that at Nottingham was not much better. On a bitter cold night the playing surface was frozen and uneven. The Italians looked the better team in the first half but failed to take their chances, but it was a different story after the break with England calling the tune. They were rewarded with the game's only goal, by Chivers on 54 minutes. The *FA Yearbook* reported, 'Young England continued to play with determination for the remainder of the game and well merited their win.'

Within a month Chivers said goodbye to homely Southampton when he moved to Tottenham. A deal which saw Frank Saul switch to The Dell was valued at £125,000, breaking the English transfer record. How Knowles would have loved to move to a high-profile club, but he was tied to Wolves by a six-year contract and manager Allen must have realised he could build a team around the talented young man.

England Under-23: Peter Springett (Sheffield Wednesday), Wright (Everton), Smith (Liverpool), Stephenson (West Ham), Hughes (Liverpool), Hollins (Chelsea), Sammels (Arsenal), Kendall (Everton), Knowles (Wolves), Kidd (Manchester United), Chivers (Southampton).

Italy Under-23: Vecchi (AC Milan), Pasetti (SPAL), Botti (Brescia), Reya (SPAL), Cresci (Varese), Tomasini (Brescia), Gori (Lanerossi), Vieri (Sampdoria) sub Vignando (Reggiana), Anastasi (Varese), Merlo (Fiorentina), Chiarugi (Fiorentina) sub Prati (AC Milan).

Knowles had every reason to feel pleased with his progress and with that of his club. He had shown he could be part of England's future, and Wolves looked like establishing themselves in mid-table, which was their main aim in their first season back in the top flight. He could hardly have guessed that Wolves were about to embark on a dismal run of seven successive defeats.

The first came on the last Saturday before Christmas when Knowles and the rest were right out of luck against Leeds at Elland Road. Knowles was much in evidence early on and made chances for Alun Evans and Pat Buckley which both wasted. Three minutes from the break Derek Dougan fired Wolves deservedly ahead with a cross-shot; however, the big man was then so badly injured he could not return for the second half, John Farrington having to replace him. Dave Wagstaffe and David Woodfield were also hampered by knocks, but Wolves held out until four minutes from time. Mick Jones sliced his shot, but it still beat Evan Williams, and another goalmouth scramble saw centre-half Jack Charlton net a minute from the end. It was an unlucky defeat and would set a pattern. For Leeds it was the first of six successive League wins.

If Wolves wanted to bounce back quickly they could hardly have had a tougher task – two matches with high-riding Manchester United who were enjoying their best form of the season. These were the games Knowles savoured, treading the same turf as true footballing greats like Bobby Charlton, George Best and Denis Law in front of huge crowds. The double header attracted a total of 117,390. Those were the days!

United completely outclassed Wolves in the Boxing Day game at Old Trafford, cantering home 4–0 with George Best (two), Brian Kidd and Charlton scoring the goals. Only consolation for Wolves fans was that their side prevented United from adding to their total for the last 40 minutes of the match. As for Knowles, he managed to catch the eye even in such exalted company, Phil Morgan writing that some of his footwork and control were superb. Knowles had been given the number-nine shirt because Dougan had been injured in the game at Elland Road and provided more evidence that he was close to becoming the finished football article, capable not just of holding his own at the top level but playing a leading role.

For the return four days later, Saturday 30 December 1967, Knowles was back wearing number-eight with little Pat Buckley the unlikely wearer of the number-nine. There was a newcomer at number-10 in the shape of former Wolverhampton Grammar School lad Stewart Ross. It was the toughest opposition possible for a debutant and Ross, a latecomer at 22, did not do too badly, though he was never granted a starting place again. Buckley had Wolves fans among the 53,940 roaring their delight when he scored after only 36 seconds, but Bobby Charlton levelled at the start of the second half with a goal that came even more swiftly after the kick-off. His was timed at 15 seconds and John Aston (49 minutes) and Kidd

(62) put the visitors in charge before Mike Bailey (67) reduced the arrears. Despite the closeness of the scoreline, Knowles did not shine as brightly as he had done at Old Trafford, and it was one of his idols, George Best, who virtually controlled proceedings.

Wolves needed to strengthen their squad, and Ronnie Allen did so by signing Frank Munro, the man who had so impressed for Aberdeen against them in the US. It cost Wolves a fee of £55,000 though Munro, who would settle down to become one of the best centre-halves in the country, was initially played in midfield when Everton visited Molineux on Saturday 6 January 1968. It was an unhappy start to the New Year as Wolves went down 3–1, Knowles scoring Wolves' goal. Dave Wagstaffe and Munro laid it on for him, but by then Everton were two up thanks to first-half goals from Joe Royle and Mike Trebilcock. Royle struck again in the final minute.

Maybe it was the depressing form of the team or the fact he had been named in a 35-strong England training party and was being unsettled by meeting men from top teams, but out of the blue there were rumours that once again Knowles had wander-lust. Just three months earlier he had written about seeing his future nowhere else but with Wolves. Now, it was revealed that Knowles was again restless. Manager Ronnie Allen confirmed Knowles had talked to him about the possibility of a move but added, 'Our supporters need not worry. So far as we are concerned Peter is here for six years, and any club who approach us about the possibility of his transfer will get a flat refusal. Far from letting Peter go, we are in the position of wanting new players – and we could do with two or three like him.'

Before the next match there was, indeed, a new face when winger Mike Kenning was bought from Norwich for £40,000. He was a decent enough player but hardly in the Knowles class; however, Allen had needed a replacement for Wharton, and Kenning marked his debut on a snow-covered Filbert Street pitch by giving Wolves the lead against Leicester City after 26 minutes. There was again a change of shirt for Knowles, number-11, in the absence of the injured Dave Wagstaffe. Leicester equalised within eight minutes and went on to win 3–1. Knowles had little chance to shine, while Alun Evans continued to find the going tough after his early promise.

Phil Morgan wrote, 'Peter Knowles promised much in the first half, and I wondered whether in the second he might have been more effective if he had switched with Alun Evans, who ran around such a lot without being allowed to achieve anything apart from the risk of having his confidence further blunted.' Morgan was always gentle in his criticism, and this was his sympathetic way of saying Evans needed a rest. Allen realised that, too, but before he named his next side there was an off-field distraction.

While it was known that Knowles would love to move to a higher profile club, there now came a suggestion that Derek Dougan was about to leave Wolves. The source was Peter Batt, one of those football writers who always professed to have inside knowledge. In the *People* he claimed that Coventry chief scout Bob Dennison had watched Dougan against Leicester and Coventry were ready to make a bid. He also reckoned Stoke were in the market for the Irishman. Batt wrote, 'You can expect denials from Wolves manager Ronnie Allen but I understand that as far as the Wolves board is concerned it is now just a question of timing.' There was an immediate denial from chairman John Ireland who said Dougan had just signed a new three-year contract. Doog was quoted in the *Express & Star*, 'If my career lasts another 10 weeks, 10 months or 10 years it will be with Wolves.' Dougan proved true to his word and Batt's 'exclusive' went the way of so many others.

Knowles and Dougan did their best to lift a sluggish Wolves in their next home game but found Bobby Moore in commanding form as West Ham triumphed 2–1 with goals early in the second half from Brian Dear and Geoff Hurst before Dougan hit a consolation for Wolves three minutes from time. Six successive League defeats and now in a relegation battle – perhaps the FA Cup would provide some respite for Wolves. It ought to have done, as their third-round task was a trip to Rotherham, then managed by Tommy Docherty, reviving his managerial career after parting company with Chelsea. It was a chance for Knowles to impress in the area where he had grown up, but even Rotherham, then struggling in the Second Division, proved too good for them. A goal on the hour by former Leeds striker Jim Storrie proved the only one of the match, and Wolves were out of the Cup and had lost seven games in a row. Not even the return of Dave Wagstaffe could get Wolves out of their rut. Knowles was one of the few to emerge with any credit as a crowd of nearly 15,000 enjoyed the occasion. It was indeed a rare moment of cheer for the Yorkshire club as they were relegated at the end of the season.

David Burnside, Knowles's one-time rival, had not done too well in the number-10 shirt at Rotherham, and for the visit to Burnley a week later he was dropped, Frank Munro coming into the side with skipper Mike Bailey taking Burnside's shirt. That proved to be the end of the road for the former Albion man. He never made another first-team appearance for Wolves and was sold to Plymouth within a few weeks. The days of the 'Peter Knowles, Burnside' chants were just a memory. At last Wolves stopped the rot, though the 1–1 draw at Turf Moor ought to have been a win. With David Woodfield and John Holsgrove controlling the threat of the lively Burnley forwards, Wolves deserved the lead given them by Derek Dougan just after half-time; however, Frank Casper levelled 17 minutes from time with a goal that looked clearly offside, and to compound the injustice referee V. James disallowed Knowles's effort for offside when he curled the ball into the far corner from the wing.

Wolves' poor run may have affected Knowles's international progress even though his form may not have dipped that much, however, players like Queen's Park Rangers' Rodney Marsh and Manchester City's Colin Bell were pushing their claims, and so there was no place for Knowles in the England side for the Under-23 game against Scotland at Hampden Park. He, Howard Kendall and Jon Sammels were omitted from the team who had played against Italy. England beat the Scots with Marsh and Martin Chivers the scorers. One could imagine that Knowles's feeling at the time was that if he was with a higher-profile club maybe he would have been displaying his talents at Hampden Park.

While the restless Knowles had not been granted his wish to leave Molineux, there had been plenty of departures. Now would come an arrival which would add to the quality of the side. Wolves paid Huddersfield £80,000 on Valentine's Day 1968 for 20-year-old Derek Parkin, a record fee at the time for a full-back. Parkin would go on to make a club record 501 League appearances and become a firm favourite with the Molineux fans.

Parkin's debut in the all-gold strip came in the place of his birth, Newcastle, though Wolves' display at St James' Park was one of their worst of the season. They went down 2–0 and took a rare verbal lashing from Phil Morgan in the *Express & Star*. He wrote, 'From the crow's nest heights of the St James' Park press box, which reveals so clearly the pattern of the play, it was difficult to see just what plan they had in mind. How on earth they hoped to break down one of the best defences in the country – Newcastle have conceded only 10 goals – was quite beyond me. Occasionally in midfield they played the ball around well but that was as far as it went and I wondered who among Peter Knowles, Bailey and Munro was supposed to be doing what, which is a pity when you consider their individual talent.'

That was probably the low point of Wolves' season, and with Alun Evans recalled to partner Derek Dougan up front Knowles and Mike Bailey could resume their midfield partnership for the visit to Molineux of Liverpool on Saturday 2 March 1968. It was Knowles who contrived with Dave Wagstaffe to lay on a centre for Derek Dougan to head Wolves in front three minutes from half-time. Such was the way Knowles and Bailey controlled midfield that Wolves ought to have had more goals. They did not, and Liverpool's late surge made them pay when Tony Hateley back-headed an Ian Callaghan corner for Roger Hunt to equalise 11 minutes from the end.

Knowles's temperament had led to a series of bookings, and the result was a suspension which caused him to miss the home game with Sunderland a week later when another new name arrived to help the fight against relegation. Former England centre-forward Frank Wignall was signed from Nottingham Forest for £50,000 which meant Evans's immediate future lay once more in the reserves. Frank Munro deputised for Knowles as Wolves gained their first win since 16 December, winning 2–1 thanks to a first-half goal from Derek Dougan and a second-half penalty from Mike Kenning before George Herd grabbed a late consolation for the Wearsiders.

An immediate return after his suspension saw Knowles help Wolves to another pressure-easing win, 2–0 against Arsenal at Highbury. Once again he impressed on the big stage, though there were fewer than 26,000 there, evidence of a Gunners slump which had seen them without a win in eight matches. Mike Bailey was the star of the show, but Phil Morgan said Knowles and Bailey got a grip on the midfield proceedings with devastating effect. A short corner routine saw John Holsgrove head the visitors in front on 31 minutes, and a minute from time Wignall got his first goal for the club, slamming home a fierce shot after one of Bailey's long throw-ins.

Two wins in a row should have been the platform for Wolves to climb to mid-table safety, especially as there followed successive home games against Sheffield opposition. Both teams from the steel city were, like Wolves, battling against relegation. First it was Wednesday on Monday, and the Owls rocked Wolves with a second-minute goal from Jack Whitham. That merely fired up Wolves, and Knowles was in the thick of the action, hitting two fierce volleys, one of which flattened Wednesday right-back Wilf Smith. A Mike Bailey shot hit the post, though Whitham also saw an effort hit the bar. It was Knowles and Dave Wagstaffe who eventually engineered a deserved equaliser for Wignall. Within seconds, 20-year-old Brian Woodhall restored the visitors' lead, despite protests from Wolves defenders that he had handled the ball first. Holsgrove headed home Wagstaffe's in-swinging corner to make it 2–2 five minutes into the second half, but things went wrong for Wolves' highly-effective left-wing pairing. Wagstaffe was slowed by a bad foul on him by Woodhall, who earned a booking, and Knowles hurt himself in what Phil Morgan described as 'a do-or-die blast for goal.' Despite the injuries Wolves looked like hanging on only for Woodhall, in only his second game, to hit an 85th-minute winner.

That match could have been viewed as a mere blip if Wolves had quickly made amends when Sheffield's other side, United, came to Molineux the following Saturday. Derek Dougan had played against Wednesday despite being unwell, but he finally succumbed to flu, and so Alun Evans was given a recall. That change, however, was no excuse for an abject display which saw the Blades win 3–1, and Phil Morgan give Knowles & Co another verbal blast, pulling no punches this time. In his *Express & Star* report, Morgan wrote, 'This was the last straw, the nadir for the once proud Wolves, who, in five days, spurned a chance to gain comparative First Division safety and left themselves with an even grimmer and not particularly hopeful fight to avoid relegation. In nearly 20 years I have watched the club reach the heights and plumb the depths, but I have never seen anything quite so depressing, so soulless, so miserable or so utterly foreign to such a famous name, as this.' It was Knowles who gave United their opening goal on 30 minutes. He lost possession on the edge of his own penalty area to let in Frank Barlow. Colin Addison made it two on 37 minutes, and Welsh winger Gil Reece struck a third on 67 before John Farrington revived home hopes two minutes later.

These were tough times for Ronnie Allen, and he decided in the continued absence of Derek Dougan to drop Alun Evans and put Mike Bailey in the number-10 shirt once more and recall Frank Munro to midfield for the trip to Coventry. The team did a bit better but lost to a Neil Martin penalty eight minutes from time. It was awarded for handball by John Holsgrove, who insisted afterwards the ball had struck his shoulder.

Wolves desperately needed a win to avoid slipping closer to relegation and got it in their next match on a sunny Molineux afternoon as they beat Nottingham Forest 6–1 to make it a nightmare second League outing for 19-year-old goalkeeper Mick Harby. With Dougan fit again, Knowles was able to resume his left-wing partnership with Dave Wagstaffe. They and the rest of the forwards had a field day, with Dougan collecting a hat-trick and Frank Wignall two goals. Wolves opened the score on 18 minutes and by 37 were 4–0 up. While the club gave Dougan three goals, it could so easily have been just one, Knowles being denied a place on the score sheet for goal number-four. His shot struck the underside of the bar, and many thought the ball had bounced down over the line before Dougan headed it in to make sure. Phil Morgan reckoned it was Knowles's goal, and he also thought Derek Parkin had lobbed in the fifth on 68 minutes, only for the club to say afterwards that the ball had glanced off Dougan's head. Barry Lyons had pulled one back for Forest just before that, but Mike Kenning hit Wolves' sixth in the final minute. Young Harby made one more League appearance and never played for Forest again.

If Knowles had been denied a goal against Forest, there was no stopping him at the Victoria Ground a week later when Wolves further eased their troubles with a 2–0 victory over Stoke. He was the star of the show and opened the scoring on 37 minutes. Wignall made it two five minutes after the break as Wolves could at last breathe more easily. Wolves looked like keeping up the revival when they visited Sunderland on Easter Monday, 15 April 1968, but somewhat against the run of play the home side scored when George Herd tapped a free-kick to Colin Todd, who fired home after 27 minutes. Wolves continued to impress, and Knowles appeared to be pushed off the ball in front of goal and then squandered Wolves' best chance by driving his shot over the bar. That was as good as it got for him and the rest, as Sunderland called the tune in the second half. Herd made it 2–0 after 80 minutes. Decisions like the one against Knowles prompted manager Ronnie Allen in a BBC *Sports Report* interview after the game to criticise referee Don Payne of Sheffield. Asked by the reporter to go into detail, Allen spelled out the letters H O M E R.

Five days later, a crowd of nearly 40,000 were at Molineux to see Wolves take on Manchester City who were closing in on rivals United for the First Division title. They had the promising Colin Bell in midfield, but he certainly did not outshine Knowles in the 0–0 draw which saw few chances created. Bell's rapid progress may have reinforced Knowles's view that he needed to be with a higher profile club as Bell's Championship success with City saw him win his first full England cap just over a month later. The draw saw City on 50 points from 38 games with United on 54 from 39; however, City would snatch the title by winning their last four games, while United lost two of their final three, including a 6–3 hammering at The Hawthorns which has gone into Albion folklore.

Wolves' attention, meanwhile, was focused on the other end of the table, and when they drew 1–1 against Southampton at The Dell it kept them clear of the bottom two places, though they had enough chances to have won, Knowles being one of those who wasted good openings. His general play impressed Phil Morgan, who wrote that he did some 'sterling work' in midfield along with the in-form Mike Bailey. Wolves ought to have built on the 11th-minute goal gifted them when home 'keeper Eric Martin turned a Dave Wagstaffe corner into his own net. Centre-forward Ron Davies, whose 28 First Division goals that season was equalled only by George Best, levelled for the Saints a minute before half-time. Near the end of the game Mike Kenning almost snatched victory for Wolves, but his diverted shot struck the bar.

Three games to go, and Wolves were still not safe, and two of those games would be against Chelsea. The first, on the Monday night after the Southampton trip, saw Wolves beaten at Stamford Bridge by the only goal when Peter Osgood struck with just a few seconds to go. One Knowles effort skimmed the bar, but Wolves clearly missed Frank Wignall, who had been injured at Southampton. Into his place in a striking role came 18-year-old John McAlle. It was an unlikely debut for a man who became a highly dependable central-defender for the club. McAlle began as he would go on, giving 100 per cent and threatening on several occasions, once being thwarted only by a last-ditch Eddie McCreadie tackle.

Wignall was back for the return with Chelsea, at Molineux on Saturday 4 May 1968, and had a field day with a hat-trick that saw Wolves beat the Londoners 3–0. So Wolves could relax when they wound up the season a week later by beating Tottenham 2–1 before 40,929 fans at Molineux. Knowles had come off second best in the clash of the brothers when Wolves visited White Hart Lane earlier in the season, but this time it was Cyril who tasted defeat. Phil Morgan summed it up in the *Express & Star*, 'Revelling in it all was Peter Knowles as though to prove international brother Cyril is not the only footballer in the family.' Knowles loved such games against the glamour sides, and Spurs were still one of those with Alan Mullery, Dave Mackay, Jimmy Greaves and Alan Gilzean in their line up. Frank Wignall had continued his scoring vein by hitting home a left-foot shot 10 minutes after the break, but there was late drama when Derek Parkin scored his first goal for the club only for Greaves to reply within a minute.

It was a rousing end to the match and to a season which had seen Wolves under-achieve but at least survive in their first campaign back in the top flight. Knowles had made considerable progress, starting 35 of a possible 42 League games and hitting 12 goals, but he was still restless to be with a bigger club. He had lost his place in the England Under-23 side, who would play four games at the end of the season and not call upon his services. He would watch one of his idols, George Best, sparkle at Wembley as Manchester United at last won the European Cup with a 4–1 extra-time win over Benfica, and he would watch England finish third in the European Championship, or Nations Cup, as it was then known. This was the high-profile action of which Knowles wanted a slice. It was something on which he no doubt dwelled during a close season, which for once saw Wolves without a foreign tour.

Molineux regular John Lalley recalls well the progress made by Knowles during that first season back in the top flight. 'Peter was a better player in the First Division and, as Wolves struggled to re-establish themselves, he really blossomed as a complete player. Sad to say it, but had he left Wolves to join a more successful club around 1968, he could have become a top-class international. Of that, I have no doubt.'

Still Restless

During the summer of 1968 Knowles's thoughts were probably still about moving to a top club and about his chances of making England's World Cup squad two years hence. It would not be long, however, before such ambitions were banished. When Knowles was first visited by the Jehovah's Witnesses I do not know, but certainly his devotion to Christianity grew during the 1968–69 season and by the end of the campaign had such a meaning for him that it would change his life.

Such was his new-found faith that no end of jibes or mickey-taking would shake Knowles as he found something that would shape his future and bring him to his ultimate decision to leave football fame behind. A significant step in his progress to maturity and different priorities in his life undoubtedly came when he and fiancée Jean Hipkins were married. A straightforward wedding would not have fitted in with the Knowles story, however, and so it was no ordinary occasion when the couple were wed at the Wolverhampton Register Office on Thursday 4 July 1968. For a start, he kept it quiet from his teammates, and only Phil Parkes and John McAlle were there, having learned about it just an hour earlier. Explained Parkes at the time, 'We knew he was getting married but we did not know when. He really took us by surprise.' The *Express & Star* reported that Knowles, who at the time was living at East Croft Road on the Warstones Estate, was one of the few footballers with a fan club but that even they were unaware of the impending occasion.

Neither was the bride's outfit ordinary. In its own way it was stunning, being described as a 'micro-mini white lace crochet dress with long sleeves and silver sandals.' Jean had flowers in her long dark ringlets and carried a bouquet of red and white roses. The report added, 'Miss Hipkins works at GKN Laboratories, Birmingham New Road,

Wolverhampton, and is the only daughter of Mr and Mrs R.C. Hipkins of Hilton Road, Parkfields. After a reception at the bride's home the couple are leaving for a touring honeymoon.'

A picture of them on their wedding day appeared in the programme for Wolves' first home game of the season – against Queen's Park Rangers – and showed the happy couple seated on the bonnet of their sports car, Jean wearing that miniest of mini wedding dresses. The programme reported that they had a honeymoon in Bournemouth and when they returned settled into the house which had once been the home of Knowles's erstwhile teammate Dave Burnside.

Talking to Knowles in 1994, Rogan Taylor pointed out, 'So here you are in the 60s, wages are quite good in those days, certainly compared with going down the mine. You had the money, the birds, the Beatle haircut...what happened? What went wrong?' Knowles replied, 'Nothing, because I liked all that. I liked football. I liked all the trimmings that went with it. It was just that I came into contact with the Jehovah's Witnesses and that totally then changed my whole outlook on life. I wasn't at all religious and then one night I was in my house and a Jehovah's Witness knocked at my door and I asked him one or two questions that I had been wanting an answer to from many years ago and he answered them, and I told my wife and then we both started to get into the Bible together with this Jehovah's Witness.' He added that when his teammates found out his new interest they were far from supportive. 'They would not believe it. Here was Peter, this arrogant individual and they just started to crack jokes.'

Religion would come to play a huge part in the lives of Mr and Mrs Peter Knowles, but that stage had clearly not been reached when the new season began. Most of Knowles's thoughts were on trying to get Wolves off to a winning start when they visited Ipswich Town. Just promoted from the Second Division and under the managership of the disciplinarian Bill McGarry, Town proved too good for Wolves, winning 1–0. An injury to David Woodfield in a clash with former colleague Ray Crawford early in the second half did not help Wolves' cause, with John McAlle having to come on as substitute. Within minutes John O'Rourke had scored from a Crawford lob. Although Wolves rallied and Knowles was among several players to go close to an equaliser, the nearest Wolves got was a Derek Parkin shot which hit a post. For most of the game goalkeeper Phil Parkes was the busiest man on the field.

Wolves also rallied against Manchester City four days later, two late Frank Wignall goals making the score a more respectable 3–2. Yet, it was still another defeat, and Knowles and several others were below their best. Things then got better with that first home game of the season, QPR being beaten even though Ian Morgan cancelled out Frank Wignall's seventh-minute opener. Mike Bailey seven minutes after half-time and Derek Dougan six minutes from time saw Wolves home 3–1. Wolves ought to have made it two home wins running when Arsenal came to town in midweek but were defied by Gunners goalkeeper Bob Wilson, who just a few years earlier had been an amateur on Wolves' books. Several Wolves players were denied by him, and Knowles went close with long-range snap shots which were fast becoming his speciality. During his spell at Wolves, Wilson had used the same digs, near Molineux, as Knowles and in his autobiography referred to him as a 'fabulous talent.'

It was one of those Knowles hot shots which brought Wolves' goal at The Dell as they went down 2–1 to Southampton. Goalkeeper Eric Martin could not hold on to the ball, such was the power of Knowles's drive, and when he spilled it Dave Wagstaffe was on the spot to take advantage. That came a minute after Terry Paine had put Saints 2–0 up, Fred Kemp, another man who had once been a fellow lodger with Knowles, having opened the scoring on 24 minutes.

Another goalkeeper stole the limelight in Wolves' next midweek game as a teenage Peter Shilton kept Leicester in the match, only being beaten once when Derek Dougan scrambled the ball in right on half-time after a long throw-in by Mike Bailey had caused a goalmouth melee. Knowles and Bailey had controlled things in midfield. In this game an injury to Dave Wagstaffe meant Mike Kenning had partnered Knowles on the left, and he benefited from Knowles's promptings.

An injury to Derek Dougan in the Leicester game let Alun Evans make a 20-minute appearance as substitute. A year earlier Evans and Knowles looked liked being cornerstones in Wolves' future but Evans, unlike Knowles, was not showing signs of fulfilling his potential. A section of fans did not help Evans when he came into the team in Dougan's absence for the home game with Stoke. He was not alone in being out of touch, Frank Wignall also being off form at centre-forward; however, it was Evans who came in for most stick. 'Alun Evans must have thought the whole business a nasty dream, especially when the crowd picked on him,' wrote Phil Morgan in the *Express & Star*. Mike Bailey's goal on 61 minutes was cancelled out by a rare one from Stoke full-back Alex Elder 20 minutes later.

It was no surprise when Evans was dropped for the 1–0 home win over Southend in the League Cup but, unexpectedly, Knowles was then left out for the First Division trip to Leeds in favour of Frank Munro. This was how Phil Morgan saw it, 'The decision to substitute Munro for Knowles seems to suggest the hope of stronger midfield support for the in-form Mike Bailey.' Knowles would quickly bounce back, but Evans had played his last senior game for Wolves. Munro gave Wolves the lead after only eight minutes at Elland Road, but Terry Cooper levelled 22 minutes from time, and big Jack Charlton won it for the home side four minutes from the end. Knowles turned out for the reserves at Molineux and helped them beat their Leeds opposite numbers 4–1.

Derek Dougan was injured in midweek helping Northern Ireland to a 3–2 friendly win over Israel in Tel-Aviv and that paved the way for Knowles to make an immediate return when Sunderland visited Molineux on Saturday 14 September to hold Wolves to a 1–1 draw. Frank Wignall's late goal cancelled out one from Billy Hughes just before the break. Finishing promising attacks was still Wolves' problem and Knowles, though close with two long shots, could not find the net. The game saw the debut of Alan Boswell, an eccentric goalkeeper bought from Shrewsbury. Ronnie Allen's judgement in signing him may have been questioned, and one also had to wonder if he did the right thing when he then let Alun Evans go. The youngster had been struggling, but clearly Liverpool boss Bill Shankly saw something in him and took him to Anfield for £100,000, at the time the biggest fee ever paid for a teenager. Those unfeeling fans who had jeered Evans may have been glad to see him go, but Evans would return very quickly to wipe the smile off their faces.

More to the point, Knowles must have wished it was he, not Evans, who was moving to a top club, and there is every reason to believe that Shankly would have loved to have him at Anfield. Freelance sports writer Ron Warrilow recalls, 'Word was that Shankly would have paid £150,000 for Peter, a huge fee in those days, but Wolves told them that no way would they sell.'

There was no doubt Knowles was desperate to leave Wolves at this time, and there was continued speculation about him in the national press. Being dropped after the Stoke game and then seeing Evans get a glamour move would only have added to his restlessness. There was a reference to this when Knowles helped Wolves draw 0–0 against Albion at The Hawthorns. Ray Matts wrote in the *Express & Star*, 'Peter Knowles, for all his apparent discontent at Molineux, still persists in being one of the most dangerous long-shots in the business. Most of Wolves' goalscoring efforts stemmed from him but with the exception of one shot, brilliantly saved by John Osborne, they were mainly off target.' This was a useful point for Wolves, who were still without Derek Dougan and had Dave Wagstaffe injured in the first minute. Frank Munro continued in the number-10 shirt with Frank Wignall at centre-forward.

This display must have cemented Knowles's ranking with Sir Alf Ramsey, who named him in the Under-23 side to face Wales. Knowles was a rising star and again appeared to have itchy feet, something reflected by renewed speculation in the national papers. It brought him censure from his club, Phil Morgan reporting in the *Express & Star* that not only had Knowles had his transfer request refused, but he had been 'severely cautioned by the club directors for inspiring press articles regarding his request.'

Although he was the only home forward not to score, Knowles continued his good form when Millwall were brushed aside 5–1 at Molineux in the third round of the League Cup. It was not all plain sailing, though, despite fit-again Derek Dougan heading a first-minute goal. Eamonn Dunphy put the Londoners level 10 minutes after half-time, but Frank Munro restored Wolves' lead within three minutes. A foul on Derek Parkin on a foray into the visitors' penalty area brought a penalty, which Mike Kenning fired home, and right-winger John Farrington hit two late goals, one from a defence-splitting pass by Knowles.

His displays against Albion and Second Division Millwall may have been impressive, but Knowles and his teammates were about to get a reality check. Wolves suffered one of the most infamous home defeats in their history as Liverpool looked different class in winning 6–0 at Molineux. Alun Evans showed his detractors his true potential as he helped himself to two goals, as did England World Cup hero Roger Hunt and outside-left Peter Thompson. Along with John Holsgrove and Les Wilson, Knowles was praised for his effort by Phil Morgan, whose verdict was that Liverpool gave Wolves a lesson in teamwork. How Knowles would have loved to be in such a team who also included Tommy Smith and Emlyn Hughes, the masterly Ian St John and England winger Ian Callaghan.

After that drubbing Knowles must have relished the chance to get away from it all and team up with England's young hopefuls for the Under-23 clash with Wales at Wrexham on Wednesday 2 October 1968. It was at such gatherings that players would talk to those at bigger clubs, and this would fan the flames of ambition. Certainly, watching managers who wanted to prise Knowles away from Molineux would have been impressed by his display, even though England did not exactly sparkle as they beat their Welsh counterparts 3–1 with Knowles hitting the final goal, his first of the season. The Welsh lads got off to a flying start when Stoke midfielder John Mahoney scored in the second minute, and it took some 25 minutes before an equaliser came courtesy of a diving header by Jimmy Greenhoff to a John Sissons cross. Knowles had an increasing influence on the game as the second half wore on, but it took an own-goal from future Arsenal central-defender John Roberts to give England the lead. In the final minute Knowles made the match safe when he drove in a goal from 18 yards out. It was one of the highlights of the game and must have registered with the watching Ramsey who admitted afterwards, 'There was a lot of good football but not much excitement.'

The teams were:

Wales: Walker (Watford), Thomas (Swindon), Collins (Tottenham), Yorath (Leeds), Roberts (Northampton), Page (Birmingham), Screen (Swansea), Mahoney (Stoke), Hawkins (Leeds), Humphreys (Everton), Jones (Swansea).

Goal: Mahoney (2).

England: Shilton (Leicester), Bonds (West Ham), Cattlin (Coventry) sub Whitham (Sheffield Wednesday), Kendall (Everton), Ellis (Sheffield Wednesday), Hurst (Everton), Radford (Arsenal), Knowles (Wolves), Greenhoff (Birmingham), Todd (Sunderland), Sissons (West Ham).

Goals: Greenhoff (27), Roberts own-goal (85), Knowles (89).

Attendance: 11,084. Referee: W. Mullan (Scotland).

More evidence of Knowles's unhappiness at Molineux came in a few paragraphs in popular weekly magazine *Soccer Star*, whose Midlands correspondent Brian Marshall wrote that Knowles was disturbed that the club had turned down Liverpool's joint offer for Evans and him. According to Marshall, Knowles felt his future lay elsewhere, saying, 'I am worried about my game, and I think I need a change of club.' Marshall said manager Allen was far from happy that the press had suggested Knowles was unsettled. The boss may not have been happy with the newspaper publicity, but the reporters were merely telling it how it was.

Three days after the Under-23 game, Knowles met up with another former colleague, Ernie Hunt, as Wolves tried to banish the Liverpool blues with a visit to Coventry, whom Hunt had joined from Everton in March that year. Hunt was out of luck as he saw a shot hit a post before Derek Dougan scored the only goal of the game on 59 minutes. Knowles continued his good work from the Under-23 game but was not at his best in the midweek game at Filbert Street where Wolves lost 2–0 to Leicester City. As Phil Morgan put it, 'Peter Knowles, after some promising early moves, faded and much of the midfield work was wrecked on a series of bad passes that gave Leicester the liberties they never expected.' Knowles was not alone. Morgan said nobody played really well.

Knowles collected his first Wolves goal of the season when he snatched a dramatic equaliser in the game against Chelsea at Molineux. England 'keeper Peter Bonetti had defied Wolves for most of the match before Bobby Tambling hit a rocket shot to give the Londoners the lead only two minutes from time. That was the signal for home fans to make for the exits, but Knowles popped up a minute later to volley the ball home after Dougan had back-headed Mike Bailey's long throw-in. Tambling was an interesting character as he was a

Jehovah's Witness. Unlike Knowles, Tambling saw no conflict of interest between football and religion and enjoyed a full career with Chelsea before moving to Crystal Palace and then to Ireland, where he progressed into football management.

Wolves' form had still not picked up and they were ushered out of the League Cup 2–1 by Second Division Blackpool at Bloomfield Road before Knowles helped the team to a welcome win – over Sheffield Wednesday at Hillsborough. He showed no nerves when he was asked to take a penalty after Man of the Match Derek Dougan had been brought down by Wednesday centre-half Sam Ellis on 18 minutes. Knowles stepped up to blast home the spot-kick and earned praise in the *Express & Star* as John Dee wrote, 'Until he went off with a leg injury, Knowles was distributing the ball well and was always ready to help out his defence.' Dougan was on the spot to prod home a second goal just before half-time after 'keeper Peter Springett had failed to hold a Dave Wagstaffe corner.

There was more praise, another goal and another early exit for Knowles when Wolves were beaten 2–1 at home by Everton. Knowles was thwarted after only five minutes when Colin Harvey looked to have used his hand to stop the ball reaching him, yet Knowles was not to be denied and wiped out a first-half goal by Joe Royle. As John Dee put it, '[The] biggest thrill was undoubtedly Knowles's equaliser five minutes into the second half – a great 25-yard volley that gave West not a hope of saving. Knowles, in fact, showed just how good a player he is when the mood takes him. It was a great pity that a leg injury took him off with a quarter of an hour remaining.' Everton controversially won the match with an Alan Ball penalty. Ball had appeared merely to collide with Derek Parkin as they chased the ball. Referee Roy Capey, having ignored Wolves' earlier claims, incurred more wrath from the home fans when he said yes to Everton's.

Knowles had scored in three successive League games and was clearly maturing as a player, even if he and the rest of the team missed a host of chances when Wolves were held 0–0 by Nottingham Forest at the City Ground at the beginning of November. His form had certainly impressed Sir Alf Ramsey, who again named him in the Under-23 team, this time for the game against Holland Under-23s. Few could have guessed that it would be his last appearance in an England shirt. Before that match, Wolves got back to winning ways with a 2–0 home success over West Ham thanks to first-half goals from Mike Bailey and winger John Farrington. Once again John Dee sang Knowles's praises. 'Up front Peter Knowles again showed he has regained the golden touch,' wrote Dee. On the debit side, Knowles got himself booked for arguing with the referee who had penalised him for a tackle on his old England Youth teammate Harry Redknapp.

A goal down at half-time, England hit back to draw 2–2 in the Under-23 clash with the Dutch at St Andrew's, Birmingham, on Wednesday 13 November 1968, where Knowles yet again showed he had the potential to be a full international. Eddie Griffiths wrote in the *Express & Star* that England opened well, adding, 'Football flowed from Everton pair Kendall and Hurst and on to Coates, Peter Knowles and Greenhoff.' After Rensenbrink had laid on the centre for Geels to head the Dutch in front on 34 minutes, it was Knowles who helped make the equaliser on the hour. Jimmy Greenhoff laid on the chance for John Radford to head home. It came, as Griffiths put it, 'following one of innumerable corners by Knowles which were always played with pinpoint accuracy and caused a lot of trouble in the Dutch goalmouth.' Once level, England pressed for a second goal, and Griffiths again sang Knowles's praises. 'In this period Knowles delighted with some superb ball control and slide rule passes.'

It was against the run of play when Klijnjan hit a 20-yard volley to put Holland ahead once more on 63 minutes. A minute later a low centre from Alun Evans was turned back by Greenhoff to John Hurst whose ground shot found the net. That was apparently the best moment for Knowles's former clubmate Evans who, Griffiths reported, looked like a little boy lost for most of the game.

England: Shilton (Leicester), Bonds (West Ham), Cattlin (Coventry), Kendall (Everton) sub Todd (Sunderland), McFarland (Derby), Hurst (Everton), Radford (Arsenal), Coates (Burnley), Greenhoff (Birmingham), Knowles (Wolves), Evans (Liverpool).

Goals: Radford, Hurst.

Holland: Treijtel (Feyenoord), Drost (Twente Enschede), Dijkstra (DWS Amsterdam), Pijlman (DWS Amsterdam), Schneider (Go Ahead Deventer), Veenstra (Go Ahead Deventer), Achterberg (NAC Breda), Geels (Feyenoord), Klijnjan (Sparta Rotterdam), van Dijke (Twente Enschede), Rensenbrink (Twente Enschede).

Goals: Geels, Klijnjan.

Attendance: 24,258.

Referee: J. Callaghan (Scotland).

Those Were The Days author Clive Corbett confirms that to most fans at the time it seemed Knowles was destined for great things. 'I remember the pride of seeing Peter play for the Under-23s at St Andrew's – my first international match – and I was certain he would figure in England's defence of the World Cup in Mexico.' Corbett was not alone in that view. How, wrong we all were!

Evidence of Knowles's status, his standing with the fans and of his continued unrest came in just a few words in *Goal* magazine, which carried his picture on its front page in November

1968. He was described as, 'The youngster Wolves fans love to hate. Reason – he can be brilliant one week and off-touch the next. But young Knowles on form is a devastating scorer and a considerable schemer in midfield, as was proved by his selection for the England Under-23 side. Not the happiest of players at Molineux, Knowles and transfer talk have been inseparable lately.'

Back in League action, Knowles took the limelight again as Wolves drew 1–1 at Burnley. Because Mike Bailey was injured, Knowles found himself at the centre of Wolves' midfield and made the most of it, creating a host of chances which should have brought victory. It was a Catch-22 situation, as Wolves could have done with Knowles in a striker role, too. As John Dee explained, 'It was a pity Mike Bailey was absent for Peter Knowles, now playing with tremendous confidence, was setting up most of the Wolves attacks from a deep-lying position. Had Bailey been there to do the job, Knowles might have been a little nearer to the Burnley goal and prevented all those scoring opportunities going astray. As it was, the Under-23 international made one superb attempt from 20 yards when Burnley were being run off their feet and only a great save by Thomson prevented Wolves going ahead.' Frank Casper duly put Burnley one up before Derek Dougan levelled three minutes from the break with a typical header to a Mike Kenning corner. 'We let them off the hook' was Ronnie Allen's verdict afterwards, in what proved to be the last time he would face the press as Molineux manager.

It was a very good point against an in-form Burnley side who had reeled off eight successive wins, including a 5–1 demolition of League leaders Leeds. Despite good results like this one since the Liverpool drubbing, Allen was a man on borrowed time, and the last thing he needed as the knives were being sharpened was some extra hassle, but extra hassle was what he got, courtesy of Knowles. A Sunday newspaper the following day carried a story claiming Knowles was so desperate to get away to a more successful club that he was prepared to take a wage cut of £20 a week. The story claimed he would even consider emigrating if he could not get a move. Allen, a man under pressure, responded to the story in the Monday edition of the *Express & Star*, saying, 'If he wants a successful club he should buckle down to his job here and help bring back success to Wolves.'

Enter McGarry

Knowles and his problems would soon be none of Ronnie Allen's concern. He was sacked on Wednesday 20 November 1968, and one suspects that not even a win at Turf Moor could have saved him. The die was cast; Wolves had at last prised their long-term target Bill McGarry from Ipswich, and he was duly comfirmed as the new boss. McGarry was a totally different character from Allen and made it clear from day one that he did not necessarily want to be liked but that his word was law. The Wolves response to the change in managership was to beat Newcastle 5–0 at Molineux. The score flattered Wolves, however, and goalkeeper Phil Parkes was one of the busiest men on the pitch in the first half. McGarry must have been impressed with reports he may have received on Knowles who scored twice, the second with a scissors-kick. Frank Wignall was also on target, while the other two came from Derek Dougan, who, in coming years, would grow to dislike the autocratic McGarry with a burning intensity.

Fan Clive Corbett rates the Knowles second goal in this game as his best – 'It was a spectacular overhead-kick and left McFaul [Newcastle's goalkeeper] clutching at air.' The verdict of the *Sunday Times* man Malcolm Winton confirms Corbett's view. He wrote, 'Knowles scored Wolves' fourth goal with the kind of audacity that has made him famous. From a Wagstaffe throw on the left Dougan chipped a pass in the direction of the Newcastle penalty spot. Knowles, with his back to the goal, volleyed straight over his left shoulder and inside the far post.'

When McGarry took charge of his new team for the first time it was a much tougher assignment as Wolves went to Old Trafford. It was made tougher by an early injury which robbed them of centre-half David Woodfield. Manchester United won 2–0 thanks to second-half goals from George Best and Denis Law. It was a star-studded United team, with Pat

Crerand, Nobby Stiles and Bobby Charlton in their line up, yet the desire of Knowles to be among such an array of talent was starting to diminish; however, he would surely have been up for the visit of Spurs a week later, who, as well as his brother Cyril, included Terry Venables, Jimmy Greaves and Alan Gilzean in their team. And Peter had the bragging rights over his brother as the top-form Derek Dougan inspired Wolves to a 2–0 victory. The Doog powered through to open the score on 63 minutes and three minutes later played Frank Wignall through for the second.

Despite his penalty success against Sheffield Wednesday, Knowles did not retain the spot-kick duties when Wolves met Chelsea at Stamford Bridge. Mike Kenning was back in the team, and it was not surprising that he was given the chance to put Wolves ahead in the first half after Frank Wignall had been fouled by Ron Harris. Kenning was a penalty expert and made no mistake on 36 minutes. He had missed his first-ever spot-kick when with Charlton but had not failed since. He made no mistake this time to make it 20 successful penalties in a row. Two minutes later Gerry Taylor handled, but goalkeeper Alan Boswell saved Peter Osgood's resultant kick. It did not put off Osgood, however, and when Chelsea were awarded a second penalty in the final minute he stepped up to level the score.

Boswell was certainly not the hero in the final game before Christmas as Sheffield Wednesday won 3–0 at Molineux as he was at fault with two of the goals, which came from John Ritchie (two) and Archie Irvine. Boswell's brief career at Molineux was virtually over. He never made another first-team appearance. Knowles's form and that of the team had taken a dip, but the new year would bring a welcome win when they played Second Division Hull City in the third round of the FA Cup. The match at Boothferry Park is often recalled by Wolves players of that era but not because Wolves won it 3–1. It was the build-up to the game which stood in their memories. It was the first overnight stay of McGarry's reign. After some days training in Southport the squad travelled to a hotel near Hull on the Friday before the game. At the evening meal defender John Holsgrove, down to play centre-half next day, ordered himself a prawn cocktail as a starter. McGarry heard him and hit the roof. 'What do you think this is, Butlin's?' roared McGarry, who reckoned that such food was bad for footballers.

Dave Wagstaffe recalled the incident well. 'We all sat there absolutely amazed, looking down like chastised school kids. McGarry walked over and stood at the end of the table. "I'll tell you what you can f***ing eat," he growled. "Soup to start, steak or chicken for the main course and fresh fruit salad for dessert." Believe it or not, that menu of soup, steak or chicken and fruit salad was to stand wherever we went in this country or in the world for the whole of McGarry's days as manager of Wolves. It was pre-ordered whenever possible when the hotel rooms were booked.'

Whether it was the right sort of diet or not, something set up Wolves to brush aside Second Division Hull, with two goals from Dougan and one from Wignall after Chris Chilton had given the Tigers an early lead. Knowles, despite a bout of flu, got back in the scoring groove a week later when he hit the only goal of the game against Nottingham Forest at Molineux. With another player whose skills Knowles admired, Jim Baxter, marshalling their attacks, Forest gave Wolves a tough workout. The cheeky chappie personality which had helped endear Knowles to his fans was mirrored in the *Sunday Express* verdict of John Cooke: 'Peter Knowles, the artful dodger of modern soccer, flitted across the Molineux stage for one brief moment two minutes before the interval to score the goal and take both points from the desperately unlucky Nottingham Forest. In the 74th minute Knowles left the field still suffering from the after-effects of flu and was replaced by Frank Munro. But his goal had been enough. He took his chance, which was a third-time-lucky affair, superbly. Both Mike Bailey and Mike Kenning had hard shots blocked by defenders before the ball came back to Knowles, who shot in a flash on the turn to beat the diving Peter Grummitt.'

A waterlogged Upton Park pitch meant the scheduled trip to West Ham a week later was postponed, giving Knowles plenty of time to savour the build-up to a trip to White Hart Lane to face Spurs in the fourth round of the FA Cup. The competition still had magic in those days, and to add to the big game atmosphere it meant another meeting of the footballing Knowles brothers. It was obviously a special occasion as far as Jane Knowles was concerned, and she was there to see her sons in action.

The match, on Saturday 25 January 1969, proved a typical Cup tie with thrills and controversy. Dave Wagstaffe gave Wolves a shock seventh-minute lead, and Knowles thought he had scored a second only for referee Norman Burtenshaw to penalise Dougan for handball. Knowles told Phil Morgan afterwards he had seen no hint of hands when the Doog put the ball back to him. After Neil Johnson's equaliser on 53 minutes Wolves felt hard done by again five minutes later. What they thought was a goal-kick was deemed a corner by Burtenshaw, and from it Jimmy Greaves hit the winner. As for Mrs Knowles, who had her young son Richard with her, she did not find it as exciting as the rest of the 48,985 spectators. 'I didn't really enjoy it,' she said afterwards, adding, 'but I must say this is one day when I would like our Peter to have won. I'd love to see him at Wembley.' Cyril had, of course, appeared at the stadium in Spurs's 1967 Final win over Chelsea, as well as playing there for England.

Mrs Knowles's hopes for her younger footballing son would never be realised, and it was after the Spurs Cup tie that Peter's religious beliefs were brought into the open. The *Daily Mail* reported that Knowles had become a Jehovah's Witness, but manager McGarry denied that there was any possibility of it affecting Knowles's football career. With hindsight the boss's remarks were way off beam, but he stated categorically, 'You can take it from me that he won't be packing in football; however, it is true that Knowles has taken a real interest in Jehovah's Witnesses, but what he does in his spare time is his own business as long as it does not interfere with his work. He has talked to me about religion but leaving the game was never suggested. Like everyone else, he's earning a good living from the game. He is not likely to give it up.'

When he arrived at Molineux that morning Knowles had been confronted by eight reporters, and his first comments were, 'I have not said I am packing in football have I? It's my living isn't it?' but, tellingly, he added, 'I may or may not give up football.' Knowles agreed that the national paper had not misquoted him when it reported, 'I shall continue to play football for the time being, but I have lost my ambition. Though I'll still do my best on the field, I need more time to learn about the Bible and may give up football.'

Jane Knowles had expressed the wish to see her son at Wembley, and Knowles confirmed that he too wanted to go to the famous stadium. Significantly, though, he wanted to go there for a big Jehovah's Witnesses convention in the summer. It was ample evidence that his priorities had changed and would, by the end of the year, lead him to make a life-changing choice.

For the moment, though, football was still playing a prominent part in his life. He had done well at White Hart Lane and was also a lone success at Goodison Park, despite an emphatic 4–0 midweek defeat at the hands of Everton. Wolves stopped the rot on the first day of February 1969, and though they were held 1–1 by Burnley Knowles was again on top of his game, overshadowing the arrival of striker Hugh Curran, a £65,000 capture from Norwich. Knowles's goal on 31 minutes was cancelled out seven minutes later by Doug Collins, but his display was summed up by Phil Morgan who wrote, 'Bill [McGarry] is too experienced a boss to comment publicly on individual failings but he was happy to acknowledge the fine performance of Peter Knowles who, I thought, showed the touch of class Wolves lacked as a complete unit. It was the third successive high-class show from the former stormy petrel and this time it was capped by as smart a goal as you could wish to see. He swung on a free-kick from Mike Bailey and Greaves-wise steered it wide of Harry Thomson.' Morgan added, 'What a pity Wolves did not all live up to the Knowles standard.'

Sir Alf Ramsey was at the game, probably to run the rule over Burnley inside-left Ralph Coates, but Morgan reckoned the England boss could not have failed to be impressed by a 'tip-top show' from Knowles.

That view was endorsed in the *Sunday Express* by John Cooke who wrote, 'Peter Knowles proved himself a real revivalist with a brilliant performance in sheets of rain on a paddyfield pitch. And he scored an astute goal before the soccer-wise presence of England team manager Sir Alf Ramsey.'

A cold snap meant the trip to Newcastle was cancelled, so it was two weeks later when Knowles kept up the good work before a crowd of just over 44,000 at Molineux to see Wolves build up a two-goal first-half lead against Manchester United, only for Bobby Charlton and George Best to wipe it out in the second half. It was touch and go whether the conditions were playable, but Knowles did not let it bother him, Phil Morgan reporting, 'With Peter Knowles showing admirable control on the frozen, tricky and treacherous surface, they wore United down to the error-making stage and this let in Dougan and Curran.' Such had been Wolves' first-half dominance that their fans were chanting 'We want six' – but it all changed after half-time.

February ended with yet another meeting of the Knowles brothers and this time the spoils were shared at White Hart Lane. Tottenham were parading their £100,000 signing from QPR, Roger Morgan, and he marked his arrival with a goal after eight minutes which Hugh Curran cancelled out 14 minutes later when he slid home a Derek Dougan cross. Morgan did not look half as impressive in his left-wing role as Wolves' masterly Dave Wagstaffe, and if late efforts from Curran and Mike Bailey had not struck the woodwork the Knowles family bragging rights would have belonged to Peter. It was a Knowles incident in this game that was featured on BBC's *Match of the Day* and was described in the *Sunday Express* by Bob Ferrier thus: 'Peter Knowles contrived to have his name taken in rather naïve circumstances. In what might have been called a discussion with referee Dawes, Knowles suddenly hurled the ball to the ground. Since Dawes was only about 3ft away it was rather less than judicial. Knowles has far too much talent for this kind of thing.'

On the first day of March, Ipswich, under the new managership of Bobby Robson, came to Molineux, and Wolves again drew 1–1 as substitute Mike Kenning scored a late goal to cancel out the one by John O'Rourke which had put Town ahead on 10 minutes. It was another disappointing result for Wolves, and the only note in Phil Morgan's meticulously kept records read, 'Wolves shocking.'

If Knowles was formulating his plans, Wolves boss Bill McGarry was also preparing for the future. Wolves won at Queen's Park Rangers a week after the Ipswich game thanks to a third-minute Derek Dougan goal, some fine goalkeeping by Phil Parkes and some poor finishing by the home side, particularly by Rodney Marsh. That would prove the last game in a gold shirt for former England full-back Bobby Thomson. He joined his old boss Stan Cullis at Birmingham City. Winger Mike Kenning also left during March, returning to his old club Charlton. McGarry was about to mould the side to the way he wanted them to play, but it would take time. From looking like top-half finishers at one stage Wolves slipped to a final placing of 16th in the First Division.

A goalless home draw with Southampton was followed by a 4–1 drubbing at Stoke despite Hugh Curran giving Wolves the lead. Former Blackburn inside-forward Peter Dobing took centre stage in the second half, making goals for Terry Conroy and David Herd and, in between, scoring two himself. Stoke in those days, under the managership of Tony Waddington, was a home for players whom many had thought past their best. As well as Dobing, the Potters that day included former Manchester United centre-forward Herd, ex-Burnley full-back Alex Elder and former Arsenal midfielder George Eastham, plus ex-Liverpool half-back Willie Stevenson as a second-half substitute. In contrast, injuries meant Wolves had to look to youngsters, giving debuts to one of the many Clarke brothers, Derek, in attack and Dave Galvin in defence.

Another teenager, Jimmy Seal, was given his chance a couple of days later when Wolves, without Woodfield, Wagstaffe and Curran, lost 3–1 at West Ham where Martin Peters (two) and Trevor Brooking hit the home goals before Les Wilson hit a late Wolves consolation.

He had not been able to make much impression against Bobby Moore & Co, but Knowles did show a revival in form when League leaders Leeds United came to Molineux at the end of March. Don Revie's team had won seven League games in a row and were on their way to becoming champions with a then record 67 points. Wolves held them to a goalless draw and could easily have won. Phil Morgan wrote in the *Express & Star* that Wolves had created more chances than Leeds and added, 'Much of the credit for Wolves' attacking accent after Leeds' fiery start must go to Peter Knowles. He kept things moving and might well have been a scorer with his quick-thinking back flick.' Don Hardisty of the *Sunday Express* was also impressed: 'Peter Knowles's tremendous appetite for work brought Wolves' attack into the game more strongly after half an hour and his skill and stamina kept them in with a chance throughout the second half.'

147

Knowles may now have become a calmer more mature person and was playing better than ever, but there were still occasional lapses which harked back to his reckless early days. So it proved when Wolves lost 1–0 at Liverpool on 5 April 1969, Easter Saturday. The only goal of the match came from World Cup hero Roger Hunt, who, just a few weeks earlier, had announced he no longer wished to play international football. He beat Knowles in the centre circle but, rather than let him get away, the Wolves man grabbed hold of Hunt and so conceded a free-kick, from which the home side duly scored. Tommy Smith's kick was turned in by Hunt. After that Knowles lifted his game but could not atone for his error.

Easter Monday saw Wolves beaten again, this time 3–1 by Arsenal at Highbury, where wingers John Robertson and George Armstrong gave the Gunners a half-time lead. Then Knowles laid on a goal with a neat centre which Les Wilson headed home only for George Graham to clinch the points with a spectacular scissor-kick. Wolves needed a lift and got it the following night despite Francis Lee giving FA Cup finalists Manchester City the lead at Molineux after a mere 30 seconds. Knowles started the revival which ended in a 3–1 home win. A typical Derek Dougan burst of speed took him to the bye-line and his centre, according to Phil Morgan, 'Knowles met full pelt for a tremendous jack-knife headed goal.' That was on 47 minutes, and 12 minutes later Dougan put Wolves ahead before Knowles raced away to lay on the third goal for Frank Munro.

Maybe the win gave Knowles a renewed appetite for the game, and he was in good form against old rivals Albion at Molineux but found visiting goalkeeper John Osborne at his best. As Ray Matts put it in the *Express & Star*, 'It was left to Peter Knowles to provide the goalpunch for Wolves, and some of his long-range efforts from outside the penalty area brought the best from Albion goalkeeper John Osborne. Just before half-time, Osborne had to dive full length to palm a sizzler from Knowles over the bar and after the break he showed fine anticipation to collect a couple more efforts from the inside-forward.' The match was settled in the 25th minute. Clive Clark came on for injured Dick Krzywicki and scored within 60 seconds to spark the inevitable *Sporting Star* headline, 'Wolves sunk by a sub.' That match also saw the first taste of First Division football for young Ken Hibbitt, the last player signed by Ronnie Allen. The former Bradford Park Avenue midfielder, who came on as sub for John Farrington for the last 20 minutes, would in time prove a fine Wolves servant.

Knowles was obviously still a force, but he would play only one more game that season and signed off with a goal when Coventry came to Molineux to play a rearranged fixture towards the end of April. Former teammate Ernie Hunt put the Sky Blues ahead on 30 minutes, but Knowles rescued a point for Wolves 20 minutes from time. Hard-man Maurice

Setters, who had given Derek Dougan little scope all night, fouled the Wolves centre-forward, and Knowles fired the free-kick home, giving Bill Glazier in the visitors' goal no chance. It was a rare highlight in another low-key Wolves display which ought to have ended in defeat. Luck was on their side, however, when Willie Carr, a future Molineux purchase, hit the bar with Phil Parkes stranded and then Jeff Blockley fired the rebound high over.

That proved to be the end of Knowles's League season, as the day before Wolves were due to play Sunderland at Roker Park he sustained a foot injury in a five-a-side game. There was evidence McGarry was looking to strengthen the team, but bids for Millwall's Keith Weller and Ipswich's Danny Hegan were rejected. The fee involved was reported as £70,000 in both cases. McGarry was looking to the future and in doing so gave teenager Jimmy McVeigh his debut in the game with Sunderland, the home side winning 2–0. Two days later Wolves completed a disappointing end to the season when they were beaten 4–1 by Newcastle at a muddy St James' Park. Knowles had scored only nine goals in 39 League games, but he had rarely been played as a striker. He was now looking the complete player. That fact would heighten the sense of loss when he decided to call an end to his career.

The Final Curtain

Wolves' summer tournament in the US would have special significance for Knowles as it would be his last footballing adventure abroad. His mind was made up that he would have to leave the game, and his plans for doing so were well advanced. Before Wolves set off across the Atlantic, they visited Portman Road to play Ipswich Town in a testimonial game for Ray Crawford, the man alongside whom Knowles had made his Wolves debut nearly six years earlier. The home side won 6–0, though Crawford himself did not get on the score sheet. Knowles did not start the match but replaced Frank Munro late on. Guest of honour at the game was Sir Alf Ramsey, and it was afterwards that he and Knowles had that brief exchange which signified so much for the young player as it ended with the England boss turning his back on him.

Ramsey would have seen Knowles as part of England's future, and there was every chance he could have gained a place in the 1970 World Cup squad in Mexico. Ramsey had named him in the party for the Under-23 team's end-of-season tour, which would include matches against Holland, Belgium and Portugal. If Knowles still had the desire to be a full international it would have been an ideal platform to stake a claim. Wolves' trip would take place during May with the England trip scheduled for the end of that month; however, Knowles was no longer interested and had told Ramsey so at Portman Road. It was reported briefly that Knowles had withdrawn from the tour, saying he preferred to attend a Jehovah's Witnesses convention. Birmingham City's Jimmy Greenhoff was called-up to replace him. The squad included such future full internationals as Peter Shilton, Emlyn Hughes, David Nish, Roy McFarland, Ralph Coates and Joe Royle.

Based in Kansas City, Wolves made a losing start to the USA tournament when they were beaten 3–2 in Baltimore by West Ham, despite Knowles giving them a half-time lead thanks to a low shot from 25 yards. Trevor Brooking levelled for the Hammers, and then a header from half-back Peter Bennett was judged to have crossed the line even though Phil Parkes had pushed the ball out. The third goal came from an 18-year-old youngster from the Bahamas, Clyde Best, who went on to have a highly successful career at Upton Park. A late Wolves consolation came from Mike Bailey.

When Wolves played their first 'home' game they beat Dundee United 4–2, and again Knowles was in scoring mood, blasting home a shot from the edge of the penalty area after Alex Gordon had put the Scots in front and collecting a second from close range after Gordon had cancelled out a Les Wilson goal. Mike Bailey made the game safe in the final minute. Knowles wore the number-nine shirt in this game and again when West Ham came to Kansas City. Wolves gained revenge over the Londoners 4–2 and John McAlle, a rare scorer for Wolves, gained a sort of hat-trick. He struck twice to put Wolves in command and then conceded an own-goal. His second was a header from a high centre by Knowles. Mike Bailey and Hugh Curran hit two more late in the match, but there was enough time left for Trevor Brooking to narrow the margin.

Hugh Curran (two) and John Farrington were the scorers when Wolves made it three wins in a row by beating Kilmarnock 3–2 in Kansas City. The Scots fought back from two down to level through Eddie Morrison and Tommy McLean before Farrington won it for Wolves. Again Knowles started in the centre-forward role, but he would have to give way in the next match as Derek Dougan joined the team after being involved in the Home International series which for the first time had been played in the last week of the season. Both Knowles and Dougan were on target as Wolves beat Aston Villa 2–1 in Atlanta. Knowles scored from the penalty spot and, after Brian Godfrey had equalised for Villa, Dougan hit the winner. Knowles would have enjoyed playing against Peter Broadbent, the man on whom he had modelled himself as a player. Broadbent was having an Indian summer with Villa, who had signed him from Third Division Shrewsbury, added evidence that Andy Beattie got it wrong in letting him leave Wolves four years earlier.

While Dougan may have been impressed by Knowles's football, the Irishman was angered by a gesture from him before the game when Knowles refused to stand up for the national anthems. Dougan wrote in his book *Doog*, 'Peter remained seated on the bench and this rankled with me. I asked my teammates how long this had been going on and they said, "Since we arrived here to play." I called to Bill McGarry to get him to stand but he didn't or couldn't. A little of my respect for both of them died out there. Whatever his religious convictions, Peter should have stood for the national anthem.'

Jehovah's Witnesses believe that in God's Kingdom their allegiance is to Him, and while conforming to a country's laws they do not believe they should salute the flag or sing nationalistic songs.

Knowles wore the number-seven shirt against Villa and did so again when Wolves beat Kilmarnock 3–0 in St Louis. Dougan opened the scoring when he headed in a Mike Bailey long throw and also claimed the second when he said he got the final touch to a Hugh Curran lob; however, the club credited the goal to the Scotsman. There was no doubting the final goal was Curran's as he headed home a Bailey centre.

In the return game with Villa at Kansas City, Knowles and Dougan were both on target again as Wolves ran out 5–0 winners to clinch the North American Soccer League title with a game to spare. Hugh Curran (two) and David Woodfield were the other scorers. Knowles hit the fourth goal from a Dougan pass. It mattered little that the last game in the USA saw Dundee United win 3–2 in Dallas, with Dougan scoring both goals for the losers. With six points for a win and a bonus for each goal up to three, Wolves ended with 57 points, followed by West Ham on 52, Dundee United 31, Villa 28 and Kilmarnock 26.

Home for what remained of the summer Knowles could busy himself with planning for his exit from football. That the new season would see England building up to their defence of the World Cup in Mexico was of no concern to him. He was building up to a new life and had found the gateway to contentment. If one Wolves career was ending, another was about to begin. A young man from Warrington joined the club and would in time set new goalscoring records. John Richards signed for Wolves in July 1969 and would be given his first-team debut the following February before becoming a regular choice in the 1971–72 season.

Richards became a Wolves legend but once recalled, 'If I had one regret it was that I never had the opportunity to play alongside Peter Knowles. When I joined the club Peter was recognised as one of the best young players in the country. He had already played at England Under-23 level, and he was without doubt one of the most skilful and destined for more international honours. I can remember watching him in some of the first-team matches, and he was absolutely magnificent. He scored one goal, a volley, which was absolutely breathtaking. It was a shock to everyone, not just the supporters but the players themselves, when out of the blue Peter decided to pack in football. I've spoken to a lot of people since Peter left, and a lot of them are critical of Peter, but I think that you have got to give him a lot of credit for the decision he took. At least he had the courage of his convictions and his beliefs, and he stuck to what he actually felt and believed he should be doing. For my own selfish point of view I wish I had had the opportunity to play alongside Peter. I got into the team about two years later, and he would have been about 25 or 26 when supposedly players are coming to their peak. I think it was a shame. I think Wolves, and football, missed a great talent.'

McGarry prepared for the season by spending £70,000 on Jim McCalliog, who had helped Scotland beat World Cup holders England at Wembley in 1967. His role was to play wide right in midfield. Knowles figured in all three pre-season friendlies, coming on as substitute against Bristol City and scoring from the penalty spot in a 1–1 draw. He played alongside McCalliog in a home friendly with Kilmarnock a week before the season began, with Derek Dougan scoring the only goal of the game.

Just as Knowles was preparing to pack up playing, Wolves made the best start to a season during his time at Molineux, winning their first four matches. Having ditched the all-gold strip and reverted to black shorts, the team not only looked like the Wolves of old, but they also briefly played like them. Their run began with a 3–1 home victory over Stoke, Dougan scoring on three minutes and Knowles hitting a second thanks to a deflection off former England full-back Tony Allen. Though Harry Burrows, one of Stoke's array of veterans, struck in the 35th minute, Dougan made the match safe on the hour. Four days later, 13 August 1969, Southampton came to Molineux and were beaten 2–1, though Knowles's old habit of unnecessary showmanship briefly reared its head again. Phil Morgan reported that it was his 'corner-flag fiddling' that led to Saints taking the lead on 24 minutes, a floated cross being missed by Phil Parkes and turned into his own net by Derek Parkin. Knowles atoned within two minutes, however, with a hard-hit volleyed goal after left-winger Bertie Lutton, deputising for Dave Wagstaffe, had laid on the chance. Another 10 minutes and a Mike Bailey throw was deflected into the path of Frank Munro, who shot home via a post. By that stage Munro was playing a more defensive role in the line up, and it would prove to be the making of a fine player who went on to win Scottish caps as a central-defender.

Two wins out of two became three out of three when Wolves visited Sheffield Wednesday, and again Knowles was a scorer. His goal, which put Wolves in front on 21 minutes, was his last for the club. In contrast, Jim McCalliog hit his first as a Molineux man, scoring on 13 minutes to wipe out Alan Warboys's third-minute opener. When Hugh Curran made it three on 36 minutes it looked as though the visitors would run riot; however, they wasted chances and nearly paid the price, David Ford narrowing the gap 26 minutes from the end. Ten minutes later came an incident which grabbed all the headlines as a scuffle saw Dougan and Wednesday's Peter Eustace sent off by referee Arthur Dimond.

The fourth successive win came in the return match with Southampton, Wolves winning 3–2 at The Dell, all their goals coming from defenders. Derek Parkin and Mike Bailey both had 25-yard shots deflected past home 'keeper Gerry Gurr. After substitute Mike Channon had pulled a goal back, Knowles set up number-three with a low corner-kick that found Les Wilson on the edge of the penalty area from where he fired the ball home. Welsh centre-forward Ron Davies had been well shackled by John Holsgrove but did manage a consolation for a Saints team who had beaten Manchester United 4–1 at Old Trafford three days earlier.

It was United whom Knowles would next face, and a crowd of 50,783 were at Molineux to see him parade his skills one last time on the same field as legends George Best, Denis Law and Bobby Charlton. Knowles would have loved to outshine a man whose football genius he greatly admired, but Best stole the limelight in a goalless draw. That scoreline was probably a fair reflection, even though Derek Dougan and Mike Bailey both hit the woodwork against a United side giving a debut to centre-half Ian Ure, newly signed from Arsenal for £80,000.

Knowles had his moments four days later when Wolves were held at home once more. This time Derby frustrated them, taking the lead on 17 minutes thanks to a free-kick from former Molineux favourite Alan Hinton. It was left to Derek Dougan to equalise 18 minutes from time with a classic header to a Mike Bailey cross. Another Molineux old boy, Ernie Hunt, was on target on the last weekend of August when Wolves finally tasted defeat for the first time that season, going down 1–0 to Coventry City at Highfield Road. It was a rugged game dominated by hard-men like George Curtis and Bailey and would probably have given Knowles evidence that football was hardly a place for a man of Christian values.

It was two days before this match that the *Express & Star* ran their front-page story headlined, 'Is Knowles Near a Career Crisis?' It began, 'How much longer will football and religion mix? That's the probable question facing Wolves' young inside-forward Peter Knowles, writes an *Express & Star* sports reporter. A devout sincere Jehovah's Witness for the past 18 months, Knowles, it is understood, is facing a moral crisis with his religious activities claiming more and more of his time.' This front-page item was to cover the *Express & Star*, who knew the announcement of Knowles's decision to retire was imminent.

The story that he was definitely to give up football finally broke a few days later, on Monday 1 September 1969. The evening paper quoted Knowles as saying, 'There is nothing to stop me playing football and being a Witness but I know the longer I play football the more I will drift away from being a Witness.' Manager McGarry admitted to being shocked and staggered that Knowles had decided his playing career must end so quickly. 'My feeling is that he may have been ill-advised by people outside the game because I feel he could still serve his cause as a player,' McGarry told the paper. 'I have told him and his wife any time he wants to come back to football as a player I shall welcome him with open arms. But I have had a written request from him for his release and he says he wants to give up football. My directors will have to discuss it but if a man wants to give up football what can we do?' The manager added that he had spent two hours at Knowles's home the night before trying to get him to have a change of heart.

It was all in vain, and Knowles remarked, 'Five days a week I am a Christian, but when Saturday comes and I put the shirt on I am not a Christian. You have to be a Christian every day of your life.' Asked what his immediate plans were, Knowles said, 'I shall be from door-to-door today and tomorrow after training, and later on I shall pay some attention to door-to-door visiting and talking to people and trying to convert them. Perhaps I'll get a part-time job.'

Many Wolves fans may have turned their anger on the Jehovah's Witnesses after Knowles's announcement, but the movement were quick to stress that they had in no way influenced the player. 'He has felt this is what he must do. There has been no pressure on him to give up anything,' said Ken Fletcher, the man who converted Knowles to the faith. Fletcher had been a Witness only a year when he decided to knock on Knowles's door without much hope of a successful call. 'I knew he was a footballer, and I was not sure of the reception I would get, but I decided to treat him as I would anyone else. I took a couple of magazines which he did not accept but he asked me to call the following week to discuss the Bible with him. Later, Peter agreed to have a Bible study and he became very interested, continuing with the Bible study sessions for 12 months.' Thus were the seeds sown for a major change in Knowles's life and thinking.

Fletcher added, 'Most people would think Peter was making a sacrifice, giving up a £100-a-week job, a club house and a car, but he has felt this is what he must do. In the eyes of the world he has everything already but, as we Jehovah's Witnesses know, the world cannot give you everything and the Bible holds out hope of everlasting life.' Further evidence that Knowles's decision was personal came from Maurice Simpson who was overseer of the neighbouring congregation in Wolverhampton's Blakenhall district. He said, 'There is nothing in our code which says an individual must give up football. In this respect, Knowles has made his decision entirely on his own.'

That a player of talent could still flourish despite the efforts of the cloggers was proved by Knowles himself just a few days after his retirement decision was made public. Wolves beat Tottenham 1–0 at Molineux in the second round of the League Cup, thanks to an eighth-minute goal from Jim McCalliog. Spurs paraded England men Alan Mullery, Jimmy Greaves and Martin Chivers in their line up, as well as his brother Cyril at full-back, but Knowles led the way as Wolves outplayed them. Phil Morgan wrote in the *Express & Star*, 'They gave Spurs lessons in speed and purpose, not to mention bits of isolated football brilliance from Knowles and Wagstaffe who, in the first half especially, were tormentors-in-chief of the Spurs defence. Knowles chose those first 45 minutes to reach a standard of soccer excellence which stemmed from a talent I am convinced the good Lord never intended he should keep from his fellows.'

On the front of the programme for that match was a picture of Peter and Cyril Knowles under the headline, 'Oh, brother…it's the League Cup!' Despite focusing on the clash of the brothers on the front of *Molinews*, there was no mention of it inside or of the shock announcement by the younger brother. In fairness, the programme had probably been printed before Peter's decision had been made official.

During his final week as a player, Knowles was inundated with letters from young and old asking him to think again. They were to no avail. As critical as anyone was his mother, Jane, who came to stay with him as he prepared for his exit. 'My mother has nothing against my religion. She just can't understand why I have to give up football,' he told John Dee in the *Express & Star*. 'It has broken her heart, and she would do anything to make me change my mind, but I'm old enough to think things out for myself. I haven't reached this decision overnight. I have spent some time thinking matters over, but now I have announced my retirement from the game I feel a lot better. I'm quite happy, and there will be no regrets when I leave Molineux for the last time tomorrow night.'

The *Daily Express* put the maternal visit more succinctly, reporter David Jack writing, 'Soccer idol Peter Knowles got a right ticking-off last night from the Yorkshire mum he did not consult before deciding to become a Jehovah's Witness.' Jack reckoned that Jane had hardly got her coat off after arriving at her son's home before she was telling him, 'I think you're stupid, lad.' She pointed out she had given half her life to get him where he was and that he had never been wanting, adding, with typical bluntness, 'Well if you do pack it in, you'd better get right out of Wolverhampton. I don't know how you'll dare walk down the street in this town. I give you a month, Peter, no more, and you'll be crawling back to that club on your knees.' The years would prove that mothers are not always right.

His final game, against Nottingham Forest, was on Saturday 6 September, and there was almost a carnival atmosphere about it all. On the grille in front of the home dressing-room windows facing Waterloo Road had been pinned posters asking Knowles to change his mind. One said, 'Please stay Pete', another said 'Peter please stay with us, cause we need you' (with the word 'you' underlined several times) while a third read, 'Peter, Peter, stay with the Wolves please do, we're so crazy all for the love of you, so give up this Jehovah's lark and stay with the Wanderers team, cause we can't win without help from you, so stay with us Knowles, please do, Stay with us, Knocker.'

The match programme made little of Knowles's farewell, Wolves perhaps hoping it was a gap in his career and not the end of it. So the front cover preferred to highlight the social club of the year award presented by the trade publication *Club Mirror* and carried a picture of chairman John Ireland receiving the trophy from current Miss World Penny Plummer. Apart from his name appearing in the teams and in the season's statistics, the only reference to Knowles was in manager Bill McGarry's notes, and it was a brief one: 'As far as Peter Knowles is concerned I am still hoping there will be a happy ending. His training gear will be laid out as usual on Monday morning and I will expect him to be here.'

Before the kick-off a number of fans came on to the pitch to get Knowles's autograph. Right from the start Knowles began to show what football would be losing as he began to torment a Forest side wearing unfamiliar blue shirts. He tried one of his trademark 25-yard shots which brought a good save from visiting goalkeeper Alan Hill and eventually helped set up the opening goal after 18 minutes, Hugh Curran driving the ball home from a Derek Dougan header. Five minutes from the break Knowles split the Forest defence with a pass to Curran who drew a defender before slipping a pass to Dougan, who virtually ran the ball over the line. Knowles again laid the foundations when Wolves went three up seven minutes into the second half. His pass across the penalty area was flicked into the path of Curran who slammed the ball home. Wolves were cruising, and it looked like being a glorious farewell. Then, in the space of nine minutes, starting in the 61st, Forest drew level through Henry Newton, Ronnie Rees and Newton again. Knowles could have gone out on a spectacular note when, just before Forest's equaliser, he was put through by Dougan but took too much time and placed his shot wide.

So the home fans forgot about Knowles and were far more concerned that their side had gone so close to snatching defeat from the jaws of victory. For in the final minute Rees got clean through again only to lift his shot over the bar. That night's *Sporting Star* front page headline read 'Wolves Peter out', and the lead story said that Knowles had sprayed out a hatfull of goodbye chances, only three of which had been accepted. He had gone out on a high note, though the verdict was that Wolves' best player had been left-winger Dave

Wagstaffe. Indeed, Waggy deflected some of the attention from Knowles at the final whistle. He weaved his way through only to be brought down unceremoniously. Penalty appeals were ignored and the winger ended the game flat on his back. Dougan and trainer Sammy Chung carried him from the pitch surrounded by small boys. By this time Knowles and the rest had scurried off to the dressing room.

Clive Corbett, one of the teenage fans who so closely identified with Knowles, had extra reason to recall the farewell match. 'There was the incredible collapse by Wolves, but I remember it well for other reasons as the back of the South Bank was kicked in and pieces of corrugated asbestos thrown down into the crowd by Forest fans.' In those days, of course, there was no such thing as segregation of home and away supporters. Such a recollection only endorses Knowles's concern for the way football was going both on and off the field.

After a weekend to reflect, Phil Morgan found the words in the *Express & Star* to catch the mood, writing, 'Just when there was a faint suggestion of the sacred in the secular air over Molineux, Wolves had to commit one of soccer's cardinal sins. They threw away a three-goal lead. So stunned were the crowd by this most unlikely turn of events they forgot all about a final farewell to Peter Knowles, who had chosen this match to call it a day in the interests of religious discipleship. Appropriately, I suppose, they had sung his praises in parodies on hymn tunes, but when it came to the 90th-minute crunch, and they had seen Wolves avoid defeat by a hairsbreadth, so to speak, Peter was able to go full pelt for the dressing room with hardly a follower in his wake.'

John Dee was also commissioned to write a piece for Monday's *Express & Star* and reported that Knowles had showed no emotion as he left the ground. Dee wrote, 'He told me, "People keep saying I will come back but I have convinced myself I will not. Convincing others seems the hardest now but there will be no comeback, today or any other day." Knowles left Molineux not by the main entrance in Waterloo Road but by walking across the pitch and leaving through a door opposite the players' tunnel on the Molineux Street side of the ground. He had to wait some minutes before his wife Jean brought their sports car to the door and several fans, mostly teenage girls – some of them in tears – rushed round to see him leave. Two of them, 15-year-old Lesley Skitt of Griffiths Drive, Wednesfield, and 17-year-old Jill Birt of Gregory Court, Wednesfield, gave their idol a farewell present. Written on the wrapping paper were the words "Never be forgotten. Good luck, Jill and Lesley." Inside was...a Bible.'

Dee noted that during the game fans, especially those on the North Bank, had repeatedly chanted Knowles's name while other chants included 'Goodbye, Peter, goodbye' and 'Give us a goal, Peter Knowles' and when his centre in the first half caused problems in the Forest defence there was 'Please don't leave us, Peter Knowles' to the tune of *Guide Me Oh Thou Great Jehovah*. The old Knowles would have wallowed in such adoration, but now it had little effect. 'They gave me a great reception but if I could have gone off at half-time I would have done,' he told Dee, adding, 'I have had enough of football. I wouldn't go back for a million pounds.'

Jane Knowles was at Molineux to see her son's finale and told the *Sunday Express*, 'I've done my best to make him change his mind but it's no good. He has made his decision and he is happy with it. As for his family, we are terribly upset. I think one reason is that we shall miss seeing him play.' There, too, was Knowles's wife Jean and, as a fellow Witness, she obviously backed her husband, saying, 'It's the best thing Peter ever did to get out now. His only regret is that he didn't do it two years ago. I am 100 per cent behind him.'

What finally made up Knowles's mind he was doing the right thing were two of his last games, against Southampton and Coventry. 'I was lucky to come out of those matches still walking. They were shockers,' he told the paper. 'I didn't get kicked, fortunately, but I saw my mates clobbered and knocked. Those two matches made me finally realise that I could not reconcile my principles as a Christian with my role as a footballer and the dirty play which is so much a part of today's game' He also stressed he was not ungrateful to football. 'Thousands of chaps in nine-to-five jobs would give their right arm for the material things I have got out of the game. Not that I have not been a waster and I have something put by to keep Jean and me until 1975. I have been on £100-a-week but I say here and now that £200-a-week would not make me go back. I couldn't be happier than I am tonight even if I have to go on the dole on Monday.'

Former fellow lodger Les Wilson played in Knowles's final game and was among those surprised by his pal's decision. 'I remember two days later, the BBC television and radio interviewed me,' said Wilson, 'and I stated that Peter could not live without football and that the Wolves brass needed to bring in professional help and assistance to mediate this impasse and resolve the situation. I strongly believe, and I am still convinced to this day, that Peter could have, and should have, followed his religious beliefs but at the same time played professional football – in the English First Division, even if it was not with the Wolves. If handled right and in a professional, sincere and caring manner, this impasse could have been a win, win, win, situation for all concerned.

'What a shame that Peter was lost to football forever. I have no doubt that he would have been an ever-present in the England team for many years to come. Peter was clean living, never smoked, gambled or drank to the best of my knowledge. He also was a great trainer. He and I would sometimes train three times a day, the morning session and afternoon session with the Wolves first and second-team squads and on occasions night training on Tuesdays and Thursdays. This boy had everything in his locker, for him to go out of the game the way he did was a tragedy, not only for the sport but also for Peter Knowles.'

The ironic thing was that the religious beliefs that caused him to quit football had also made him a better-adjusted and more mature person. Though Wilson would not go into details, he admits that Knowles had a touch of devilment about him in his younger days. Wilson says, 'Peter did some things off the cuff, and I believe Hugh McIlmoyle nicknamed him "Peter the Pig". Hugh was right to some extent. The way Peter behaved sometimes was deplorable; however, believe me, Peter had a very caring and kind side to him, he was very aware when he did wrong, and he certainly had a conscience and regretted some of his, let's say, uglier antics, both on and off the field of play.'

Back to the Revd John Bates, with whom as a teenager I had watched Knowles's debut at Leicester in 1963. Now a Methodist minister, he still finds it hard to understand the player's decision to quit the game. 'The Jehovah's Witnesses are coming at their religion from a very different angle, I know, but I believe talents we may possess can be used for a positive purpose. There is nothing incongruous about being a sportsman and a Christian. I would have said to him [Knowles] that if you have a gift there have to be ways of using it for good. He could have been a role model in the way Bobby Charlton was and in the way our own Ron Flowers, Billy Wright and Jimmy Mullen were. He could have influenced people's lives. It was a great shame he chose not to carry on playing.'

Fan Clive Corbett confirms Knowles's standing among Wolves followers: 'Yes, there was the famous petulance, but that didn't bother me as adolescence beckoned – it just added to the attraction, the danger. In spite of this dark side, on the occasions that I got autographs, Peter was always the complete gentleman as I fought my way through swooning ladies of all ages.'

Skipper Mike Bailey also endorsed the fans' view of Knowles's special talent, 'He was flamboyant with brilliant skills and the need to do things like sit on the ball. I used to bollock him, but I was wrong from the entertainment point of view because the crowd loved it. He has kept to his beliefs, but we missed a very talented player. He was the one who, when we were struggling, would pull some magic out. He was absolutely outstanding, quick feet and a good passer. He had something different from everybody else.'

Epilogue

So it was all over, though players and officials at Molineux did not think so. There was speculation a couple of months after his final game that Knowles might be getting back his appetite for football when he took a job with Wolverhampton Council's education department, coaching youngsters on the football fields which then formed part of Dunstall Park racecourse. This coincided with Derek Dougan collecting an eight-week ban, and Knowles admitted manager McGarry had asked him to play during the Doog's absence. Knowles told the *Express & Star's* John Dee, 'I went in to get my kit and Bill McGarry called me into his office and asked if I would consider helping the club by returning to the game during Derek Dougan's absence. He told me I needed six days to get fit and would be in the side at Liverpool on Saturday [8 November 1969]. I was prepared to go back and help out but when I got home I thought things over and had second thoughts.'

He added that he thought the business about him coming back would be a seven-day wonder and fans would let it drop. He felt the team were doing fine without him and the feelings of the players ought to be considered when fans started talking about him returning. Knowles added, 'If anyone can persuade me to return it's Bill McGarry, but he didn't succeed last week. I'm sure no-one else will make me change my mind.'

It was not only fans who had tried to get him to reconsider. Knowles told Rogan Taylor in his 1994 interview how his family had also disapproved of his decision. He said, 'My mother was very upset. She was pleased that me and my brother were footballers because she'd had to struggle to bring up six children, and now she was thinking "Peter's going to throw all this away."You see, she was upset about it. She still is today when I go and see her – she gets upset about it. I took my mother around Molineux football ground a few months ago. I said, "Come on, I'll take you and show you the football ground." So as we went round the ground, on the pitch, in the dressing rooms and the boardrooms, she said "All this could have been yours." So she still gets upset.'

Mrs Knowles's other footballing son, Cyril, continued playing until a serious knee injury forced him to retire. He had made over 500 first-team appearances in 12 seasons at White Hart Lane. Peter still followed his career, and in his fly-on-the wall book about a season with Spurs, *The Glory Game*, Hunter Davies recounts a scene in the visitors' dressing room when Spurs played Wolves on the opening day of the 1971–72 season. Davies wrote, 'There was a knock at the door. It opened and Cyril's brother came in, looking very scrubbed and neat in a short white raincoat. He stood hesitantly in a corner, looking round. He looked across at Bill Nicholson, knowing that the Spurs manager doesn't normally allow outsiders in his dressing room, but Bill recognised him. He didn't say anything, just caught his eye and looked at him, then turned back and continued talking quietly to Ralph Coates in a corner. Cyril beckoned to his brother to sit beside him and they chatted for about 10 minutes. "That your brother, then, Cyril?" said someone when Peter had gone. "Yeh," said Cyril. "Still got a lot of skill." "Must have," said Alan Gilzean. "Takes a lot of skill to read the Bible." Everybody laughed.'

That scenario summed up the attitude of most football people to what Knowles had done. For them it was something to make fun of, yet for Knowles it remained the best thing he ever did. It was for his brother that Knowles made one of his rare returns to action, playing in Cyril's testimonial game, a 2–2 draw with Arsenal in October 1975. He came on as substitute for Cliff Jones and, after a brief cameo had shown he still had his old skill, he was replaced by Terry Naylor. Sadly, tragedies beset Cyril. He lost his young son in a motorway accident and was only 47 when he died. He had gone into management with Darlington, Torquay and Hartlepool, but a brain illness caused him to quit the Hartlepool job in June 1991, and he was dead within two months. A new stand at Hartlepool's Victoria Ground was named after him.

Six years after playing in his brother's testimonial match Knowles also took part in one for Wolves stalwart Kenny Hibbitt against Derby at Molineux on Sunday 23 August 1981. He made a brief appearance as a substitute for Peter Daniel as Wolves won 2–1. Steve Powell gave Derby the lead, but then 16-year-old John Pender stole the limelight. He headed the equaliser and then made the pass from which Andy Gray hit the winner. Eddie Griffiths wrote in the *Express & Star* that Knowles gave the fans 'a reminder of the wonderful skills that delighted more than a decade ago' and added, 'The fans marvelled at the little touches of a once-great player.' Since then, Knowles has been back to Molineux a number of times, not for football but for Jehovah's Witnesses' conventions. Interestingly, Wolves retained his registration, and the club did not cancel his contract until June 1982.

Another comeback outing saw Knowles turn out for old pal Terry Wharton, who was then managing West Midlands League side Brewood, and Knowles impressed top *News of the World* sportswriter David Harrison who was then with the *Express & Star*. 'It must have been about 1983 as Graham Hawkins was manager of Wolves at the time,' said Harrison. 'He asked me to turn out for an Old Wolves side to play at Brewood. I think it was to help Terry raise funds for the club. Who should turn up for the game but Peter Knowles, and he looked immaculate, as if he'd just finished playing the day before. During the warm-up he was doing a few things with the ball, and Graham said to me, "Look at him, look at his touch, he's still better than anything I've got at the moment." Peter must have been about 37 or 38 at the time.'

Wharton was player-manager at Brewood, based in the village of that name near Wolverhampton, during a successful period and was twice named the League's player of the season, but sadly the club folded some years later. Knowles and Wharton had shared digs at one stage and remained friends after Wharton's transfer to Bolton. 'I came down to see him and we had Sunday lunch,' Wharton recalled. 'Over the washing-up, I said "I can't believe you, Knowlesy, what are you doing?" but there was no changing his mind about giving up the game.'

Of all the occasions when Knowles turned back the clock and donned his boots once more, the most significant for him must surely have been at the unlikely venue of Admiral's Park in the Shropshire village of Shifnal. He had once spoken of wishing he could have played in the same team as George Best and it finally happened, when both were pushing 40, in October 1984. A local radio man, Alan Phillips, had organised a charity game for a brain-damaged youngster, Jamie Fellows, and Best agreed to play. So did Knowles. Actor Denis Waterman, of *Minder* fame, sent his celebrity team to play against the team of old stars, but there was a worry that Best might make one of his legendary non-appearances; however, his delayed arrival was due to the illness of his own young son Callum, and so a large crowd got to see him and Knowles in action – a world legend and a local legend.

Knowles also played again to aid another old teammate Frank Munro in a testimonial game at Willenhall. Munro was not granted a benefit game by Wolves as he was there only nine years and not the 10 which is the usual criterion. Many fans felt it a harsh decision by the club, which may well have been what prompted Knowles to support this special match. Steve Daley recalled in Clive Corbett's excellent book *Those Were The Days*, 'Peter was a bit slower – but what a first touch. It used to take me three or four touches to do what he did in one. He'd got the tricks as well, a great player and very fit.' Former goalkeeper Phil Parkes also recalls that Willenhall game. 'He agreed to play for Frank because the club had never given Frank a testimonial. He said he'd play 45 minutes, but he scored a goal and didn't want to come off. I think if he hadn't have given up when he did he had the ability to be Wolves' best player ever. He certainly had the ability to be as good as Peter Broadbent and Johnny Hancocks.'

There was yet another cameo role when Knowles took part in the belated testimonial game for Ted Farmer at Molineux in 1990 and again showed the old skills were still at his disposal.

Knowles made tremendous progress in his six years as a Wolves first teamer and was the only remaining link between the promising side of 1969–70 and the one in which he had made his debut in 1963. Let us take a look at the other 10 players in the Wolves team on the night of his debut against Leicester at Filbert Street:

Fred Davies: he had the tough task of following two great goalkeepers in England international Bert Williams and brave Scotsman Malcolm Finlayson. Yet he had made the goalkeeping position his own and would play 156 League games for the club. He lost his place to Dave MacLaren but regained it to play 27 times during Wolves' 1966–67 promotion season. Later he had lengthy spells with Cardiff and Bournemouth.

George Showell: first made his name as the capable deputy to Billy Wright at centre-half, notably in the floodlit win over Real Madrid at Molineux when he faced the mighty Alfredo di Stefano. He was right-back in Wolves' 1960 FA Cup-winning side and even had some games at centre-forward. He later played a few games for Bristol City before moving to Wrexham. Injury hampered his spell with the Welsh club, but he later served them well as assistant manager when the club moved from the Fourth Division to the Second Division.

Bobby Thomson: a pacy full-back who won eight full caps for England and 15 for the Under-23 side, which he skippered on several occasions. He won his first full cap just before his 20th birthday but was unlucky to be playing at the same time as the great George Cohen and Ray Wilson. He moved to Birmingham City in March 1969. After a brief loan spell at Walsall he joined Luton, where he made over 100 League appearances.

Fred Goodwin: an enthusiastic wing-half who was given a shock debut by Stan Cullis in the 1962 FA Cup clash with Albion, along with Fred Davies and Bobby Thomson. Unlike the other two, his Molineux career was a limited one. He played only 44 League games before seeing service with his home-town club Stockport, then Blackburn, Southport and Port Vale before making a brief return to Stockport.

David Woodfield: an extremely fit player who made his debut at the end of the 1961–62 season and went on to play in 250 League games for Wolves, mostly at centre-half, though he did have a successful spell at centre-forward. He joined Watford in 1971, but injury problems meant he made only 15 League appearances for them. He then took up a coaching role at Vicarage Road.

Ron Flowers: one of the truly great players in Molineux history. He helped Wolves win the First Division Championship in 1953–54, 1957–58 and 1958–59 and the FA Cup in 1960. He made 467 League appearances for Wolves and then 61 for Northampton. Flowers won 49 England caps and captained his country on three occasions as well as being a member of England's squad of 22 for the 1966 World Cup Finals. In January 2009 he was one of the six inaugural inductees to the Wolves Hall of Fame.

Chris Crowe: signed from Blackburn by Stan Cullis, along with Villa winger Peter McParland, in 1962 when Wolves were dangerously close to relegation. He helped them escape and figured in the young side which made such a wonderful start to the 1962–63 season. That won him his only England cap, when he faced France in the European Nations Cup, as the European Championship was then known. Having started his career at Leeds, Crowe later played for Nottingham Forest, Bristol City and Walsall, after making 83 League appearances for Wolves.

Ray Crawford: signed from Ipswich shortly before Knowles made his debut. He had been a prolific goalscorer at Portman Road where his partnership with Ted Phillips was a key factor in Town's shock First Division title triumph in 1961–62 under Alf Ramsey. After 57 League games and 39 goals for Wolves, he moved to Albion before returning to Ipswich and later playing for Charlton and Colchester. In a career which began at Portsmouth, he scored 290 League goals.

Jimmy Murray: along with Flowers and Showell, was a last link with the all-conquering side of the late 1950s. He had made his debut in a friendly against Moscow Dynamo in 1955 and took over the number-nine shirt after injury ended Roy Swinbourne's career. He won two Championship medals and an FA Cup-winners' medal before joining Manchester City. He hit 155 goals in 273 League games for Wolves and 43 in 70 League games for City. He also played for Walsall, where his 13 goals in 58 games took his League scoring tally past the 200 mark. He died in 2008.

Alan Hinton: a clever left-winger with a fierce shot, who was capped for England while at Molineux but was unexpectedly transferred to Nottingham Forest where he played 108 League games. He played more than twice that number for Derby County. His Wolves goal haul was 29 goals from 75 League games. At Derby it was 64 from 253. He helped bring the First Division Championship to the Baseball Ground in 1971–72 when he was their top League scorer with 15 goals, eight of them penalties, from 38 games.

Now let us take a look at the players who lined up in Knowles's final game just over six years after his first:

Phil Parkes: a couple of years younger than Knowles, he established himself in the side during the 1966–67 Second Division promotion campaign and eventually took his League appearances to the 303 mark. He was unlucky not to win representative honours and missed the 1974 League Cup Final triumph through injury. He was also a more-than-useful club cricketer.

Les Wilson: born in Manchester but brought up in Canada, he joined Wolves as a play-anywhere player, making his debut in 1965, the first of 101 League games he figured in while with Wolves. He later played for Bristol City and Norwich.

Derek Parkin: was the costliest full-back of his day when he joined Wolves from Huddersfield in 1968 for £80,000. He went on to set a Wolves club record of 501 League appearances, bettering the previous record set by Billy Wright. He would have played even more games but for a mystery illness which sidelined him for five months in 1972–73. He won League Cup medals in 1974 and 1980 and was capped five times at Under-23 level by England. He later played for Stoke. In January 2009 he was one of the six inaugural inductees to the Wolves Hall of Fame.

Mike Bailey: in the best tradition of Wolves' old-style wing-halves. An ideal captain, he drove his team on and led by example. Tough in the tackle and a good passer of the ball, he had won two England caps with Charlton before joining Wolves. He was often in the England squad while at Molineux but never added to his England appearances.

John Holsgrove: born just three days before Knowles, he was signed from Crystal Palace, Ronnie Allen's former club. He lost his first-team place with the emergence of John McAlle and had made 180 League appearances before moving to Sheffield Wednesday.

Frank Munro: impressed for Aberdeen against Wolves in the 1967 North American tournament. He was signed as a midfielder but settled down as a central-defender, where he was nine times capped by Scotland. He had been on Chelsea's books as a youngster but made his name in Scotland with Dundee United and then Aberdeen before being signed by Wolves in January 1968. In December 1977 he moved to Celtic but stayed there only a year before having a lengthy spell in Australian football.

Jim McCalliog: a highly talented Scot who typified the sort of all-round skilful midfielders of the 1970s. He played seven League games for Chelsea as a teenager and then

150 at Sheffield Wednesday before joining Wolves in July 1969. He had scored for Wednesday in their 1966 FA Cup Final defeat by Everton and was also a scorer when Scotland famously won 3–2 at Wembley to become the first team to beat England after their 1966 World Cup triumph. After 163 League games with Wolves, he played for Manchester United, Southampton and Lincoln. He was in the Saints side who secured a surprise win over Manchester United in the 1976 FA Cup Final.

Derek Dougan: one of the game's great characters and a highly talented centre-forward. He soon became a cult figure among Wolves fans and settled down after a career which had begun at Portsmouth and taken him to Blackburn, where he famously asked for a transfer on the morning of Rovers's 1960 FA Cup Final clash with Wolves, Villa, Peterborough and Leicester. He scored goals everywhere he went and collected 43 Northern Ireland caps on the way. He died in 2007.

Hugh Curran: he had been an apprentice at Manchester United but made his breakthrough into the English game with Millwall and Norwich, joining Wolves in January 1969. He became the first Molineux player to win a Scottish cap. He later had spells with Oxford and Bolton.

Dave Wagstaffe: another who became a Molineux folk hero, Waggy was an old-style winger who created chances galore for others. Although he was only 21 when signed by Wolves on Boxing Day 1964, he had already made 144 League appearances for Manchester City. Wingers were not in fashion during Sir Alf Ramsey's spell as England boss, and the nearest Wagstaffe got to a cap was an appearance for the Football League side. In any other era, he would surely have won a host of caps.

In between Knowles's first and last first-team appearance, many other players came and went – such as gritty full-back Joe Wilson, former England midfielder Jimmy Melia, centre-forward Hughie McIlmoyle, still fondly remembered among Molineux's older fans, and chunky inside-forward Ernie Hunt, who played a big part in the 1966–67 promotion season.

The Knowles story continued to fascinate people. Singer Billy Bragg was not old enough to remember the events surrounding his shock retirement, being 11 at the time, but he discovered them when he bought a video tape celebrating 25 years of *Match of the Day*, the BBC Saturday night football show. On it he came across the interview with Knowles and was so moved by the story that he penned a song, *God's Footballer*, in praise of Knowles.

As a fan of both men, I contacted Bragg via his manager and did an interview with him about the song for the *Wolverhampton Chronicle,* which I then edited. As an added bonus, I arranged to see Bragg in concert at the Hummingbird in Birmingham. Two other Bragg fans agreed to come with me, Keith Downing, a tough man in Wolves midfield, and Rob Kelly, whose career at Molineux had been cut short by a back injury. Kelly was in the process of re-training as a journalist. This, incidentally, Kelly did before eventually returning to football to look after Wolves' youngsters when Graham Taylor was boss. Our proposed party for Brum, along with my 15-year-old daughter Helen, was reduced when Wolves won through to the third round of the League Cup which meant Downing had to turn out against Everton at Goodison Park the same night. Wolves lost 4–1 on 30 October 1991 and Downing, to his lasting regret, missed a great night at the Hummingbird. We took along with us a Wolves shirt, courtesy of Kelly, which we gave to Bragg's manager before the show. When it came to *God's Footballer*, Bragg put on the shirt, a brave move in a venue filled largely by Villa and Blues fans. He sang the song and got a rapturous reception. It was a magic moment. One can only wonder if it is some sort of record that two footballing brothers have had songs written about them as *Nice One Cyril* was based on Spurs fans' chorus for Cyril Knowles.

Billy Bragg confirmed, when I approached him about this biography, that he recalled that night at Hummingbird and putting on the Wolves shirt. He obviously has the utmost respect for Knowles and said he would be honoured if the lyrics of *God's Footballer* were included in this book. So here they are:

God's footballer hears the voices of angels
Above the choir at Molineux
God's footballer stands on the doorstep
And brings the Good News of the Kingdom to come
While the crowd sings 'Rock of Ages'
The goals bring weekly wages
Yet the glory of the sports pages
Is but the worship of false idols and tempts him not

God's footballer turns on a sixpence
And brings the great crowd to their feet in praise of him
God's footballer quotes from the Gospels
While knocking on the doors in the Black Country back streets
He scores goals on a Saturday
And saves souls on a Sunday

For the Lord says these are the last days
Prepare thyself for the judgement yet to come
His career will be over soon
And the rituals of a Saturday afternoon
Bid him a reluctant farewell
For he knows beyond the sport lies the spiritual.

The song is one of the tracks on Bragg's album *Don't Try This At Home* and it ends with a bit of commentary, presumably from BBC's *Match of the Day* with commentator Kenneth Wolstenholme yelling, '20 seconds left to play and Knowles has equalised.' This has to be from the match against Chelsea in October 1968 when Knowles's last-minute goal earned Wolves a 1–1 draw at Molineux.

In 2007 Peter Knowles was asked for a contribution to a biography of Ray Crawford and wrote to him, 'Many people couldn't cope or understand me giving up football, especially my family. Many footballers said I would be back in six months. McGarry couldn't handle it. He didn't know what advice to give me. He hadn't come across something like this before. People didn't want me to give it up. They wanted me to mix the two – my faith and football. I couldn't. It was one or the other, not both. I've never regretted it. It's one of the best moves I've ever made. People didn't agree with it but they all say they admire you because you stuck to your word. I look at videos and pictures of myself and it's like looking at another person. I cannot imagine that I ever was a footballer once. I had some good times in football but that cliché rings true, "You are only as good as your last game." Many people ask would I like to play today for the big stakes, but to me the individuality and flair has gone. Now I can see the game played at 100 miles an hour.'

Crawford himself has the utmost respect for the Knowles talent, which he believes was ahead of its time. In his book, *Curse of the Jungle Boy*, Crawford wrote, 'Peter was a born entertainer and the fans quickly came to adore him. You couldn't say the same for defenders who had to mark him. More often than not he was a total nightmare to them. As slippery as a young black-and-gold fish, right up there with the likes of George Best, a true football genius. Alf [Ramsey] once said Martin Peters was 10 years ahead of his time. I reckon Peter must have been light years ahead in comparison. He could play the game fast or slow and had a unique style. If you think the step-over was invented in the last few years by Ronaldo of Manchester United and many others who have copied him, I'm sorry but they're about 40 years too late to patent it as their own invention. I saw Peter do it time and again. He could frighten and tease the life out of defenders running at them, sometimes stopping and putting his foot on the ball, followed by a couple of step-overs inviting opponents to go for it dog-like for a toy, ready to whip the ball away in a flash if they lunged in.' Crawford won only two England caps and deserved an extended chance to prove himself at international level. Tellingly, he says of Knowles, 'I wish I'd had him alongside me when I played my two internationals instead of the selfish players I played with.'

Derek Dougan had no doubts about Knowles's potential. Wrote Dougan in his book *Doog*, 'Although he could be erratic and inclined to let a sudden flare-up of temper on the pitch upset his judgment, I am quite sure he would have matured sufficiently to have played himself into the England side. Next to George Best, he could well have been the biggest name in English football, combining looks with exceptional talent.'

Another who believed Knowles would have gone all the way is an unlikely Wolves fan, John Lloyd, the former British tennis number one. He remembered that final game well and recalled it in an interview with *The Times* in 2005. Lloyd said, 'I was 15 and such a committed supporter of Wolverhampton Wanderers that I regularly made the trip to Molineux from my home in Southend. To me, Knowles was a potential England player and the superstar who was going to make my club great. Like every other Wolves supporter, I couldn't believe he had decided to retire, aged just 24, to become a Jehovah's Witness. I didn't even know he had such strong religious beliefs; for some reason, I didn't associate that sort of thing with footballers. It was clear the club expected him to have second thoughts, because it retained his registration.

'Alas, it was not to be and we were left to speculate on what might have been. I am convinced he would have become a force as a full international. Then again, he might have suffered the same fate as so many other flair players from that period, such as Rodney Marsh, Frank Worthington, Stan Bowles and Alan Hudson. But the true loss was to Wolves. In today's transfer market, what would he be worth? Alun Evans went from Wolves to Liverpool as the first £100,000 teenager, and he was not a patch on Knowles. The styles of Doog and Knowles perfectly complemented one another; there was the big swashbuckling centre-forward who went where it hurt to win the ball, and Knowles the gloriously talented player who could produce the unexpected. He was not just a goalscorer, he was an entertainer who could stun the crowd and the opposition with a glorious flick or dummy.

'Although tennis took a huge amount of my time, I watched Wolves every time they played in London. I initially supported them at the age of eight because I loved the gold colour of their shirts and wanted to support somebody different because all my friends had fallen for Manchester United, Arsenal or Spurs. It was the early 1960s, and Wolves were in the old First Division. Billy Wright had retired, but Ron Flowers was a great servant and later I came to revere the likes of Mike Bailey and John Richards, but there's never been another Peter Knowles.'

The impact on a young fan is summed up by Jim Heath who was just 11 when Knowles announced he was leaving the game. 'I suppose it was my personal "JFK, Princess Diana, 9/11, where were you when?" moment. I was on a day out at Trentham Gardens, and at first it didn't register when I saw a newspaper billboard announce "Football Star Quits". Innocently, I wondered who it could be. As soon as I saw the paper my world was sent in a tailspin. The last match I saw him play was the League Cup tie against Tottenham at Molineux just after he had made the announcement. The atmosphere was electric, with a crowd of some 33,000 packed in the ground. Knowles was superb – all the flicks, dummies and a god-like aura that made him stand out from every other player on the pitch. We won 1–0, it was a fantastic night.'

Heath also has interesting views on what Knowles might have achieved had he continued playing. 'At the time I not only felt for Wolves' loss but also for England's. In my mind he was the perfect replacement for Bobby Charlton, bringing a bit of flamboyance and a touch of genius to the England side. To an 11-year-old it was inevitable, but with years of hindsight I now have my doubts. He just wasn't a Sir Alf Ramsey player. The more I think about it, he probably wasn't even a McGarry type of player. Just how long would the grumpy Wolves manager have tolerated the collective excesses of Dougan and Knowles? More likely, Knowles would have eventually been transferred, if rumours were right, to Liverpool. Just imagine that – he would definitely have had stronger England claims in the successful Liverpool team of the early 1970s.

'It's difficult to assess how much Wolves actually missed Knowles. The first full season after his retirement we finished fourth in Division One, our highest since the Cullis era. Would Knowles have made a difference? Part of me would like to think he could have won the Championship for Wolves. On the other hand, would we have ever seen the emergence of Kenny Hibbitt and, dare I say it, John Richards if Knowles was still a regular in the team? It would have been interesting to see all three play together.'

There is also the theory that had Knowles not found religion his name might have been added to the list of gifted players who went off the rails. It's a view which Heath can appreciate. 'Just after Knowles retired a group of outrageously talented footballers emerged – the "mavericks" of the '70s, like Tony Currie, Frank Worthington and Stan Bowles. Perhaps Peter would have been acclaimed as the godfather of the mavericks. As it transpires, he is even more "out there" than that group and probably evokes closer associations with two serious wayward rebels with untamed talent whose careers, like Knowles, were unfulfilled. I'm thinking of Luton Town's Graham French and Robin Friday [Reading and Cardiff City] whose careers were respectively cut short by a jail sentence for a shot gun incident and a decadent lifestyle dominated by class A drugs, eventually leading to premature death. In the light of what happened to those two, perhaps religion really did save Peter Knowles.'

Heath may well have a point. Knowles certainly enjoyed all the trappings of football stardom in his early days, and it would have been very easy for him to go off the rails if he had not found a meaning to his life. When Knowles looks back on the way he was, he does not like what he sees. He made that clear to Rogan Taylor in the 1994 interview:

'I loved the cars, the women and the money and the adulation. I used to love that, but when I started to study the Bible my total views changed. I look back now, and I wish I'd never have ever played football. It brings a lot of bad memories to me. I am trying to live by the Bible now and trying to do what the Bible says, but I have a battle with those years when I played football. And so I look back now and I think to myself I wish I'd never gone into the game. The way I treated people, my attitude towards life, my attitude towards people and individuals, I have got to live with that and I regret it. But I can't put the clock back and change it, so I honestly wish that I'd never have played football. I wish that I'd have met Jehovah's Witnesses the day before I went into football. My whole life would have changed, and it would have changed for the better.'

He explained the contrast in his life after he had turned his back on football. 'I wasn't a very educated person – I'd got no qualifications, so I went delivering milk, and then when I'd finished delivering milk I used to go round preaching from house to house. I did that for quite a time, and then finally I went to work for a Jehovah's Witness who owned a waste company. And that's what I've been doing. People used to invite me in, and they wanted to talk about football. They were puzzled, they were confused and they would say, "Well, why can't you mix the two?" and "Why have you become a Jehovah's Witness?" We used to talk about it, and then I used to come away and that was it. But as the years went by people now view me as the fella who gave up football to become a Jehovah's Witness, and that's how people see me now.'

Knowles stressed he had never once doubted he had made the right decision. 'Me and my wife, we're together. If I'd have carried on playing football, me and my wife wouldn't have been together. We know what the future holds. We know what we're doing is the right thing. We've got some nice friends. It's the best thing we've ever done.'

To a generation of Wolves fans, Knowles will always be special. The club have launched an official Hall of Fame, and there is a good case for Knowles being in it and not just because his story is unique. As Jim Heath says, 'I think Wolves should recognise what a great player he was, the vast contribution he made in such a short careeer and the amazing impact he had on Wolves fans. Peter Knowles is a proud and vital part of Wolves heritage. We should never be allowed to forget that.'

John Lalley is another fan with a nostalgic view of Knowles. 'For those of us in attendance at his last game, against Forest, it was a truly bizarre experience, a unique set of circumstances which will never be repeated. I don't think I saw him again until I spotted him walking to the ground for Ted Farmer's testimonial game in 1990. Nowadays, you can bump into him working in the city centre store, and he is always courteous and friendly. Amazing to think it is the same guy who signed autographs for me at Molineux such a long time ago. For the last 40 years, whenever I have driven past a Jehovah's Witnesseses' Kingdom Hall, anywhere in the world, I immediately think of Peter and will probably continue to do so until I pop my clogs. Sad to think that nobody saw him play at the peak of his ability, but he deserves every respect for refusing to be swayed in the choice he made. He certainly seems to have no doubt on that score.'

For a last word, let's turn again to Dave Wagstaffe. The former Wolves wing wizard saw Knowles, not so long ago, happily working on the garden at the Kingdom Hall in Newhampton Road, Wolverhampton. Said Waggy, 'I was in my car and wound down the window and shouted "How about helping me on my allotment, Peter?" and he just smiled and said "I did enough fetching and carrying for you on the pitch!" I sometimes see him in town and when I ask him how is he always replies "I wake up, and every day's a wonderful day." How many people can say that?'

Wolves fans will be happy that Knowles has found that contentment, but most wish he could have given them a few more wonderful days on the football field. For those days he did give us we will always be grateful.

God bless you, Peter.

Bibliography

Corbett, Clive *Those Were The Days* Geoffrey Publicatons, 2007

Crawford, Ray *Curse of the Jungle Boy* PB Publishing, 2007

Dougan, Derek *Doog* All Seasons Publishing, 1980

Farmer, Ted *The Heartbreak Game* Hillburgh Publishers, 1987

Greaves, Jimmy *The Sixties Revisited* Queen Anne Press, 1993

Goodwin, Bob *Spurs A Complete Record* Breedon Books, 1993

Hugman, Barry J. *Football League Players Record 1946–92* Tony Williams Publications, 1992

Lansley, Peter *Running With Wolves* Thomas Publications, 2004

Laschke, Ian *Rothmans Book of Football League Records 1888–89 to 1978–79* Macdonald and Jane's, 1980

Matthews, Tony *The Wolves* Breedon Books, 1989

McGuinness, Wilf *Manchester United Man and Babe* Know The Score, 2008

Morgan, Phil *The Wolverhampton Wanderers Football Book* Stanley Paul and Co, 1970

Morrison, Ian and Shury, Alan *Manchester United A Complete Record 1878–1992* Breedon Books, 1992

Mullery, Alan *In Defence Of Spurs* Stanley Paul and Co, 1969

Redknapp, Harry *'Arry* Collins Willow

Ross, Charles *We Are Wolves* Juma, 1997

Turner, Dennis and White, Alex *Football Managers* Breedon Books, 1993

Wagstaffe, David *Waggy's Tale* Breedon Books, 2008

Warsop, Keith *British and Irish Special and Intermediate Internationals* SoccerData, 2002

Wilson, Bob *Bob Wilson My Autobiography* Hodder and Stoughton, 2003

Knowles's Games for Wolves

1963–64

Appearances 14 (all League) Goals 4

Leicester City 0 Wolves 1, First Division, 14 October 1963.
Leicester City: Banks, Chalmers, Norman, McLintock, King, Appleton, Riley, Cross, Keyworth, Gibson, Stringfellow.
Wolves: Davies, Showell, Thomson, Goodwin, Woodfield, Flowers, Crowe, Knowles, Crawford, Murray, Hinton.
Attendance: 25,067. Referee: K.Howley (Middlesbrough).
Scoring: 0–1 Crawford (9).

Wolves 2 Bolton Wanderers 2, First Division, 19 October 1963.
Wolves: Davies, Showell, Thomson, Goodwin, Flowers, Kirkham, Crowe, Knowles, Crawford, Broadbent, Hinton.
Bolton Wanderers: Smith, Hartle, Hatton, Rimmer, Hulme, Lennard, Butler, Lee, Davies, Deakin, Pilkington.
Attendance 19,420. Referee: D.W. Smith (Stonehouse).
Scoring: 1–0 Knowles (14), 1–1 Butler (25), 2–1 Broadbent (40), 2–2 Pilkington (55).

Birmingham City 2 Wolves 2, First Division, 26 October 1963.
Birmingham City: Withers, Lynn, Green, Hennessey, Smith, Beard, Hellawell, Bloomfield, Harley, P.Bullock, Thwaites.
Wolves: Davies, Showell, Thomson, Goodwin, Woodfield, Flowers, Wharton, Knowles, Crawford, Broadbent, Hinton.
Attendance: 24,804. Referee: G. McCabe (Sheffield).
Scoring: 1–0 Woodfield, own-goal (5), 2–0 Harley (16), 2–1 Wharton (32), 2–2 Hinton (75).

Wolves 2 Manchester United 0, First Division, 2 November 1963.
Wolves: Davies, Showell, Thomson, Goodwin, Woodfield, Flowers, Wharton, Knowles, Crawford, Broadbent, Hinton.
Manchester United: Gregg, Dunne, Cantwell, Crerand, Foulkes, Setters, Moir, Chisnall, Quixall, Law, Charlton.
Attendance: 34,159. Referee: S.B. Stokes (Mansfield).
Scoring: 1–0 Wharton (48), 2–0 Crawford (58).

Burnley 1 Wolves 0, First Division, 9 November 1963.
Burnley: Blacklaw, Angus, Joyce, O'Neil, Talbut, Miller, Meredith, Lochhead, Robson, Harris, Connelly.
Wolves: Davies, Showell, Thomson, Goodwin, Woodfield, Flowers, Wharton, Knowles, Crawford, Broadbent, Hinton.
Attendance: 19,754. Referee: A.W. Luty (Leeds).
Scoring: 1–0 Connelly (86).

Wolves 2 Ipswich Town 1, First Division, 16 November 1963.
Wolves: Davies, Showell, Thomson, Goodwin, Woodfield, Flowers, Wharton, Knowles, Crawford, Broadbent Hinton.
Ipswich Town: Bailey, Davin, Compton, Baxter, Bolton, Elsworthy, Stephenson, Moran, Phillips, Hegan, Broadfoot.
Attendance: 17,891. Referee: L.S. Hamer (Bolton).
Scoring: 1–0 Crawford (60), 1–1 Phillips (70), 2–1 Knowles (84).

Sheffield Wednesday 5 Wolves 0, First Division, 23 November 1963.
Sheffield Wednesday: R. Springett, Johnson, Megson, McAnearney, Swan, Young, Finney, Dobson, Layne, Pearson, Holliday.
Wolves: Davies, Thomson, Harris, Goodwin, Woodfield, Flowers, Stobart, Farmer, Crawford, Knowles, Wharton.
Attendance: 22,650. Referee: R. Crossley (Lancaster).
Scoring: 1–0 Finney (42), 2–0 Layne (61), 3–0 Finney (65), 4–0 Dobson (75), 5–0 Dobson (88).

Wolves 0 Everton 0, First Division, 30 November 1963.
Wolves: Barron, Showell, Thomson, Goodwin, Woodfield, Flowers, Crowe, Knowles, Crawford, Broadbent, Wharton.
Everton: Rankin, Brown, Meagan, Harris, Heslop, Kay, Scott, Stevens, Young, Vernon, Temple.
Attendance: 25,133. Referee: N.C.H. Burtenshaw (Great Yarmouth).

Fulham 4 Wolves 1, First Division, 7 December 1963.
Fulham: Macedo, Cohen, Drake, Mullery, Keetch, Robson, Key, Cook, Leggat, Haynes, Howfield.
Wolves: Davies, Showell, Thomson, Goodwin, Woodfield, Flowers, Wharton, Knowles, Crawford, Crowe, Hinton.
Attendance: 19,305. Referee: T.W. Dawes (Norwich).
Scoring: 1–0 Haynes (5), 2–0 Cook (34), 2–1 Crawford (40), 3–1 Key (72), 4–1 Leggat (75).

Wolves 2 Arsenal 2, First Division, 14 December 1963.
Wolves: Davies, Showell, Thomson, Goodwin, Woodfield, Flowers, Wharton, Knowles, Crawford, Crowe, Hinton.
Arsenal: Furnell, Magill, McCullough, Barnwell, Ure, Sneddon, McLeod, Strong, Baker, Eastham, Armstrong.
Attendance: 18,952. Referee: R.H. Windle (Chesterfield).
Scoring: 1–0 Flowers (14), 2–0 Crowe (26), 2–1 Strong (31), 2–2 Strong (79).

Chelsea 2 Wolves 3, First Division, 8 February 1964.
Chelsea: Dunn, Hinton, McCreadie, R.Harris, Mortimore, Upton, Murray, Tambling, Bridges, Venables, Blunstone.
Wolves: Davies, Showell, Thomson, Broadbent, Woodfield, Flowers, Wharton, Knowles, Crawford, Crowe, Le Flem.
Attendance: 26,323. Referee: D. Smith (Gloucester).
Scoring: 0–1 Crawford (4), 0–2 Crawford (30), 0–3 Le Flem (32), 1–3 Tambling (58), 2–3 Murrray (89).

Wolves 0 West Ham United 2, First Division, 17 February 1964.
Wolves: Davies, Showell, Thomson, Broadbent, Woodfield, Flowers, Wharton Knowles, Crawford, Crowe, Le Flem.
West Ham: Standen, Kirkup, Bond, Bovington, Peters, Moore, Brabrook, Boyce, Byrne, Hurst, Sissons.
Attendance: 14,455. Referee: P. Bye (Bedford).
Scoring: 0–1 Hurst (23), 0–2 Byrne (66).

Wolves 4 Fulham 0, First Division, 18 April 1964.
Wolves: Davies, Showell, Thomson, Flowers, Woodfield, Woodruff, Crowe, Knowles, Crawford, Melia, Le Flem.
Fulham: Macedo, Cohen, Langley, Robson, Keetch, Callaghan, Earle, Metchick, Leggat, Haynes, O'Connell.
Attendance: 16,438. Referee: S.J. Kayley (Preston).
Scoring: 1–0 Melia (32), 2–0, Le Flem (40), 3–0 Melia (44), 4–0 Knowles (54).

Bolton Wanderers 0 Wolves 4, First Division, 24 April 1964.
Bolton: Hopkinson, Hartle, Farrimond, Rimmer, Edwards, Lennard, Davison, Bromley, Lee, Hatton, Taylor.
Wolves: Davies, Showell, Thomson, Flowers, Woodfield, Woodruff, Crowe, Knowles, Crawford, Melia, Le Flem.
Attendance: 27,579. Referee: W.M. Holland (Chesterfield).
Scoring: 0–1 Crawford (25), 0–2 Crawford (53), 0–3 Knowles (55), 0–4 Crawford (85).

1964–65
Appearances 25 (23 Lge, 2 FAC) Goals 7 (6 Lge, 1 FAC)

Leicester City 3 Wolves 2, First Division, 26 August 1964.
Leicester City: Banks, Sjoberg, Norman, McLintock, King, Appleton, Riley, Sweenie, Keyworth, Gibson, Stringfellow.
Wolves: Davies, Thomson, Harris, Goodwin, Flowers, Woodruff, Broadbent, Knowles, Crawford, Melia, Wharton.
Attendance: 25,636. Referee: S. Stokes (Nottingham).
Scoring: 0–1 Knowles (20), 1–1 McLintock (26), 2–1 Keyworth (42), 3–1 Appleton, penalty (51), 3–2 Wharton (53).

Leeds United 3 Wolves 2, First Division, 29 August 1964.
Leeds United: Sprake, Reaney, Bell, Bremner, Charlton, Hunter, Giles, Weston, Storrie, Lawson, Johanneson.
Wolves: Davies, Thomson, Harris, Goodwin, Flowers, Woodruff, Broadbent, Knowles, Crawford, Melia, Wharton.
Attendance: 34,538. Referee: K.E. Walker (Blackpool).
Scoring: 0–1 Knowles (13), 1–1 Storrie (15), 1–2 Crawford (41), 2–2 Charlton (63), 3–2 Storrie (71).

Wolves 1 Leicester City 1, First Division, 2 September 1964.
Wolves: Davies, Thomson, Harris, Goodwin, Flowers, Woodruff, Broadbent, Knowles, Crawford, Melia, Wharton.
Leicester City: Banks, Chalmers, Norman, McLintock, Sjoberg, Appleton, Riley, Sweenie, Keyworth, Gibson, Stringfellow.
Attendance: 22,907. Referee: R.H. Windle (Chesterfield).
Scoring: 1–0 Crawford (35), 1–1 McLintock (42).

Blackburn Rovers 4 Wolves 1, First Division, 12 September 1964.
Blackburn Rovers: Else, Newton, Joyce, Clayton, England, McGrath, Ferguson, McEvoy, Byrom, Douglas, Harrison.
Wolves: Barron, Thomson, Harris, Flowers, Showell, Woodruff, Thompson, Knowles, Galley, Melia, Wharton.
Attendance: 16,745. Referee: D.W.G. Brady (Rotherham).
Scoring: 1–0 McEvoy (44), 2–0 Byrom (50), 3–0 Byrom (58), 4–0 McEvoy (80), 4–1 Thompson (84).

Wolves 4 West Ham United 3, First Division, 14 September 1964.
Wolves: Davies; Thomson, Harris; Goodwin, Showell, Woodruff; Thompson, Knowles, Crawford, Broadbent, Wharton.
West Ham United: Standen; Bond, Burkett; Bovington, Peters, Moore; Sealey, Boyce, Byrne, Hurst, Brabrook.
Attendance: 19,405. Referee: F. Schofield (Morecambe).
Scoring: 1–0 Crawford (3), 2–0 Knowles (34), 2–1 Brabrook (39), 2–2 Harris own-goal (51), 2–3 Byrne, penalty (61), 3–3 Crawford (77), 4–3 Harris (86).

Wolves 1 Blackpool 2, First Division, 19 September 1964.
Wolves: Davies, Thomson, Harris, Flowers, Showell, Woodruff, Thompson, Knowles, Crawford, Broadbent, Wharton.
Blackpool: Waiters, Armfield, Thompson, Rowe, James, Green, Lea, Ball, Charnley, Oates, Horne.
Attendance: 22,260. Referee: R. Tinkler (Boston).
Scoring: 0–1 Charnley (6), 1–1 Crawford (18), 1–2 Oates (20).

Sheffield Wednesday 2 Wolves 0, First Division, 26 September 1964.
Sheffield Wednesday: R. Springett, Hill, Megson, McAnearney, Mobley, Young, Finney, Quinn, Wilkinson, Fantham, Dobson.
Wolves: Davies, Thomson, Harris, Flowers, Showell, Woodruff, Thompson, Broadbent, Ford, Knowles, Wharton.
Attendance: 19,881. Referee: L. J. Hamer (Bolton).
Scoring: 1–0 McAnearney, penalty (45), 2–0 Dobson (90).

Wolves 0 Birmingham City 2, First Division, 30 September 1964.
Wolves: Davies, Showell, Thomson, Goodwin, Flowers, Woodruff, Wharton, Broadbent, Galley, Knowles, Buckley.
Birmingham City: Schofield, Lynn, Martin, Hennessey, Foster, Beard, Hellawell, Jackson, Thomson, Leek, Auld.
Scoring: 0–1 Lynn (26), 0–2 Leek (39).
Attendance: 21,435. Referee: K. Dagnall (Bolton).

West Bromwich Albion 5 Wolves 1, First Division, 10 October 1964.
West Bromwich Albion: Potter, Cram, G. Williams, Howshall, Jones, Simpson, Clark, Kaye, Astle, Hope, Carter.
Wolves: Davies, Showell, Thomson, Flowers, Hawkins, Woodruff, Thompson, Melia, Crawford, Knowles, Buckley.
Attendance: 23,006. Referee: N.C.H. Burtenshaw (Great Yarmouth).
Scoring: 1–0 Astle (25), 2–0 Astle (49), 3–0 Kaye (60), 4–0 Kaye (65), 4–1 Knowles (73), 5–1 Cram, penalty (82).

Manchester United 3 Wolves 0, First Division, 27 February 1965.
Manchester United: P. Dunne, Brennan, A. Dunne, Crerand, Foulkes, Stiles, Connelly, Best, Herd, Law, Charlton.
Wolves: Davies, Thomson, Harris, Flowers, Woodfield, Kirkham, Wharton, Woodruff, Miller, Knowles, Wagstaffe.
Attendance: 37,018. Referee: A.W. Luty (Leeds).
Scoring: 1–0 Connelly (5), 2–0 Charlton (69), 3–0 Charlton (84).

Wolves 3 Aston Villa 1, FA Cup, fifth-round second replay, 1 March 1965.
(at The Hawthorns, West Bromwich)
Wolves: Davies, Thomson, Harris, Flowers, Woodfield, Miller, Wharton, Woodruff, McIlmoyle, Knowles, Wagstaffe.
Aston Villa: Withers, Lee, Aitken, Wylie, Pountney, Deakin, Baker, Park, Hateley, Woosnam, Macleod.
Attendance: 37,534. Referee: K. Stokes (Newark).
Scoring: 1–0 McIlmoyle (4), 1–1 Park (52), 2–1 McIlmoyle (69), 3–1 McIlmoyle (88).

Wolves 3 Manchester United 5, FA Cup sixth round, 10 March 1965.
Wolves: Davies, Thomson, Harris, Flowers, Woodfield, Miller, Wharton, Woodruff, McIlmoyle, Knowles, Wagstaffe.
Manchester United: P. Dunne, Brennan, A. Dunne, Crerand, Foulkes, Stiles, Connelly, Charlton, Herd, Law, Best.
Attendance: 53,581. Referee: L. Callaghan (Merthyr).
Scoring: 1–0 McIlmoyle (3), 2–0 McIlmoyle (15), 2–1 Law (44), 2–2 Herd (50), 2–3 Best (62), 2–4 Crerand (68), 2–5 Law (75), 3–5 Knowles (81).

Birmingham City 0 Wolves 1, First Division, 13 March 1965.
Birmingham City: Schofield, Lynn, Green, Hennessey, Foster, Beard, Jackson, Fraser, Thomson, Vowden, Thwaites.
Wolves: Davies, Thomson, Harris, Flowers, Woodfield, Miller, Wharton, Woodruff, McIlmoyle, Knowles, Wagstaffe.
Attendance: 18,860. Referee: F. Cowen (Manchester).
Scoring: 0–1 Wharton (51).

Wolves 3 West Bromwich Albion 2, First Division, 15 March 1965.
Wolves: Davies, Thomson, Harris, Kirkham, Flowers, Miller, Wharton, Woodruff, McIlmoyle, Knowles, Buckley.
West Bromwich Albion: Potter, Cram, G. Williams, Howshall, Jones, Fraser, Foggo, Astle, Kaye, Hope, Clark.
Attendance: 26,722. Referee: H. Richards (Oldham).
Scoring: 0–1 Foggo (5), 1–1 McIlmoyle (49), 1–2 Harris, own-goal (57), 2–2 Woodruff (64), 3–2 McIlmoyle (67).

Wolves 3 Stoke City 1, First Division, 20 March 1965.
Wolves: Davies, Thomson, Harris, Kirkham, Flowers, Miller, Wharton, Woodruff, McIlmoyle, Knowles, Buckley.
Stoke City: Leslie, Skeels, Allen, Palmer, Kinnell, Setters, Bebbington, McIlroy, Ritchie, Vernon, Burrows.
Attendance: 20,945. Referee: J.R. Osborne (Ipswich).
Scoring: 1–0 Buckley (7), 2–0 Woodruff (10), 2–1 Burrows (73), 3–1 Wharton (79).

Aston Villa 3 Wolves 2, First Division, 22 March 1965.
Aston Villa: Withers, Lee, Aitken, Wylie, Pountney, Deakin, Baker, Chatterley, Hateley, Woosnam, Macleod.
Wolves: Davies, Thomson, Harris, Kirkham, Flowers, Miller, Wharton, Woodruff, McIlmoyle, Knowles, Buckley.
Attendance: 28,892. Referee: K. Stokes (Newark).
Scoring: 1–0 Baker (5), 2–0 Chatterley (6), 2–1 Woodruff (21), 3–1 Chatterley (30), 3–2 McIlmoyle (84).

Tottenham Hotspur 7 Wolves 4, First Division, 27 March 1965.
Tottenham Hostpur: W. Brown, Knowles, Henry, Mullery, L. Brown, Clayton, Weller, Greaves, Allen, Gilzean, Jones.
Wolves: Davies, Thomson, Harris, Kirkham, Flowers, Miller, Wharton, Woodruff, McIlmoyle, Knowles, Buckley.
Attendance: 25,974. Referee: R. Aldous (Suffolk).
Scoring: 0–1 Buckley (10), 1–1 Allen (37), 2–1 Gilzean (49), 3–1 Clayton (53), 3–2 McIlmoyle (58), 4–2 Jones (61), 4–3 Kirkham (63), 5–3 Gilzean (69), 5–4 Wharton (74), 6–4 Jones (84), 7–4 Jones (85).

Wolves 0 Fulham 0, First Division, 30 March 1965.
Wolves: MacLaren, J. Wilson, Harris, Kirkham, Flowers, Miller, Wharton, Woodruff, McIlmoyle, Knowles, Buckley.
Fulham: Macedo, Cohen, Langley, Robson, Keetch, Brown, Key, Marsh, Stratton, Haynes, Leggat.
Attendance: 18,960. Referee: G.T. Powell (Newport).

Wolves 1 Burnley 2, First Division, 3 April 1965.
Wolves: MacLaren, J. Wilson, Harris, Kirkham, Flowers, Miller, Wharton, Woodruff, McIlmoyle, Knowles, Wagstaffe.
Burnley: Thompson, Todd, Elder, O'Neil, Talbut, Miller, Morgan, Lochhead, Coates, Harris, Latcham.
Attendance: 16,841. Referee: W.M. Holian (Chesterfield).
Scoring: 0–1 Lochhead (7), 1–1 Flowers (38), 1–2 Latcham (73).

Sheffield United 0 Wolves 2, First Division, 10 April 1965.
Sheffield United: Widdowson, Badger, G. Shaw, Kettleborough, Mallender, Matthewson, Woodward, T. Wagstaff, Allchurch, Birchenall, Hartle.
Wolves: MacLaren, J. Wilson, Thomson, Kirkham, Flowers, Miller, Wharton, Woodruff, McIlmoyle, Knowles, Wagstaffe.
Attendance: 11,850. Referee: K. Dagnall (Bolton).
Scoring: 0–1 Knowles (60), 0–2 Woodruff (61).

Sunderland 1 Wolves 2, First Division, 16 April 1965.
Sunderland: McLaughlan, Parke, Ashurst, Harvey, Hurley, McNab, Hellawell, Herd, Hood, Sharkey, Usher.
Wolves: MacLaren, J. Wilson, Thomson, Kirkham, Flowers, Miller, Wharton, Woodruff, McIlmoyle, Knowles, Wagstaffe.
Attendance: 43,328. Referee: W. Crossley (Lancaster).
Scoring: 1–0 Hellawell (1), 1–2 McIlmoyle (50), 1–2 Knowles (87).

Wolves 2 Everton 4, First Division, 17 April 1965.
Wolves: MacLaren, J. Wilson, Thomson, Kirkham, Flowers, Miller, Wharton, Woodruff, McIlmoyle, Knowles, Buckley.
Everton: West, Brown, Wright, Gabriel, Labone, Harris, Scott, Harvey, Pickering, Temple, Morrissey.
Attendance: 19,689. Referee: G.N.T. Davis (Romford).
Scoring: 0–1 Morrissey (8), 1–1 Woodruff (15), 2–1 Wharton (22), 2–2 Harris (28), 2–3 Pickering (47), 2–4 Brown, penalty (51).

Wolves 3 Sunderland 0, First Division, 20 April 1965.
Wolves: MacLaren, Knighton, Thomson, Kirkham, Flowers, Miller, Wharton, Woodruff, McIlmoyle, Knowles, Buckley.
Sunderland: McLaughlan, Irwin, Ashurst, Harvey, Rooks, McNab, Hellawell, Herd, Moore, Hood, Mulhall.
Attendance: 14,896.
Scoring: 1–0 Woodruff (15), 2–0 Woodruff (36), 3–0 Woodruff (65).

Nottingham Forest 0 Wolves 2, First Division, 24 April 1965.
Nottingham Forest: Grummitt, Hindley, Mochan, Newton, McKinlay, Whitefoot, Crowe, Addison, Wignall, Barnwell, Hinton.
Wolves: MacLaren, Knighton, Thomson, Kirkham, Flowers, Miller, Wharton, Woodruff, McIlmoyle, Knowles, Buckley.
Attendance: 18,500. Referee: R.A. Payne (Southall).
Scoring: 0–1 McIlmoyle (27), 0–2 Buckley (72).

Wolves 1 Liverpool 3, First Division, 26 April 1965.
Wolves: MacLaren, Knighton, Thomson, Kirkham, Flowers, Miller, Wharton, Woodruff, McIlmoyle, Knowles, Buckley.
Liverpool: Molyneux, Lowry, Hignett, Chisnall, Moran, Ferns, Graham, Sealey, Arrowsmith, Strong, Wallace.
Attendance: 13,839. Referee: D.W. Smith (Stonehouse, Gloucs).
Scoring: 0–1 Strong (14), 0–2 Sealey (35), 1–2 Miller (47), 1–3 Arrowsmith (70).

1965–66
Appearances 33 (31 Lge, 2 FAC) Goals 21 (19 Lge, 2 FAC)

Coventry City 2 Wolves 1, Second Division, 21 August 1965.
Coventry City: Wesson, Kearns, Harris, Farmer, Curtis, Hill, Rees, Hale, Hudson, Machin, Clements.
Wolves: MacLaren, Knighton, Thomson, Flowers, Woodfield, Miller, Wharton, Woodruff, McIlmoyle, Knowles, Wagstaffe.
Attendance: 36,722. Referee: L.J. Hamer (Bolton).
Scoring: 0–1 McIlmoyle (58), 1–1 Hudson (78), 2–1 Hudson (84).

Manchester City 2 Wolves 1, Second Division, 25 August 1965.
Manchester City: Dowd, Bacuzzi, Connor, Doyle, Cheetham, Oakes, Summerbee, Crossan, Murray, Brand, Pardoe.
Wolves: MacLaren, Knighton, Thomson, Flowers, Woodfield, Miller, Wharton, Woodruff, McIlmoyle, Knowles, Wagstaffe.
Attendance: 25,572. Referee: P. Rhodes (Yorkshire).
Scoring: 1–0 Miller, own-goal (29), 2–0 Thomson, own-goal (85), 2–1 Knowles (88).

Wolves 3 Carlisle United 0, Second Division, 28 August 1965.
Wolves: MacLaren, Knighton, Thomson, Flowers, Woodfield, Miller, Wharton, Woodruff, McIlmoyle, Knowles, Wagstaffe.
Carlisle United: Dean, Gallagher, Caldwell, McConnell, Passmoor, Harland, Blain, Evans, Large, Balderstone, Simpson.
Attendance: 18,934. Referee: L.W. Faulkner (Liverpool).
Scoring: 1–0 Knowles (29), 2–0 Knowles (54), 3–0 Knowles (89).

Wolves 2 Manchester City 4, Second Division, 30 August 1965.
Wolves: MacLaren, Thomson, Harris, Flowers, Woodfield, Miller, Wharton, Woodruff, McIlmoyle, Knowles, Wagstaffe.
Manchester City: Dowd, Bacuzzi, Sear, Doyle, Oakes, Kennedy, Summerbee (Cheetham 23), Crossan, Murray, Pardoe, Connor.
Attendance: 22,799. Referee: D.W.G. Brady (Rotherham).
Scoring: 1–0 Wagstaffe (5), 1–1 Murray (6), 1–2 Crossan (8), 1–3 Harris, own-goal (36), 2–3 Woodruff (81), 2–4 Doyle (86).

Cardiff City 1 Wolves 4, Second Division, 4 September 1965.
Cardiff City: Wilson, Coldrick, Rodrigues, Williams, Murray, Hole, Farrell, Johnston, Charles, Harkin, Lewis.
Wolves: MacLaren, J. Wilson, Thomson, Flowers, Woodfield, Miller, Wharton, Woodruff, McIlmoyle, Knowles, Wagstaffe.
Attendance: 19,949. Referee: W. Crossley (Lancaster).
Scoring: 0–1 McIlmoyle (12), 0–2 McIlmoyle (15), 0–3 Williams, own-goal (38), 1–3 Johnston, penalty (75), 1–4 Wagstaffe (89).

Rotherham United 4 Wolves 3, Second Division, 7 September 1965.
Rotherham United: Morritt, Wilcockson, Clish, Hardy, Madden, Tiler, Lyons, Chappell, Galley, Williams, Pring.
Wolves: MacLaren, J. Wilson, Thomson, Flowers, Woodfield, Miller, Wharton, Woodruff, McIlmoyle, Knowles, Wagstaffe.
Attendance: 11,370. Referee: R. Egan (Lymm).
Scoring: 1–0 Pring (20), 2–0 Lyons (46), 2–1 Wagstaffe (49), 3–1 Williams (59), 3–2 Knowles (60), 4–2 Williams (75), 4–3 Wharton, penalty (84).

Wolves 4 Derby County 0, Second Division, 11 September 1965.
Wolves: MacLaren, J. Wilson, Thomson, Flowers, Woodfield, Miller, Wharton, Woodruff, McIlmoyle, Knowles, Wagstaffe.
Derby County: Matthews, Barrowcliffe, Ferguson, Webster, Young, Parry, Hughes, Durban, Bowers, Hodgson, Cleeveley.
Attendance: 17,063. Referee: K.E. Walker (Preston).
Scoring: 1–0 Knowles (3), 2–0 Knowles (9), 3–0 Woodruff (21), 4–0 Knowles (75).

Wolves 4 Rotherham United 1, Second Division, 13 September 1965.
Wolves: MacLaren, J. Wilson, Thomson, Flowers, Woodfield, Miller, Wharton, Woodruff, McIlmoyle, Knowles, Wagstaffe.
Rotherham United: Jones, Wilcockson, Clish, Hardy, Haselden, Tiler, Lyons, Chappell, Galley, Williams, Pring.
Attendance: 20,012. Referee: K. Dagnall (Bolton).
Scoring: 1–0 McIlmoyle (4), 2–0 Wagstaffe (9), 3–0 Knowles (32), 4–0 Woodfield (40), 4–1 Pring (54).

Southampton 9 Wolves 3, Second Division, 18 September, 1965.
Southampton: Godfrey, Jones, Williams, Walker, Knapp, Huxford, Paine, O'Brien, Melia, Chivers, Sydenham.
Wolves: MacLaren, J. Wilson, Thomson, Flowers, Woodfield, Miller, Wharton, Woodruff, McIlmoyle, Knowles, Wagstaffe.
Attendance: 23,226. Referee: A.E. Dimond (Harlow).
Scoring: 0–1 Knapp, own-goal (1), 1–1 Chivers (4), 2–1 Sydenham (11), 2–2 Woodruff (12), 3–2 Paine (25), 4–2 O'Brien (30), 5–2 Chivers (33), 6–2 Chivers (47), 7–2 Chivers (50), 7–3 Knowles (54), 8–3 Sydenham (55), 9–3 Paine (60).

Wolves 3 Bury 0, Second Division, 25 September 1965.
Wolves: MacLaren, J. Wilson, Thomson, Flowers, Woodfield, Holsgrove, Wharton, Hunt, McIlmoyle, Knowles, Wagstaffe.
Bury: Harker, Bray, Eastham, Colquhoun (Claxton 22), Clunie, Leach, Henderson, Griffin, Bell, Lindsay, Roberts.
Attendance: 15,549. Referee: J.E. Carr (Sheffield).
Scoring: 1–0 Wagstaffe (14), 2–0 Knowles (54), 3–0 Wharton (70).

Norwich City 0 Wolves 3, Second Division, 2 October 1965.
Norwich City: Keelan, Stringer, Mullett, Lucas, Butler, Allcock, Mannion, Bryceland, Davies, Bolland, Punton.
Wolves: MacLaren, J. Wilson, Thomson, Flowers, Woodfield, Holsgrove, Wharton, Hunt, McIlmoyle, Knowles, Wagstaffe.
Attendance: 20,939. Referee: A.W. Sparling (Grimsby).
Scoring: 0–1 Wagstaffe (8), 0–2 Wharton (27), 0–3 Knowles (40).

Leyton Orient 0 Wolves 3, Second Division, 9 October 1965.
Leyton Orient: Rouse, Webb, Worrall, Sorrell, Nelson, Smith, Price, Gregory, Flatt, Ferry, Metchick.
Wolves: MacLaren, J. Wilson, Thomson, Flowers, Woodfield, Holsgrove, Wharton, Hunt, McIlmoyle, Knowles, Wagstaffe.
Attendance: 11,411. Referee: T.W. Dawes (Norwich).
Scoring: 0–1 Wagstaffe (6), 0–2 Ferry, own-goal (21), 0–3 Ferry, own-goal (56).

Wolves 3 Middlesbrough 0, Second Division, 16 October 1965.
Wolves: MacLaren, J. Wilson, Thomson, Flowers, Woodfield, Holsgrove, Wharton, Hunt (Goodwin 47), McIlmoyle, Knowles, Wagstaffe.
Middlesbrough: Connachan, Gates, Jones, Horner, Rooks, Davidson, Holliday, Gibson, Garbett, Irvine, Ratcliffe.
Attendance: 20,927. Referee: G.W.T. Davis (Romford).
Scoring: 1–0, Knowles (8), 2–0 Hunt (29), 3–0 Woodfield (89).

Huddersfield Town 1 Wolves 1, Second Division, 23 October 1965.
Huddersfield Town: Oldfield, Atkins, McNab, Nicholson, Coddington, Meagan, McHale, Dinsdale, Leighton, Quigley, Legg.
Wolves: MacLaren, J. Wilson, Thomson, Flowers, Woodfield, Holsgrove, Wagstaffe, McIlmoyle, Wharton, Knowles, Buckley.
Attendance: 19,122. Referee: F. Cowen (Oldham).
Scoring: 1–0 Leighton (52), 1–1 Wharton (54).

Wolves 1 Crystal Palace 0, Second Division, 30 October 1965.
Wolves: MacLaren, J. Wilson, Thomson, Flowers, Woodfield, Holsgrove, Wharton, Hunt, McIlmoyle, Knowles, Wagstaffe.
Crystal Palace: Jackson, Long, Howe, Payne, Stephenson, Bannister, Whitehouse, Lawson, Burnside, Kevan, Yard.
Attendance: 21,623. Referee: D.N.H. Payne (Sheffield).
Scoring: 1–0 Knowles (51).

Preston North End 2 Wolves 2, Second Division, 6 November 1965.
Preston North End: Barton, Ross, Smith, Spavin, Singleton, Kendall, Hannigan, Ashurst, Dawson, Lawton, Lee.
Wolves: MacLaren, J. Wilson, Thomson, Flowers, Woodfield, Holsgrove, Wharton, Hunt, McIlmoyle, Knowles, Wagstaffe.
Attendance: 15,971. Referee: E. Crawford (Doncaster).
Scoring: 0–1 Knowles (12), 0–2 Wharton (19), 1–2 Lee (62), 2–2 Kendall (86).

Wolves 2 Charlton Athletic 2, Second Division, 13 November 1965.
Wolves: Davies, J. Wilson, Thomson, Flowers, Woodfield, Holsgrove, Wharton, Hunt, McIlmoyle, Knowles, Wagstaffe.
Charlton Athletic: Rose, Bonds, Kinsey (Halom 20), Bailey, Haydock, Tocknell, Kenning, Campbell, Saunders, Myers, Glover.
Attendance: 20,944. Referee: J. Mitchell (Prescott).
Scoring: 1–0 McIlmoyle (33), 1–1 Bailey (57), 1–2 Saunders (71), 2–2 Hunt (73).

Plymouth Argyle 2 Wolves 2, Second Division, 20 November 1965.
Plymouth Argyle: Leiper, Book, Baird, Williams, Nelson, Hore, Jones, Newman, Reynolds, Trebilcock, Jennings.
Wolves: Davies, J. Wilson, Thomson, Flowers, Woodfield, Holsgrove, Wharton, Hunt, McIlmoyle, Knowles, Wagstaffe.
Attendance: 17,685. Referee: H.D. Davies (Wenvoe).
Scoring: 1–0 Reynolds (48), 1–1 McIlmoyle (60), 2–1 Wilson, own-goal (86), 2–2 McIlmoyle (88).

Wolves 4 Ipswich Town 1, Second Division, 11 December 1965.
Wolves: Davies, J. Wilson, Thomson, Flowers (Knighton 51), Hawkins, Woodruff, Wharton, Hunt, McIlmoyle, Knowles, Wagstaffe.
Ipswich Town: Hancock, Davin, McNeil, Lea, Baxter, Thompson, Spearritt, Hegan, Bolton, Kellard, Brogan.
Attendance: 19,072. Referee: P.R. Walton (Bridgwater).
Scoring: 0–1 Hegan (1), 1–1 Hunt (4), 2–1 Woodruff (27), 3–1 McIlmoyle (38), 4–1 Wharton (66).

Middlesbrough 3 Wolves 1, Second Division, 18 December 1965.
Middlesbrough: McPartland, Gates, Jones, Anderson, Rooks, Davidson, Townsend, McMordie, Horsfield, Gibson, Holliday.
Wolves: Davies, J. Wilson, Thomson, Woodruff, Woodfield, L. Wilson, Wharton, Hunt, McIlmoyle, Knowles, Wagstaffe.
Attendance: 13,419. Referee: H. Richards (Oldham).
Scoring: 1–0 Rooks (8), 2–0 Gibson (9), 2–1 Knowles (19), 3–1 Horsfield (22).

Wolves 1 Bristol City 1, Second Division, 27 December 1965.
Wolves: Davies, J. Wilson, Thomson, Woodruff, Woodfield, Holsgrove, Wharton, Hunt, McIlmoyle, Knowles, Buckley.
Bristol City: Gibson, Ford, Briggs, Parr, Connor, Low, Savino, Atyeo, Bush, Clark, Peters.
Attendance: 32,526. Referee: L.W. Faulkner (Liverpool).
Scoring: 1–0 Buckley (59), 1–1 Atyeo (77).

Bristol City 0 Wolves 1, Second Division, 28 December 1965.
Bristol City: Gibson, Ford, Showell, Parr (Bartley HT), Connor, Low, Sharp, Atyeo, Bush, Clark, Peters.
Wolves: Davies, J. Wilson, Thomson, Woodruff, Woodfield, Holsgrove, Wharton, Hunt, McIlmoyle, Knowles, Buckley.
Attendance: 36,183. Referee: J. Finney (Hereford).
Scoring: 0–1 Knowles (78).

Wolves 2 Leyton Orient 1, Second Division, 1 January 1966.
Wolves: MacLaren, J. Wilson, Thomson, Woodruff, Woodfield, Holsgrove, Wharton, Hunt, McIlmoyle, Knowles, Buckley.
Leyton Orient: Rouse, Forsyth, Webb, Smith, Ferry, Sorrell, Price, Allen, Flatt, Metchick, Nicholas.
Attendance: 20,857. Referee: C.F. Duxbury (Preston).
Scoring: 1–0 Wharton (9), 2–0 Hunt (76), 2–1 Metchick (81).

Wolves 3 Sheffield United 0, FA Cup, fourth round, 12 February 1966.
Wolves: MacLaren, J. Wilson, Thomson, Flowers, Woodfield, Holsgrove, Wharton, Hunt, McIlmoyle, Knowles, Wagstaffe.
Sheffield United: Hodgkinson, Badger, Mallender, Matthewson, J. Shaw, B. Wagstaff, Woodward, T. Wagstaff, Birchenall, Fenoughty, Reece.
Attendance: 32,456. Referee: A.E. Dimond (Harlow).
Scoring: 1–0 McIlmoyle (31), 2–0 Knowles (65), 3–0 Knowles (67).

Wolves 2 Cardiff City 1, Second Division, 19 February 1966.
Wolves: MacLaren, J. Wilson, Thomson, Flowers, Woodfield, Holsgrove, Wharton, Hunt, McIlmoyle, Knowles, Wagstaffe.
Cardiff City: Davies, Carver, Ferguson, Williams, Murray, Hole, Lewis, Johnston, Andrews, King, Bird.
Attendance: 24,179. Referee: G.D. Roper (Cambridge).
Scoring: 1–0 Wharton (44), 2–0 Wharton (47), 2–1 Andrews (67).

Derby County 2 Wolves 2, Second Division, 26 February 1966.
Derby County: Matthews, Richardson, Daniel, Webster, Saxton, Upton, Hughes, Thomas, Buxton, Durban, Hodgson.
Wolves: MacLaren, J. Wilson, Thomson, Flowers, Woodfield, Holsgrove, Wharton, Hunt, McIlmoyle, Knowles, Wagstaffe.
Attendance: 27,265. Referee: P. Baldwin (Middlesbrough).
Scoring: 0–1 Hunt (17), 1–1 Thomas (24), 1–2 McIlmoyle (62), 2–2 Thomas (77).

Wolves 2 Manchester United 4, FA Cup fifth round, 5 March 1966.
Wolves: MacLaren, J. Wilson, Thomson, Flowers, Woodfield, Holsgrove, Wharton, Hunt, McIlmoyle, Knowles, Wagstaffe.
Manchester United: Gregg, Brennan, A. Dunne, Crerand, Foulkes, Stiles, Best, Law, Charlton, Herd, Connelly.
Attendance: 53,428. Referee: K. Howley (Middlesbrough).
Scoring: 1–0 Wharton, penalty (2), 2–0 Wharton, penalty (9), 2–1 Law (23), 2–2 Law (62), 2–3 Best (73), 2–4 Herd (89).

Wolves 1 Southampton 1, Second Division, 12 March 1966.
Wolves: MacLaren, J. Wilson, Thomson (Woodfield 76), Bailey, Flowers, Holsgrove, Wharton, Hunt, McIlmoyle, Knowles, Wagstaffe.
Southampton: Forsyth, Webb, Williams, Walker, Knapp, Huxford, Paine, Chivers, Dean, Melia, Sydenham (Wimshurst 80).
Attendance: 26,876. Referee: L.J. Hamer (Bolton).
Scoring: 0–1 Webb (51), 1–1 Hunt (62).

Bury 1 Wolves 0, Second Division, 19 March 1966.
Bury: Ramsbottom, Bray, Eastham, Leech, Turner, Parry, Lowes, Maltby, Aimson, G. Kerr, J. Kerr.
Wolves: MacLaren, J. Wilson, Harris, Bailey, Flowers, Holsgrove, Wharton, Hunt, Woodfield, Knowles, Wagstaffe.
Attendance: 9,211. Referee: N. Callender (Richmond).
Scoring: 1–0 Aimson (41).

Wolves 2 Birmingham City 0, Second Division, 12 April 1966.
Wolves: MacLaren, J. Wilson, Thomson, Bailey, Hawkins, Flowers, Knowles, Hunt, Woodfield, McIlmoyle, Wagstaffe.
Birmingham City: Herriot, Fraser, Martin, Wylie, Foster, Beard, Jackson, Vincent, Thomson, Vowden, Hockey.
Attendance: 32,511. Referee: R. Harper (Sheffield).
Scoring: 1–0 McIlmoyle (30), 2–0 Hunt (67).

Wolves 0 Plymouth Argyle 0, Second Division, 16 April 1966.
Wolves: MacLaren, J. Wilson, Thomson, Bailey, Hawkins, Flowers, Knowles, Hunt, Woodfield, McIlmoyle, Wagstaffe.
Plymouth Argyle: Leiper, Book, Baird, Piper, Nelson, Newman, Corbett, Brimscombe, Reynolds, Jackson, Jones.
Attendance: 20,792. Referee: K.J. Seddon (Southport).

Wolves 3 Bolton Wanderers 1, Second Division, 30 April 1966.
Wolves: MacLaren, J. Wilson (Woodfield 65), Thomson, Bailey, Hawkins, Flowers, Wharton, Hunt, McIlmoyle, Knowles, Wagstaffe.
Bolton Wanderers: Hopkinson, Rimmer, Farrimond, Beech, Hulme, Lennard, Lee, Hatton, Davies, Hill, Taylor.
Attendance: 14,770. Referee: I. Rhodes (York).
Scoring: 0–1 Taylor (57), 1–1 Knowles (58), 2–1 McIlmoyle (80), 3–1 Wharton (88).

Ipswich Town 5 Wolves 2, Second Division, 7 May 1966.
Ipswich Town: Hancock, Mills, McNeil, D.Harper, Baxter, Lea, Spearritt, Hegan, Crawford, Baker, Brogan.
Wolves: MacLaren, Woodfield, Thomson (Knighton 65), Bailey, Hawkins, Flowers, Wharton, Hunt, McIlmoyle, Knowles, Buckley.
Attendance: 14,236. Referee: M.A. Fussey (Retford).
Scoring: 1–0 Crawford (2), 1–1 Buckley (10), 1–2 Knowles (13), 2–2 Baker (19), 3–2 Hawkins, own-goal (30), 4–2 Crawford (43), 5–2 Hegan (51).

1966–67
Appearances 26 + 2 sub (21 Lge + 2 sub, 4 FAC, 1 LC) Goals 8 (8 Lge)

Wolves 1 Birmingham City 2, Second Division, 20 August 1966.
Wolves: MacLaren, Knighton, Thomson, Bailey, Flowers, Holsgrove, Farrington, Knowles, McIlmoyle, Hunt, Wagstaffe.
Birmingham City: Herriot, Martin, Green, Wylie, Foster, Beard, Hockey, Thomson, Vowden, Bridges, Murray.
Attendance: 26,800. Referee: J. Finney (Knighton).
Scoring: 0–1 Murray (52), 0–2 Murray (67), 1–2 McIlmoyle (77).

Ipswich Town 3 Wolves 1, Second Division, 27 August 1966.
Ipswich Town: Hancock, Mills, Houghton, Harper, Baxter, Lea, Spearritt, Hegan, Crawford, Baker, Brogan.
Wolves: Davies, Knighton (L. Wilson 24), Thomson, Bailey, Woodfield, Holsgrove, Farrington, Hunt, McIlmoyle, Knowles, Wagstaffe.
Attendance: 17,210. Referee: A.R. Weller (Bromley).
Scoring: 1–0 Hegan (2), 2–0 Hegan (8), 2–1 McIlmoyle (9), 3–1 Brogan (20).

Cardiff City 0 Wolves 3, Second Division, 31 August 1966.
Cardiff City: John, Carver, Ferguson, Williams, Murray, Coldrick, Farrell, King, Andrews, Toshack, Lewis.
Wolves: Davies, J. Wilson, Thomson, Bailey, Woodfield, Holsgrove, Buckley, Knowles, McIlmoyle, Hunt, Wagstaffe.
Attendance: 13,951. Referee: R.F. Pritchard (Salisbury).
Scoring: 0–1 McIlmoyle (75), 0–2 McIlmoyle (85), 0–3 Buckley (88).

Wolves 1 Bristol City 1, Second Division, 3 September 1966.
Wolves: Davies, L. Wilson, Thomson, Bailey, Woodfield, Holsgrove, Wagstaffe, Hunt, McIlmoyle, Knowles, Buckley.
Bristol City: Gbson, Ford, Briggs, Parr, Connor, Low, Peters, Derrick, Clarke, Sharpe, Bartley.
Attendance: 17,952. Referee: K.E. Walker (Blackpool).
Scoring: 0–1 Peters (49), 1–1 Knowles (68).

Bolton Wanderers 0 Wolves 0, Second Division, 24 September 1966.
Bolton Wanderers: Hopkinson, Cooper, Farrimond, Rimmer, Napier, Hatton, Lee, Hill, Davies, Bromley, Taylor.
Wolves: Davies, J. Wilson, Thomson, Bailey, Woodfield, Hawkins, Wharton, Knowles, McIlmoyle, Burnside (Holsgrove 57), Wagstaffe.
Attendance: 20,927. Referee: G.W. Hill (Scunthorpe).

Wolves 1 Charlton Athletic 0, Second Division, 1 October 1966.
Wolves: Davies, J. Wilson, Thomson, Bailey, Woodfield, Hawkins, Wharton, Knowles, McIlmoyle, Burnside, Wagstaffe.
Charlton Athletic: Wright, Bonds, Kinsey, Reeves, King, Burridge (Peacock 21), Kenning, Gregory, Matthews, Campbell, Glover.
Attendance: 20,728. Referee: E.D. Wallace (Swindon).
Scoring: 1–0 McIlmoyle (61).

Fulham 5 Wolves 0, Football League Cup third round, 5 October, 1966.
Fulham: McClelland, Cohen, Dempsey, Robson, Callaghan, Conway, Haynes, Brown, Earle, Clarke, Barrett.
Wolves: Davies, J. Wilson, Thomson, Bailey, Woodfield, Hawkins, Wharton, Knowles, McIlmoyle, Burnside, Wagstaffe.
Attendance: 14,321. Referee: H.G. New (Portsmouth).
Scoring: 1–0 Earle (10), 2–0 Clarke (43), 3–0 Conway (59), 4–0 Clarke (64), 5–0 Barrett (69).

Norwich City 1 Wolves 2, Second Division, 10 December 1966.
Norwich City: Keelan, Stringer, Mullett, Kelly, Brown, Allcock, Bolland, Bryceland, Sheffield, Curran, Anderson.
Wolves: Davies, Hawkins, Thomson, Bailey, Woodfield, Flowers, Wharton, Hunt, Knowles, Burnside, Wagstaffe.
Attendance: 15,423. Referee: M.V. Sinclair (Guildford).
Scoring: 1–0 Bolland (2), 1–1 Knowles (15), 1–2 Wagstaffe (78).

Birmingham City 3 Wolves 2, Second Division, 17 December 1966.
Birmingham City: Herriot, Murray, Green, Thomson, Sharples, Beard, Hockey, Vincent, M.Bullock, Vowden, Bridges.
Wolves: Davies, Flowers, Thomson, Bailey, Woodfield, Hawkins, Wharton, Hunt, Knowles, Burnside, Wagstaffe.
Attendance: 27,527. Referee: K. Dagnall (Bolton).
Scoring: 0–1 Wagstaffe (1), 0–2 Bailey (35), 1–2 Bridges (68), 2–2 Bullock (77), 3–2 Vowden (86).

Wolves 1 Carlisle United 1, Second Division, 14 January 1967.
Wolves: Davies, Taylor, Thomson, Bailey, Woodfield, Holsgrove, Wharton, Hunt, McIlmoyle, Knowles, Wagstaffe.
Carlisle United: Ross, Neil, Caldwell, McConnell, Passmore, Garbutt, Welsh, Carlin, Wilson, Balderstone, McVitie.
Attendance: 23,522. Referee: R. Darlington (Runcorn).
Scoring: 1–0 Hunt (61), 1–1 McVitie (84).

Blackburn Rovers 0 Wolves 0, Second Division, 21 January 1967.
Blackburn Rovers: Barton, Ferguson, Wilson, Sharples, Clayton, Hole, Connelly, Newton, Lord, McEvoy, Harrison.
Wolves: Davies, Taylor, Thomson, Bailey, Woodfield, Holsgrove, Wharton, Hunt, Hatton, Knowles, Wagstaffe.
Attendance: 15,489. Referee: K. Styles (Barnsley).

Oldham 2 Wolves 2, FA Cup third round, 28 January 1967.
Oldham: Best, Ledger, Knighton (Wood 17), Stevens, Asprey, Bowie, Bebbington, Collins, Frizzell, Towers, Blore.
Wolves: Davies, Taylor, Thomson, Bailey, Woodfield, Holsgrove, Wharton, Hunt, McIlmoyle, Knowles, Wagstaffe.
Attendance: 24,969. Referee: P. Bye (Bedford).
Scoring: 1–0 Bebbington (19), 2–0 Bebbington (77), 2–1 Bailey (88), 2–2 Thomson (89).

Wolves 4 Oldham 1, FA Cup third-round replay, 1 February 1967.
Wolves: Davies, Taylor, Thomson, Bailey, Woodfield, Holsgrove, Wharton, Hunt (L. Wilson 73), McIlmoyle, Knowles, Wagstaffe.
Oldham: Best, Ledger, Knighton, Stevens, Asprey, Bowie, Bebbingotn, Towers, Frizzell, Collins, Blore.
Attendance: 29,772. Referee: P. Rhodes (York).
Scoring: 1–0 Hunt (25), 2–0 Woodfield (30), 2–1 Bebbington (54), 3–1 Wharton (59), 4–1 McIlmoyle (70).

Wolves 5 Bolton Wanderers 2, Second Division, 4 February 1967.
Wolves: Davies, Taylor, Thomson, Bailey, Woodfield, Holsgrove, Wharton, Hunt, Hatton, Knowles, Wagstaffe.
Bolton Wanderers: Hopkinson, Farrimond, Cooper, Rimmer, Hulme, Hatton, Bromley, Byrom, Lee, Lennard, Taylor.
Attendance: 24,015. Referee: J.P. Jones (Glamorgan).
Scoring: 0–1 Bromley (1), 1–1 Hunt (10), 2–1 Hatton (30), 3–1 Hunt (70), 3–2 Bromley (74), 4–2 Hatton (79), 5–2 Wagstaffe (87).

Charlton Athletic 1 Wolves 3, Second Division, 11 February 1967.
Charlton Athletic: Wright, Bonds, Kinsey, Reeves, King, Appleton, Gregory, Tees, Green, Campbell, Glover.
Wolves: Davies, Taylor, Thomson, Bailey, Woodfield, Holsgrove, Wharton, Hunt, Hatton, Knowles, Wagstaffe.
Attendance: 17,865. Referee: L.J. Hamer (Bolton).
Scoring: 1–0 Tees (17), 1–1 Hatton (27), 1–2 Woodfield (61), 1–3 Knowles (78).

Wolves 1 Everton 1, FA Cup fourth round, 18 February 1967.
Wolves: Davies, Taylor, Thomson, Bailey, Woodfield, Holsgrove, Wharton, Hunt, Hatton, Knowles (McIlmoyle 60), Wagstaffe.
Everton: West, Wright, Wilson, Hurst, Labone, Harvey, Young, Ball, Gabriel, Husband, Morrissey.
Attendance: 53,439. Referee: G. McCabe (Sheffield).
Scoring: 1–0 Wharton (29), 1–1 Ball, penalty (78).

Everton 3 Wolves 1, FA Cup fourth-round replay, 21 February 1967.
Everton: West, Wright, Wilson, Hurst, Labone, Harvey, Young, Ball, Temple, Husband, Morrissey.
Wolves: Davies, Taylor, Thomson, Bailey, Woodfield, Holsgrove, Wharton, Hunt, Hatton, Knowles, Wagstaffe
Attendance: 60,020. Referee: L. Callaghan (Merthyr).
Scoring: 1–0 Husband (11), 2–0 Temple (35), 2–1 Wharton (41), 3–1 Husband (80).

Portsmouth 2 Wolves 3, Second Division, 25 February 1967.
Portsmouth: Milkins, Pack, Tindall, Gordon, Radcliffe, Harris, Portwood, Hiron, Pointer, Kellard, Jennings.
Wolves: Parkes, Taylor, Thomson, Bailey, Woodfield, Holsgrove, Wharton, Hunt, Burnside, Knowles, Wagstaffe.
Attendance: 23,144. Referee: R. Johnson (Lowestoft).
Scoring: 1–0 Portwood (15), 2–0 Portwood (27), 2–1 Bailey (71), 2–2 Knowles (79), 2–3 Hunt (83).

Wolves 1 Northampton Town 0, Second Division, 4 March 1967.
Wolves: Parkes, Taylor, Thomson, Bailey, Woodfield, Holsgrove, Wharton (Burnside 84), Hunt, Hatton, Knowles, Wagstaffe.
Northampton Town: Harvey, Foley, Everitt, Mackin, Branston, Kurila, Walden, Brown, Large, Moore, Lines.
Attendance: 25,672. Referee: J. Finney (Hereford).
Scoring: 1–0 Wagstaffe (71).

Plymouth Argyle 0 Wolves 1, Second Division, 18 March 1967.
Plymouth Argyle: Dunne, Sillett, Everitt, Piper, Nelson, Hore, Etheridge, Banks. Buckle, Bloomfield, Mitten.
Wolves: Parkes, Taylor, Thomson, Bailey (Hawkins 89), Woodfield, Holsgrove, Wharton, Hunt, Dougan, Knowles, Wagstaffe.
Attendance: 18,389. Referee: D.N.Smith (Stonehouse).
Scoring: 0–1 Knowles (55).

Wolves 4 Hull City 0, Second Division, 25 March 1967.
Wolves: Parkes, Taylor, Thomson, Bailey, Woodfield, Holsgrove, Wharton, Hunt (Burnside 59), Dougan, Knowles, Wagstaffe.
Hull City: McKechnie, Davidson, D. Butler, Greenwood, Milner, Simpkin, Henderson, Wagstaff, Chilton, Jarvis, Young.
Attendance: 30,991. Referee: D. Laing (Preston).
Scoring: 1–0 Dougan (37), 2–0 Dougan (60), 3–0 Dougan (73), 4–0 Knowles (84).

Huddersfield Town 0 Wolves 1, Second Division, 27 March 1967.
Huddersfield Town: Oldfield, Parkin, Cattlin, Nicholson, Coddington, Meagan, Hellawell, Clark, Harper, Dobson, Hill.
Wolves: Parkes, Taylor, Thomson, Bailey, Woodfield, Holsgrove, Wharton (Hawkins 60), Burnside, Dougan, Knowles, Wagstaffe.
Attendance: 28,829. Referee: K. Howley (Billingham).
Scoring: 0–1 Wharton (7).

Wolves 1 Huddersfield Town 0, Second Division, 28 March 1967.
Wolves: Parkes, Taylor, Thomson, Bailey, Woodfield, Holsgrove, Farrington, Burnside, Dougan, Knowles, Wagstaffe.
Huddersfield Town: Oldfield, Parkin, Cattlin, Nicholson, Ellam, Meagan, Hellawell, Harper, Leighton, Smith, Hill.
Attendance: 40,929. Referee: R.F. Pritchard (Salisbury).
Scoring: 1–0 Knowles (44).

Millwall 1 Wolves 1, Second Division, 1 April 1967.
Millwall: Leslie, Gilchrist, Cripps, James, Snowden, Plume, Armstrong, Hunt, Neil, Julians, Dunphy.
Wolves: Parkes, Taylor, Thomson, Bailey, Woodfield, Holsgrove, Farrington, Knowles (L. Wilson 75), Dougan, Burnside, Wagstaffe.
Attendance: 23,908. Referee: W.J. Gow (Swansea).
Scoring: 1–0 Julians (57), 1–1 Dougan (89).

Preston North End 1 Wolves 2, Second Division, 15 April 1967.
Preston North End: Kelly, Ross, Smith, Cranston, Singleton, McNab, Hannigan, Lyall, Forrest, Spavin, Godfrey.
Wolves: Parkes, Taylor, Thomson, Bailey, Woodfield (Wharton 84), Holsgrove, Knowles, Hunt, Dougan, Burnside, Wagstaffe.
Attendance: 18,790. Referee: V.J. Batty (Cheshire).
Scoring: 0–1 Hunt (2), 0–2 Hunt (42), 1–2 Hannigan (56).

Wolves 4 Bury 1, Second Division, 22 April 1967.
Wolves: Parkes, Taylor (Knowles 60), Thomson, Bailey, Hawkins, Holsgrove, Wharton, Hunt, Dougan, Burnside, Wagstaffe.
Bury: Ramsbottom, Bain, Tinney, Kerr, Turner, Lindsay, Farrell, Jones, Dawson, Collins, Aimson.
Attendance: 30,893. Referee: J.E. Thacker (Scarborough).
Scoring: 1–0 Wharton, penalty (12), 2–0 Dougan (18), 2–1 Jones (39), 3–1 Burnside (54), 4–1 Dougan (67).

Coventry City 3 Wolves 1, Second Division, 29 April 1967.
Coventry City: Glazier, Kearns, Bruck, Lewis, Curtis, Clements, Key, Machin, Tudor, Gibson, Rees.
Wolves: Parkes, Bailey, Thomson, Hunt, Hawkins, Holsgrove, Wharton, Knowles, Dougan, Burnside, Wagstaffe.
Attendance: 51,445. Referee: N. Callander.
Scoring: 0–1 Knowles (42), 1–1 Machin (60), 2–1 Gibson (64), 3–1 Rees (85).

Crystal Palace 4 Wolves 1, Second Division, 13 May 1967.
Crystal Palace: Parsons, Sewell, Presland, Payne, Stephenson, Bannister, Light, Byrne, Dyson, Woodruff, Jackson.
Wolves: Parkes, Taylor, Thomson, Hawkins, Woodfield, Holsgrove, Wharton (Knowles HT), Hunt, Dougan, Burnside, Wagstaffe.
Attendance: 26,930. Referee: E.D. Wallace (Swindon).
Scoring: 1–0 Light (3), 2–0 Woodruff (28), 3–0 Bannister (64), 3–1 Hunt (69), 4–1 Dyson (84).

1967–68

Appearances 37 + 1 sub (35 + 1 Lge, 1 FAC, 1 LC) Goals 12 (12 Lge)

West Bromwich Albion 4 Wolves 1, First Division, 30 August 1967.
West Bromwich Albion: Osborne, Fairfax, Williams, Fraser, Colquhoun (Kaye 81), Talbut, Stephens, Brown, Astle, Hope, Clark.
Wolves: Parkes, Taylor, L. Wilson, Bailey, Woodfield, Holsgrove, Wharton Hunt (Knowles HT), Dougan, Burnside, Wagstaffe.
Attendance: 38,454. Referee: I.P. Jones (Treharris).
Scoring: 1–0 Astle (11), 1–1 Bailey (17), 2–1 Clark (37), 3–1 Stephens (73), 4–1 Kaye (86).

Tottenham Hotspur 2 Wolves 1 First Division, 6 September 1967.
Tottenham: Jennings, Kinnear, Knowles, Mullery, England, Beal, Robertson, Greaves, Gilzean, Venables, Saul.
Wolves: Davies, Taylor, Thomson, Bailey, Woodfield, Holsgrove, Wharton (L. Wilson 67), Hunt, Dougan, Burnside, Knowles.
Attendance: 44,408. Referee: P. Walters (Somerset).
Scoring: 1–0 Greaves (7), 1–1 Hunt (31), 2–1 Robertson (40).

Wolves 1 Leicester City 3, First Division, 9 September 1967.
Wolves: Davies, Taylor, Thomson, Bailey, Woodfield, Holsgrove, Wagstaffe, Knowles, Dougan, Burnside, Buckley.
Leicester City: Williamson, Rodrigues, Norman, Roberts, Woollett, Cross, Sinclair, Nish, Sjoberg, Gibson, Stringfellow.
Attendance: 31,278. Referee: C. Thomas (Treorchy).
Scoring: 0–1 Nish (16), 0–2 Sinclair (20), 1–2 Knowles (57), 1–3 Stringfellow (81).

Huddersfield Town 1 Wolves 0, Football League Cup second round,
12 September 1967.
Huddersfield Town: Oldfield, Parkin, Cattlin, Nicholson, Ellam, Cherry, Hellawell, Clark, Harper, Dobson, Hill.
Wolves: Parkes, Taylor, L. Wilson, Bailey, Woodfield, Holsgrove, Farrington, Knowles, Dougan, Burnside, Wagstaffe.
Attendance: 11,850. Referee: R. Tinkler (Boston).
Scoring: 1–0 Dobson (13).

West Ham United 1 Wolves 2, First Division, 16 September 1967.
West Ham United: Standen, Charles, Kitchener, Peters, Cushley, Moore, Redknapp, Boyce, Brooking, Hurst, Sissons.
Wolves: Parkes, Taylor, Thomson, Bailey, Woodfield, Holsgrove, Wharton, Evans, Dougan, Knowles, Wagstaffe.
Attendance: 30,780. Referee: R. Johnson (Lowestoft).
Scoring: 0–1 Dougan (35), 1–1 Hurst (36), 1–2 Dougan (87).

Wolves 3 Burnley 2, First Division, 23 September 1967.
Wolves: Parkes, Taylor, Thomson, Bailey, Woodfield, Holsgrove, Wharton, Evans, Dougan, (L. Wilson 85), Knowles, Wagstaffe.
Burnley: Thomson, Smith, Latcham, O'Neil, Ternent, Bellamy, Morgan, Casper, Dobson, Harris, Coates (Buxton 66).
Attendance: 28,151. Referee: C.H. Nicholls (Plymouth).
Scoring: 1–0 Knowles (17), 1–1 Harris, penalty (34), 2–1 Knowles (53), 2–2 Harris, penalty (85), 3–2 Evans (88).

Sheffield Wednesday 2 Wolves 2, First Division, 30 September 1967.
Sheffield Wednesday: P. Springett, Smith, Megson, Mobley, Ellis, Young, Usher, Fantham (Quinn 53), Ritchie, McCalliog, Eustace.
Wolves: Parkes, Taylor, Thomson, Bailey, Woodfield, Holsgrove, Wharton, Knowles, Dougan, Evans, Wagstaffe.
Attendance: 35,177. Referee: L.J. Hamer (Bolton).
Scoring: 0–1 Knowles (5), 1–1 Mobley (18), 2–1 Ritchie (64), 2–2 Evans (90).

Wolves 2 Newcastle United 2, First Division, 7 October 1967.
Wolves: Parkes, Taylor, Thomson, Bailey, Woodfield, Holsgrove, Wharton, Knowles, Dougan (Hawkins 77), Evans, Wagstaffe.
Newcastle United: Marshall, Burton, Guthrie, Elliott, McNamee, Moncur, B. Robson, Bennett, Davies, Iley, T. Robson.
Attendance: 32,386. Referee: S.J. Kaylor (Preston).
Scoring: 0–1 T.Robson (7), 1–1 Holsgrove (17), 2–1 Wharton (26), 2–2 B Robson (73).

Manchester City 2 Wolves 0, First Division, 14 October 1967.
Manchester City: Mulhearn, Book, Pardoe, Doyle, Heslop, Oakes, Lee, Bell, Summerbee, Young, Coleman.
Wolves: Parkes, Taylor, Thomson, Bailey, Woodfield, Holsgrove, Wharton, Knowles, Dougan, Evans, Wagstaffe.
Attendance: 36,276. Referee: P. Partridge (Middlesbrough).
Scoring: 1–0 Doyle (10), 2–0 Young (22).

Wolves 3 Arsenal 2, First Division, 23 October 1967.
Wolves: Williams, Taylor, Thomson, Bailey, Woodfield, Holsgrove, Wharton, Knowles, Dougan, Evans, Wagstaffe.
Arsenal: Furnell, Storey, McNab, McLintock, Neill, Ure, Radford, Addison, Graham, Sammels, Armstrong.
Attendance: 36,664. Referee: H. Richards (Oldham).
Scoring: 1–0 Dougan (4), 1–1 Graham (36), 2–1 Evans (60), 3–1 Dougan (70), 3–2 Armstrong (77).

Sheffield United 1 Wolves 1, First Division, 28 October 1967.
Sheffield United: Hodgkinson, Badger, G.Shaw, Munks, Mallender, Barlow, Woodward, Carlin, Hill, Birchenall, Reece.
Wolves: Williams, Taylor, Thomson, Bailey, Woodfield, Holsgrove, Wharton, Knowles, Dougan, Evans, Wagstaffe.
Attendance: 19,207. Referee: V.J. Batty (Cheshire).
Scoring: 1–0 Woodward (46), 1–1 Dougan (55).

Wolves 2 Coventry City 0, First Division, 4 November 1967.
Wolves: Williams, Taylor, Thomson, Bailey, Woodfield, Holsgrove, Farrington, Knowles, Dougan, Evans, Wagstaffe (Hawkins HT).
Coventry City: Glazier, Coop, Kearns, Hill, Clements, Morrissey, Key, Carr, Tudor, Machin, Rees.
Attendance: 38,659. Referee: A.E. Dimond (Harlow).
Scoring: 1–0 Knowles (36), 2–0 Knowles (42).

Nottingham Forest 3 Wolves 1, First Division, 11 November 1967.
Nottingham Forest: Grummitt, Hindley, Winfield, Hennessey, McKinlay, Newton, Taylor, Barnwell, Baker, Wignall, Chapman.
Wolves: Williams, Taylor, Thomson, Bailey, Woodfield, Holsgrove, Farrington, Knowles, Dougan, Evans, Hawkins (Buckley 83).
Attendance: 36,522. Referee: M. Sinclair (Guildford).
Scoring: 1–0 Newton (15), 1–1 Thomson (38), 2–1 Wignall (70), 3–1 Barnwell (89).

Wolves 3 Stoke City 4, First Division, 18 November 1967.
Wolves: Williams, Taylor, Thomson, Bailey, Woodfield, Holsgrove, Farrington, Knowles, Dougan, Evans, Buckley.
Stoke City: Banks, Elder, Bentley, Skeels, Bloor, Allen, Mahoney, Palmer, Dobing, Eastham, Burrows.
Attendance: 34,544. Referee: K. Dagnall (Bolton).
Scoring: 0–1 Mahoney (5), 0–2 Palmer (10), 0–3 Burrows (33), 1–3 Holsgrove (38), 2–3 Knowles, penalty (39), 3–3 Buckley (70), 3–4 Bloor (89).

Wolves 2 Southampton 0, First Division, 2 December 1967.
Wolves: Williams, L. Wilson, Thomson, Bailey, Woodfield, Holsgrove, Farrington, Evans, Dougan, Burnside, Knowles.
Southampton: Forsyth, Jones, Hollywood, Gabriel, Webb, Walker, Paine, Chivers, Davies, Melia, Channon.
Attendance: 29,488. Referee: L. Callaghan (Merthyr).
Scoring: 1–0 Dougan (84), 2–0 Knowles (88).

Wolves 3 Fulham 2, First Division, 16 December 1967.
Wolves: Williams, L. Wilson, Thomson, Bailey, Woodfield, Holsgrove, Farrington, Knowles, Dougan, Burnside, Wagstaffe.
Fulham: Macedo, Conway, Dempsey, Brown, Callaghan, Pearson, Haynes, Moss, Earle, Gilroy, Barrett.
Attendance: 25,950. Referee: N. Burtenshaw (Great Yarmouth).
Scoring: 0–1 Gilroy (27), 1–1 Knowles (36), 2–1 Woodfield (44), 2–2 Moss (60), 3–2 Knowles (87).

Leeds United 2 Wolves 1, First Division, 23 December 1967.
Leeds United: Sprake, Reaney, Cooper, Bremner, Charlton, Hunter, Greenhoff, Lorimer (Madeley 64), Jones, Gray Giles.
Wolves: Williams, L. Wilson, Thomson, Bailey, Hawkins, Holsgrove, Evans, Knowles, Dougan (Farrington HT), Burnside, Buckley.
Attendance: 28,376. Referee: H. Richards (Oldham).
Scoring: 0–1 Dougan (42), 1–1 Jones (86), 2–1 Charlton (89).

Manchester United 4 Wolves 0, First Division, 26 December 1967.
Manchester United: Stepney, A. Dunne, Burns, Crerand, Foulkes, Sadler, Best, Kidd, Charlton, Law, Aston.
Wolves: Williams, Taylor, Thomson, Bailey, Hawkins, Holsgrove, L. Wilson, Evans, Knowles, Burnside, Wagstaffe.
Attendance: 63,450. Referee: K. Styles (Barnsley).
Scoring: 1–0 Best (11), 2–0 Kidd (33), 3–0 Best (42), 4–0 Charlton (50).

Wolves 2 Manchester United 3, First Division, 30 December 1967.
Wolves: Williams, L. Wilson, Thomson, Bailey, Hawkins (Taylor 50), Holsgrove, Evans, Knowles, Buckley, Ross, Wagstaffe.
Manchester United: Stepney, A. Dunne, Burns, Crerand, Foulkes, Sadler, Best, Kidd, Charlton, Law, Aston.
Attendance: 53,940. Referee: K.E. Watkins (Maidstone).
Scoring: 1–0 Buckley (1), 1–1 Charlton (46), 1–2 Aston (49), 1–3 Kidd (62), 2–3 Bailey (67).

Wolves 1 Everton 3, First Division, 6 January 1968.
Wolves: Williams, L. Wilson, Thomson, Bailey (Ross 75), Woodfield, Holsgrove, Munro, Knowles, Dougan, Evans, Wagstaffe.
Everton: West, Wright (Brown 77), Wilson, Kenyon, Labone, Harvey, Hunt, Ball, Royle, Hurst, Trebilcock.
Attendance: 37,802. Referee: R.V. Spittle (Great Yarmouth).
Scoring: 0–1 Royle (34), 0–2 Trebilcock (36), 1–2 Knowles (68), 1–3 Royle (89).

Leicester City 3 Wolves 1, First Division, 13 January, 1968.
Leicester City: Shilton, Rodrigues, Bell, Roberts, Sjoberg, Nish, Gibson, Large, Stringfellow, Cross, Glover.
Wolves: Parkes, Taylor, L. Wilson, Munro, Woodfield, Holsgrove, Kenning, Evans, Dougan, Burnside, Knowles
Attendance: 21,463. Referee: M. Fussey (Retford).
Scoring: 0–1 Kenning (26), 1–1 Glover (34), 2–1 Gibson (51), 3–1 Large (60).

Wolves 1 West Ham United 2, First Division, 20 January 1968.
Wolves: Williams, Taylor, L. Wilson, Bailey, Woodfield, Holsgrove, Kenning, Knowles, Dougan, Munro, Farrington.
West Ham United: Ferguson, Bonds, Lampard, Peters, Cushley, Moore, Dear, Boyce, Brooking, Hurst, Sissons.
Attendance: 32,273. Referee: G. McCabe (Sheffield).
Scoring: 0–1 Dear (47), 0–2 Hurst (52), 1–2 Dougan (87).

Rotherham United 1 Wolves 0, FA Cup third round, 27 January 1968.
Rotherham United: Hill, Watson, Hague, Quinn, Swift, Tyler, Wilson, Chappell, Storrie, Shepherd, Bentley.
Wolves: Parkes, Taylor, L. Wilson, Bailey, Woodfield, Holsgrove, Kenning, Knowles, Dougan, Burnside, Wagstaffe.
Attendance: 14,841. Referee: G.W. Hill (Leicester).
Scoring: 1–0 Storrie (59).

Burnley 1 Wolves 1, First Division, 3 February 1968.
Burnley: Thompson, Ternent, Latcham, Todd, Waldron, Blant, Morgan, Lochhead, Casper, Bellamy, Coates.
Wolves: Parkes, Taylor, L. Wilson, Munro, Woodfield, Holsgrove, Kenning, Knowles, Dougan, Bailey, Wagstaffe.
Attendance: 12,620. Referee: V. James (York).
Scoring: 0–1 Dougan (47), 1–1 Casper (73).

Newcastle United 2 Wolves 0, First Division, 24 February 1968.
Newcastle United: Marshall, Burton, Clark, Elliott, McNamee, Moncur, Sinclair, Scott, Davies, B. Robson, T. Robson.
Wolves: Parkes, Parkin, Thomson, Munro, Woodfield, Holsgrove, Kenning, Knowles, Dougan, Bailey, L. Wilson.
Attendance: 35,420. Referee: K. Styles (Barnsley).
Scoring: 1–0 Elliott (50), 2–0 T.Robson (86).

Wolves 1 Liverpool 1, First Division, 2 March 1968.
Wolves: Parkes, Parkin, Thomson, Bailey, Woodfield, Holsgrove, Kenning, Evans (Farrington 72), Dougan, Knowles, Wagstaffe.
Liverpool: Lawrence, Lawler, Byrne, Smith, Yeats, Hughes, Callaghan, Hunt, Hateley, St. John, Thompson.
Attendance: 33,207. Referee: R.A. Paine (Hounslow).
Scoring: 1–0 Dougan (42), 1–1 Hunt (79).

Arsenal 0 Wolves 2, First Division, 16 March 1968.
Arsenal: Wilson, Storey, McNab, McLintock, Simpson (Davidson 31), Neill, Radford, Gould, Graham, Sammels, Armstrong.
Wolves: Parkes, Parkin, Thomson, Bailey, Woodfield, Holsgrove, Kenning, Wignall, Dougan, Knowles, Wagstaffe.
Attendance: 25,983. Referee: J.R. Osborn (Ipswich).
Scoring: 0–1 Holsgrove (31), 0–2 Wignall (89).

Wolves 2 Sheffield Wednesday 3, First Division, 19 March 1968.
Wolves: Parkes, Parkin, Thomson, Bailey, Woodfield, Holsgrove, Kenning, Wignall, Dougan, Knowles, Wagstaffe.
Sheffield Wednesday: P. Springett, Smith, Megson, Young, Mobley, Eustace, Usher, McCalliog, Ritchie, Whitham, Woodhall.
Attendance: 32,869. Referee: W. Gow (Swansea).
Scoring: 0–1 Whitham (2), 1–1 Wignall (37), 1–2 Woodhall (38), 2–2 Holsgrove (50), 2–3 Woodhall (85).

Wolves 1 Sheffield United 3, First Division, 23 March 1968.
Wolves: Parkes, Parkin, L. Wilson, Bailey, Woodfield, Holsgrove, Farrington, Wignall (Kenning HT), Evans, Knowles, Wagstaffe.
Sheffield United: Hodgkinson, Badger, G. Shaw, Munks, Mallender, Barlow, Woodward, Carlin, Addison, Currie, Reece.
Attendance: 25,106. Referee: R. Prichard (Salisbury).
Scoring: 0–1 Barlow (30), 0–2 Addison (37), 0–3 Reece (67), 1–3 Farrington (69).

Coventry City 1 Wolves 0, First Division, 30 March 1968.
Coventry City: Glazier, Bruck, Cattlin, Lewis, Setters, Clements, Hannigan (Coop 62), Hunt, Martin, Tudor, Carr.
Wolves: Parkes, Parkin, Thomson, Munro, Woodfield, Holsgrove, Kenning, Knowles, Wignall, Bailey, Wagstaffe.
Attendance: 36,084. Referee: A.E. Dimond (Harlow).
Scoring: 1–0 Martin, penalty (82).

Wolves 6 Nottingham Forest 1, First Division, 6 April 1968.
Wolves: Parkes, Parkin, Thomson, Bailey, Woodfield, Holsgrove, Kenning, Wignall (Munro 72), Dougan, Knowles, Wagstaffe.
Nottingham Forest: Harby, Hindley, Winfield, Hennessey, McKinlay, Newton, Lyons, Barnwell, Chapman, Baxter, Storey-Moore.
Attendance: 28,198. Referee: L. J. Hamer (Bolton).
Scoring: 1–0 Dougan (18), 2–0 Wignall (24), 3–0 Wignall (30), 4–0 Dougan (37), 4–1 Lyons (67), 5–1 Dougan (68), 6–1 Kenning (89).

Stoke City 0 Wolves 2, First Division, 13 April 1968.
Stoke City: Banks, Skeels, Allen, Moore, Bloor, Stevenson, Mahoney (Bentley HT), Barnard, Dobing, Eastham, Burrows.
Wolves: Parkes, Parkin, Thomson, Bailey, Woodfield, Holsgrove, Kenning, Wignall, Dougan, Knowles, Wagstaffe.
Attendance: 26,290. Referee: R. Harper (Sheffield).
Scoring 0–1 Knowles (37), 0–2 Wignall (50).

Sunderland 2 Wolves 0, First Division, 15 April 1968.
Sunderland: Forster, Harvey, Ashurst, Hurley, Kinnell, Todd, Harris, Herd, Brand, Suggett, Mulhall.
Wolves: Parkes, Parkin, Thomson, Bailey, Woodfield, Holsgrove, Kenning, Wignall, Dougan, Knowles, Wagstaffe.
Attendance: 34,026. Referee: D. Payne (Sheffield).
Scoring: 1–0 Todd (27), 2–0 Herd (80).

Wolves 0 Manchester City 0, First Division, 20 April 1968.
Wolves: Parkes, Parkin, Thomson, Bailey, Woodfield, Holsgrove, Kenning, Wignall, Dougan, Knowles, Wagstaffe.
Manchester City: Mulhearn, Book, Pardoe, Doyle, Heslop, Oakes, Lee, Bell, Summerbee, Young, Connor.
Attendance: 39,622. Referee: H. Davies (Cardiff).

Southampton 1 Wolves 1, First Division, 27 April 1968.
Southampton: Martin, Kirkup, Hollywood, Fisher, McGrath, Gabriel, Paine, Channon, Davies, Melia, Sydenham (Saul 85).
Wolves: Parkes, Parkin, Thomson, Bailey, Woodfield, Holsgrove, Kenning, Wignall, Dougan, Knowles, Wagstaffe.
Attendance: 23,436. Referee: D.H. Counsell (Blagdon).
Scoring: 0–1 Wagstaffe (11), 1–1 Davies (44).

Chelsea 1 Wolves 0, First Division, 29 April 1968.
Chelsea: Bonetti, Hinton, McCreadie, Hollins, Webb, Boyle, Cooke, Baldwin, Osgood, Birchenall (Thomson 68), Houseman.
Wolves: Parkes, Parkin, Thomson, Bailey, Woodfield, Holsgrove, Kenning, McAlle (Evans 77), Dougan, Knowles, Wagstaffe.
Attendance: 28,447. Referee: P. Bye (Bedford).
Scoring: 1–0 Osgood (89).

Wolves 3 Chelsea 0, First Division, 4 May 1968.
Wolves: Parkes, Parkin, Thomson, Bailey, Woodfield, Holsgrove, Kenning (McAlle 77), Wignall, Dougan, Knowles, Wagstaffe.
Chelsea: Bonetti, Hinton, McCreadie, Hollins, Webb, Boyle, Cooke, Baldwin (Thomson 35), Osgood, Birchenall, Houseman.
Attendance: 35,600. Referee: F. Cowen (Manchester).
Scoring: 1–0 Wignall (13), 2–0 Wignall (27), 3–0 Wignall (48).

Wolves 2 Tottenham Hotspur 1, First Division, 11 May 1968.
Wolves: Parkes, Parkin, Thomson, Bailey, Woodfield, Holsgrove, Kenning, Wignall, Dougan, Knowles, Wagstaffe.
Tottenham Hotspur: Jennings, Beal, Knowles, Mullery, England, Mackay (Jones 73), Robertson, Greaves, Chivers, Venables, Gilzean.
Attendance: 40,929. Referee: K. Dagnall (Bolton).
Scoring: 1–0 Wignall (55), 2–0 Parkin (88), 2–1 Greaves (89).

1968–69
Appearances 44 (39 Lge, 2 FAC, 3 LC) Goals 9 (9 Lge)

Ipswich Town 1 Wolves 0, First Division, 10 August 1968.
Ipswich Town: Hancock, Carroll, Houghton, Morris, Baxter, Jefferson, Hegan, Viljoen, Crawford, O'Rourke, Brogan,
Wolves: Parkes, Parkin, Thomson, Bailey, Woodfield (McAlle 65), Holsgrove, Kenning, Wignall, Dougan, Knowles, Wagstaffe.
Attendance: 25,940. Referee: B. Homewood (Sunbury-on-Thames).
Scoring: 1–0 O'Rourke (59).

Manchester City 3 Wolves 2, First Division, 14 August 1968.
Manchester City: Mulhearn, Kennedy, Pardoe, Doyle, Heslop, Oakes, Lee, Bell, Summerbee, Owen, Young.
Wolves: Parkes, Parkin, Thomson, Bailey, Woodfield, Holsgrove, Kenning, Wignall, Dougan (McAlle 85), Knowles, Wagstaffe.
Attendance: 35,853. Referee: V. James (York).
Scoring: 1–0 Lee (31), 2–0 Summerbee (44), 3–0 Summerbee (51), 3–1 Wignall (56), 3–2 Wignall (73).

Wolves 3 Queens Park Rangers 1, First Division, 17 August 1968.
Wolves: Parkes, Parkin, Thomson, Bailey, Woodfield, Holsgrove, Kenning, Wignall, Dougan, Knowles, Wagstaffe.
Queens Park Rangers: Kelly, Watson, Harris, Keen, Keetch, Hazell, I. Morgan, Sibley, Leach, Wilks, R. Morgan.
Attendance: 30,858. Referee: D. Counsell (Blagdon).
Scoring: 1–0 Wignall (7), 1–1 I.Morgan (25), 2–1 Bailey (52), 3–1 Dougan (84).

Wolves 0 Arsenal 0, First Division, 21 August 1968.
Wolves: Parkes, Parkin, Thomson, Bailey, Woodfield, Holsgrove, Kenning, Wignall, Dougan, Knowles, Wagstaffe.
Arsenal: Wilson, Storey, McNab, McLintock, Neill, Simpson, Radford, Sammels, Gould, Court, Jenkins.
Attendance: 36,006. Referee: R. Tinkler (Boston).

Southampton 2 Wolves 1, First Division, 24 August, 1968.
Southampton: Martin, Kirkup, Hollywood, Kemp, McGrath, Gabriel, Paine, Channon, Saul, Melia, Judd.
Wolves: Parkes, Parkin, L. Wilson, Bailey, Woodfield, Holsgrove, Kenning, Wignall, Dougan, Knowles, Wagstaffe.
Attendance: 19,746. Referee: D. Smith (Stonehouse).
Scoring: 1–0 Kemp (24), 2–0 Paine (57), 2–1 Wagstaffe (58).

Wolves 1 Leicester City 0, First Division, 28 August 1968.
Wolves: Parkes, Parkin, L. Wilson, Bailey, Woodfield, Holsgrove, Farrington, Wignall, Dougan (Evans 70), Knowles, Kenning.
Leicester City: Shilton, Woollett, Bell, Mackay, Sjoberg, Manley, Tewley, Clarke, Roberts, Gibson, Glover.
Attendance: 33,472. Referee: G. Jones (Bowerham).
Scoring: 1–0 Dougan (45).

Wolves 1 Stoke City 1, First Division, 31 August 1968.
Wolves: Parkes, Parkin, L. Wilson, Bailey, Woodfield, Holsgrove, Farrington, Evans, Wignall, Knowles, Kenning (D. Clarke 85).
Stoke City: Farmer, Marsh, Elder, Allen, Bloor, Stevenson, Bridgwood (Skeels 76), Mahoney, Conroy, Dobing, Eastham.
Attendance: 31,034. Referee: P. Harper (Sheffield).
Scoring: 1–0 Bailey (61), 1–1 Elder (81).

Wolves 1 Southend United 0, Football League Cup second round,
4 September 1968.
Wolves: Parkes, Parkin, L. Wilson, Bailey, Woodfield, Holsgrove, Farrington Wignall, Dougan, Knowles, Kenning.
Southend United: Leslie, Bentley, Birks, Beesley, McMillan, Kurila, Clayton, Best, Smillie, Chisnall, McKinven.
Attendance: 18,667. Referee: I. Jones (Treharris).
Scoring: 1–0 Farrington (89).

Wolves 1 Sunderland 1, First Division, 14 September 1968.
Wolves: Boswell, Parkin, L. Wilson, Bailey, Woodfield, Holsgrove, Farrington, Knowles, Wignall, Munro, Wagstaffe.
Sunderland: Montgomery, Palmer, Harvey, Hurley, Todd, Porterfield, Herd, Harris, Hughes, Suggett, Mulhall. (Ashurst HT).
Attendance: 27,212. Referee: R. Kirkpatrick (Leicester).
Scoring: 0–1 Hughes (42), 1–1 Wignall (84).

West Bromwich Albion 0 Wolves 0, First Division, 21 September 1968.
West Bromwich Albion: Osborne, Fraser, Williams, Brown, Talbut, Kaye, Rees, Lovett, Krzywicki (Merrick 35), Hartford, Clark.
Wolves: Boswell, Parkin, L. Wilson, Bailey, Woodfield, Holsgrove, Kenning, Knowles Wignall, Munro, Wagstaffe (Ross 9).
Attendance: 35,790. Referee: B. Daniel (Rainham).

Wolves 5 Millwall 1, Football League Cup third round, 25 September 1968.
Wolves: Williams, Parkin, L. Wilson, Bailey, Woodfield, Holsgrove, Farrington, Knowles, Dougan, Munro, Kenning.
Millwall: King, Gilchrist, Cripps, Jones, Kitchener, Burnett, Possee, Weller, Conlon, Jacks, Dunphy.
Attendance: 17,046. Referee: K. Styles (Barnsley).
Scoring: 1–0 Dougan (1), 1–1 Dunphy (55), 2–1 Munro (58), 3–1 Kenning, penalty (66), 4–1 Farrington (83), 5–1 Farrington (84).

Wolves 0 Liverpool 6, First Division, 28 September 1968.
Wolves: Boswell, Parkin, L. Wilson, Bailey, Woodfield, Holsgrove, Farrington (Thomson 57), Knowles, Dougan, Munro, Kenning.
Liverpool: Lawrence, Lawler, Wall, Smith, Yeats, Hughes, Callaghan, Hunt, Evans, St. John, Thompson.
Attendance: 39,203. Referee: J.G. Lewis (Swansea).
Scoring: 0–1 Hunt (15), 0–2 Thompson (26), 0–3 Evans (29), 0–4 Evans (62), 0–5 Hunt (73), 0–6 Thompson (79).

Coventry City 0 Wolves 1, First Division, 5 October 1968.
Coventry City: Glazier, Coop, Bruck, Machin, Curtis, Hill, Hunt, Tudor, Hateley, Gibson, Clements.
Wolves Boswell, Parkin, Thomson, Bailey, Woodfield, Holsgrove, L. Wilson, Knowles, Dougan, Wignall, Kenning.
Attendance: 39,271. Referee: A.E. Dimond (Harlow).
Scoring: 0–1 Dougan (59).

Leicester City 2 Wolves 0, First Division, 9 October 1968.
Leicester City: Shilton, Potts, Bell, Nish, Manley, Cross, Glover, Clarke, Fern, Gibson, Stringfellow.
Wolves: Boswell, Parkin, Thomson, Bailey, Woodfield, Holsgrove, L. Wilson, Knowles, Dougan, Wignall, Kenning.
Attendance: 27,048. Referee: M. Sinclair (Guildford).
Scoring: 1–0 Stringfellow (5), 2–0 Fern (14).

Wolves 1 Chelsea 1, First Division, 12 October 1968.
Wolves: Boswell, Parkin, L. Wilson, Bailey, Woodfield, Holsgrove, Farrington, Knowles, Dougan, Wignall, Wagstaffe.
Chelsea: Bonetti, Hinton, McCreadie, Hollins, Webb, Harris, Cooke, Tambling, Baldwin, Birchenall, Houseman.
Attendance: 27,803. Referee: H. Williams (Sheffield).
Scoring: 0–1 Tambling (88), 1–1 Knowles (89).

**Blackpool 2 Wolves 1, Football League Cup fourth round,
16 October 1968.**
Blackpool: Taylor, Armfield, Thompson, Rowe, James, McPhee, Skirton, Green, Marsden, Suddick, Hutchison.
Wolves: Williams, Parkin, L. Wilson, Bailey, Woodfield, Holsgrove, Farrington, Knowles, Dougan, Wignall, Wagstaffe.
Attendance: 16,466. Referee: K. Howley (Billingham).
Scoring: 1–0 Suddick (51), 1–1 Wagstaffe (64), 2–1 Marsden (72).

Sheffield Wednesday 0 Wolves 2, First Division, 19 October 1968.
Sheffield Wednesday: P. Springett, Smith, Megson, Ellis, Mobley, Young, Whitham, McCalliog, Warboys, Ford, Eustace.
Wolves: Boswell, Parkin, Thomson, Bailey, Woodfield, Holsgrove, Farrington Knowles (McAlle), Dougan, L. Wilson, Wagstaffe.
Attendance: 23,928. Referee: P. Baldwin (Middlesbrough).
Scoring: 0–1 Knowles, penalty (18), 0–2 Dougan (44).

Wolves 1 Everton 2, First Division, 26 October 1968.
Wolves: Boswell, Parkin, Thomson, Bailey, Woodfield, Holsgrove, Farrington, Knowles (Kenning 75), Dougan, L. Wilson, Wagstaffe.
Everton: West, Wright, Brown, Kendall, Labone, Harvey, Humphreys, Ball, Royle, Hurst, Morrissey.
Attendance: 34,744. Referee: R. Capey (Madeley Heath, Cheshire).
Scoring: 0–1 Royle (20), 1–1 Knowles (50), 1–2 Ball, penalty (62)

Nottingham Forest 0 Wolves 0, First Division, 2 November 1968.
Nottingham Forest: Marshall, Hindley, Winfield, Hennessey, McKinlay, Newton, Hall, Barnwell, Baker, Chapman, Moore.
Wolves: Parkes, Parkin (McAlle), Thomson, Bailey, Woodfield, Holsgrove, Farrington, Knowles, Dougan, L. Wilson, Wagstaffe.
Attendance: 19,470. Referee: F. Allott (Sheffield).

Wolves 2 West Ham United 0, First Division, 9 November 1968.
Wolves: Parkes, Parkin, Thomson, Bailey, Woodfield, Holsgrove, Farrington, Knowles, Dougan, L. Wilson, Wagstaffe.
West Ham United: Ferguson, Bonds, Charles, Peters, Stephenson, Moore, Redknapp, Boyce, Brooking, Hurst, Hartley.
Attendance: 29,704. Referee: F. Nicholson (Manchester).
Scoring: 1–0 Farrington (40) 2–0 Bailey (14).

Burnley 1 Wolves 1, First Division, 16 November, 1968.
Burnley: Thomson, Smith, Latcham, Dobson, Waldron, Blant, Thomas, Murray, Casper, Coates, Kindon.
Wolves: Parkes, Parkin, Thomson, Wignall, Woodfield, Holsgrove, Kenning (Munro), Knowles, Dougan, L. Wilson, Wagstaffe.
Attendance: 20,848. Referee: V. James (York).
Scoring: 1–0 Casper (20), 1–1 Dougan (42).

Wolves 5 Newcastle United 0, First Division, 23 November 1968.
Wolves: Parkes, Parkin, Thomson, Bailey, Woodfield, Holsgrove, Wignall (Kenning), Knowles, Dougan, L. Wilson, Wagstaffe.
Newcastle United: McFaul, Craig, Clark, Gibb, Burton, Moncur, Scott, B. Robson, Davies, Elliott, Dyson.
Attendance: 25,495. Referee: R.V. Spittle (Great Yarmouth).
Scoring: 1–0 Knowles (11), 2–0 Wignall (43), 3–0 Dougan (48), 4–0 Knowles (52), 5–0 Dougan (77).

Manchester United 2 Wolves 0, First Division, 30 November 1968.
Manchester United: Stepney, Kopel, Dunne, Crerand, Sadler, Stiles, Morgan, Sartori, Charlton, Law, Best.
Wolves: Parkes, Parkin, Thomson, Bailey, Woodfield (Kenning), Holsgrove, Wignall, Knowles, Dougan, L. Wilson, Wagstaffe.
Attendance: 50,165. Referee: N. Graham (Northumberland).
Scoring: 1–0 Best (59), 2–0 Law (84).

Wolves 2 Tottenham Hotspur 0, First Division, 7 December 1968.
Wolves: Parkes, Parkin, Thomson, Bailey, Holsgrove, L. Wilson, Kenning, Knowles, Dougan, Wignall, Wagstaffe.
Tottenham Hotspur: Jennings, Kinnear, Knowles, Mullery, Collins, Beal, Jenkins, Greaves, England, Venables, Gilzean.
Attendance: 30,846. Referee: J. Gow (Swansea).
Scoring: 1–0 Dougan (63), 2–0 Wignall (66).

Chelsea 1 Wolves 1, First Division, 14 December 1968.
Chelsea: Bonetti, Collins, McCreadie, Osgood, Webb, Harris, Birchenall, Tambling, Baldwin, Boyle, Cooke.
Wolves: Boswell, Parkin, Thomson, Bailey, Holsgrove, Taylpr, L. Wilson, Knowles, Dougan, Wignall, Kenning.
Attendance: 26,194. Referee: J. Osborne (Ipswich).
Scoring: 0–1 Kenning, penalty (36), 1–1 Osgood, penalty (89).

Wolves 0 Sheffield Wednesday 3, First Division, 21 December 1968.
Wolves: Boswell, Parkin, Thomson, Bailey, Holsgrove, L. Wilson, Kenning, Knowles, Dougan, Wignall, Wagstaffe.
Sheffield Wednesday: P. Springett, Smith, Megson, Ellis, Mobley, Young, Irvine, McCalliog, Ritchie, Eustace, Ford.
Attendance: 24,724. Referee: V. Batty (Cheshire).
Scoring: 0–1 Ritchie (34), 0–2 Irvine (38), 0–3 Ritchie (47).

Hull City 1 Wolves 3, FA Cup third round, 4 January 1969.
Hull City: McKechnie, Greenwood, Beardsley, Pettit, Wilson, Simkin, Jarvis, Wagstaff, Chilton, Houghton, Butler.
Wolves: Parkes, Parkin, Thomson, Bailey, Holsgrove, L. Wilson, Kenning, Knowles, Dougan, Wignall, Wagstaffe.
Attendance: 27,526. Referee: A. W. Jones (Ormskirk).
Scoring: 1–0 Chilton (14), 1–1 Dougan (21), 1–2 Wignall (31), 1–3 Dougan (85).

Wolves 1 Nottingham Forest 0, First Division, 11 January 1969.
Wolves: Parkes, Parkin, Thomson, Bailey, Holsgrove, L. Wilson, Kenning, Knowles (Munro 74), Dougan, Wignall, Wagstaffe.
Nottingham Forest: Grummitt, Hindley, Winfield, Newton, Hennessey, Baxter, Lyons, Richardson, Hall, Chapman, Moore.
Attendance: 24,659. Referee: A. W. Jones (Ormskirk).
Scoring: 1–0 Knowles (43).

Tottenham Hotspur 2 Wolves 1, FA Cup fourth round, 25 January 1969.
Tottenham Hotspur: Jennings, Beal, Knowles, Mullery, England, Collins, Johnson, Greaves, Gilzean, Venables, Jenkins.
Wolves: Parkes, Parkin, Thomson, Bailey, Woodfield, McAlle, Kenning (Wignall 73), Knowles, Dougan, L. Wilson, Wagstaffe.
Attendance: 48,985. Referee: N. Burtenshaw (Norfolk).
Scoring: 0–1 (Wagstaffe (7), 1–1 Johnson (53), 2–1 Greaves (58).

Everton 4 Wolves 0, First Division, 28 January 1969.
Everton: West, Wright, Wilson, Kendall, Labone, Brown, Husband, Ball, Royle, Hurst, Morrissey.
Wolves: Parkes, Parkin, Thomson, Bailey, Holsgrove, L. Wilson, Farrington, Knowles, Dougan, Munro, Wagstaffe (Kenning 62).
Attendance: 48,057. Referee: R. Harper (Sheffield).
Scoring: 1–0 Royle, penalty (20), 2–0 Morrissey (43), 3–0 Husband (68), 4–0 Royle (82).

Wolves 1 Burnley 1, First Division, 1 February 1969.
Wolves: Parkes, Parkin, Thomson, Bailey, Holsgrove, L. Wilson, Farrington (Munro 63), Knowles, Dougan, Curran, Wagstaffe.
Burnley: H. Thomson, Smith, Latcham, Bellamy, Waldron, Blant, Thomas, Collins, Casper, Coates, J. Thomson.
Attendance: 27,733. Referee: L. Callaghan (Merthyr).
Scoring: 1–0 Knowles (31), 1–1 Collins (38).

Wolves 2 Manchester United 2, First Division, 15 February 1969.
Wolves: Parkes, Parkin, Thomson, Bailey, Woodfield, Taylor, L. Wilson, Knowles, Dougan, Curran, Wagstaffe.
Manchester United: Stepney, Fitzpatrick, Dunne, Crerand, James, Sadler, Morgan, Kidd, Charlton, Sartori (Foulkes 24), Best.
Attendance: 44,023. Referee: B. Homewood (Sunbury-on-Thames).
Scoring: 1–0 Dougan (28), 2–0 Curran (44), 2–1 Charlton (47), 2–2 Best (67).

Tottenham Hotspur 1 Wolves 1, First Division, 22 February 1969.
Tottenham Hotspur: Jennings, Beal, Knowles, Mullery, England, Collins, Pearce (Johnson 74), Greaves, Gilzean, Venables, Morgan.
Wolves: Parkes, Parkin, Thomson, Bailey, Woodfield, Holsgrove, L. Wilson, Knowles, Dougan, Curran, Wagstaffe.
Attendance: 35,912. Referee: T. Dawes (Norwich).
Scoring: 1–0 Morgan (8), 1–1 Curran (22).

Wolves 1 Ipswich Town 1, First Division, 1 March 1969.
Wolves: Parkes, Parkin, Thomson, Bailey, Woodfield, Holsgrove, L. Wilson (Kenning 75), Knowles, Dougan, Curran, Wagstaffe.
Ipswich Town: Best, Mills, Houghton, Viljoen, Baxter, Jefferson, Hegan, Barnard, Crawford, O'Rourke, Woods.
Attendance: 25,600. Referee: F. Cowan (Oldham).
Scoring: 0–1 O'Rourke (10), 1–1 Kenning (88).

Queens Park Rangers 0 Wolves 1, First Division, 8 March 1969.
Queens Park Rangers: Spratley, Watson, Gillard, Hazell, Hunt, Keetch, Morgan, Glover, Clarke, Marsh, Wilks.
Wolves: Parkes, Parkin, Thomson, Bailey, Woodfield, Holsgrove, L. Wilson, Knowles, Dougan, Curran, Kenning.
Attendance: 17,901. Referee: I.P. Jones (Glamorgan).
Scoring: 0–1 Dougan (3).

Wolves 0 Southampton 0, First Division, 15 March 1969.
Wolves: Parkes, Taylor, Parkin, Bailey, Woodfield (Farrington 8), Holsgrove, L. Wilson, Knowles, Dougan, Curran, Wagstaffe.
Southampton: Gurr, Jones, Hollywood, Kemp, McGrath, Gabriel, Paine, Channon, Davies, Walker, Judd.
Attendance: 24,322. Referee: A.E. Dimond (Harlow).

Stoke City 4 Wolves 1, First Division, 22 March 1969.
Stoke City: Banks, Marsh, Elder, Skeels (Stevenson HT), Bloor, Barnard, Herd, Dobing, Conroy, Mahoney, Eastham.
Wolves: Parkes, Taylor, Parkin, Bailey, Galvin, Holsgrove, L. Wilson, Knowles, Dougan, Curran (McAlle 74), D. Clarke.
Attendance: 19,514. Referee: H.G. New (Portsmouth).
Scoring: 0–1 Curran (39), 1–1 Conroy (46), 2–1 Dobing (53), 3–1 Dobing (58), 4–1 Herd (74).

West Ham United 3 Wolves 1, First Division, 24 March 1969.
West Ham United: Ferguson, Charles, Howe, Peters, Stephenson, Moore, Bonds, Boyce, Brooking, Hurst, Sissons.
Wolves: Parkes, Taylor, Parkin, Bailey, Holsgrove, McAlle, L. Wilson, Knowles, Dougan, Seal, Farrington.
Attendance: 25,221. Referee: C.H. Nicholls (Plymouth).
Scoring: 1–0 Peters (31), 2–0 Brooking (55), 2–1 Peters (60), 3–1 Wilson (80).

Wolves 0 Leeds United 0, First Division, 29 March 1969.
Wolves: Parkes, Taylor, Parkin, Bailey, Holsgrove, McAlle, Farrington, Knowles, Dougan, L. Wilson, Munro.
Leeds United: Sprake, Reaney, Cooper, Bremner, Charlton, Hunter, O'Grady, Madeley (Lorimer HT), Jones, Giles, Gray.
Attendance: 27,987. Referee: R.V. Spittle (Great Yarmouth).

Liverpool 1 Wolves 0, First Division, 5 April 1969.
Liverpool: Lawrence, Lawler, Strong, Smith, Yeats, Byrne, Callaghan, Hunt, Evans, St. John, Thompson.
Wolves: Parkes, Taylor, Parkin, Galvin, Holsgrove, McAlle, Farrington (D. Clarke 68), Knowles, Dougan, L. Wilson, Munro.
Attendance: 45,399. Referee: H. Wilson (Sheffield).
Scoring: 1–0 Hunt (20).

Arsenal 3 Wolves 1, First Division, 7 April 1969.
Arsenal: Wilson, Storey, McNab, McLintock, Ure, Graham, Robertson, Sammels, Court, Gould, Armstrong.
Wolves: Parkes, Taylor, Parkin, Galvin (D. Clarke), Holsgrove, McAlle, Farrington, Knowles, Dougan, L. Wilson, Munro.
Attendance: 31,011. Referee: D.W. Smith (Stonehouse, Gloucs).
Scoring: 1–0 Robertson (28), 2–0 Armstrong (44), 2–1 Wilson (59), 3–1 Graham (63).

Wolves 3 Manchester City 1, First Division, 8 April 1969.
Wolves: Parkes, Taylor, Parkin, L. Wilson, Holsgrove, McAlle, Farrington, Knowles, Dougan, Munro, Lutton.
Manchester City: Dowd, Book, Pardoe, Doyle, Booth, Oakes, Summerbee, Bell, Lee, Young, Coleman.
Attendance: 28,533. Referee: R.A. Paine (Hounslow).
Scoring: 0–1 Lee (1), 1–1 Knowles (47), 2–1 Dougan (59), 3–1 Munro (83).

Wolves 0 West Bromwich Albion 1, First Division, 12 April 1969.
Wolves: Parkes, Taylor, Parkin, L. Wilson, Holsgrove, McAlle, Farrington (Hibbitt 70), Knowles, Dougan, Munro, Lutton.
West Bromwich Albion: Osborne, Fraser, Wilson, Brown, Talbut, Kaye, Krzywicki (Clark 25), Lovett, Martin, Hope, Hartford.
Attendance: 37,920. Referee: H. New (Portsmouth).
Scoring: 0–1 Clark (25).

Wolves 1 Coventry City 1, First Division, 15 April 1969.
Wolves: Parkes, Taylor (Munro 37), Parkin, L. Wilson, Holsgrove, McAlle, Lutton, Knowles, Dougan, Curran, Wagstaffe.
Coventry City: Glazier, Coop, Cattlin, Machin, Setters, Bruck, Hannigan, Hunt, Martin, Carr, Blockley.
Attendance: 32,535. Referee: T. Hill (Macclesfield).
Scoring: 0–1 Hunt (30), 1–1 Knowles (70).

1969–70
Appearances 9 (8 Lge, 1 LC) Goals 3 (3 Lge)

Wolves 3 Stoke City 1, First Division, 9 August, 1969.
Wolves: Parkes, Taylor, Parkin, Bailey, Holsgrove, Munro, McCalliog, Knowles, Dougan, Curran, Wagstaffe (L. Wilson 71).
Stoke City: Banks, Skeels, Elder, Bloor, Smith, Allen, Dobing, Greenhoff, Ritchie, Eastham, Burrows (Barnard 67).
Attendance: 32,260. Referee: P. Walters (Bridgwater).
Scoring: 1–0 Dougan (3), 2–0 Knowles (18), 2–1 Burrows (35), 3–1 Dougan (60).

Wolves 2 Southampton 1, First Division, 13 August 1969.
Wolves: Parkes, Taylor (L. Wilson 75), Parkin, Bailey, Holsgrove, Munro, McCalliog, Knowles, Dougan, Curran, Lutton.
Southampton: Gurr, Jones, Hollywood, Fisher, McGrath, Gabriel, Paine, Stokes, Davies, Byrne, Judd.
Attendance: 32,485. Referee: W.J. Gow (Swansea).
Scoring: 0–1 Parkin, own-goal (24), 1–1 Knowles (26), 2–1 Munro (36).

Sheffield Wednesday 2 Wolves 3, First Division, 16 August 1969.
Sheffield Wednesday: P. Springett, Branfoot, Burton, Young, Mobley, Craig, Fantham, Eustace, Warboys, Prendergast, Ford.
Wolves: Parkes, L. Wilson, Parkin, Bailey, Holsgrove (McAlle 12), Munro, McCalliog, Knowles, Dougan, Curran, Walker.
Attendance: 23,167. Referee: A.E. Dimond (Harlow).
Scoring: 1–0 Warboys (3), 1–1 McCalliog (13), 1–2 Knowles (21), 1–3 Curran (36), 2–3 Ford (64).

Southampton 2 Wolves 3, First Division, 20 August 1969.
Southampton: Gurr, Jones, Hollywood, Fisher, McGrath, Gabriel, Paine, Saul, Davies, Byrne (Channon 27), Sydenham.
Wolves: Parkes, L. Wilson, Parkin, Bailey, Holsgrove, Munro, McCalliog, Knowles, Dougan (McAlle 86), Curran, Walker.
Attendance: 25,792. Referee: I. Jones (Glamorgan).
Scoring: 0–1 Parkin (17), 0–2 Bailey (23), 1–2 Channon (52), 1–3 Wilson (67), 2–3 Davies (87).

Wolves 0 Manchester United 0, First Division, 23 August, 1969.
Wolves: Parkes, L. Wilson, Parkin, Bailey, Holsgrove, Munro, McCalliog, Knowles, Dougan, Curran, Walker.
Manchester United: Stepney, Fitzpatrick, Burns, Crerand, Ure, Sadler, Morgan, Kidd, Charlton, Law (Givens 84), Best.
Attendance: 50,783. Referee: T.W. Dawes (Norwich).

Wolves 1 Derby County 1, First Division, 27 August, 1969.
Wolves: Parkes, L. Wilson, Parkin, Bailey, Holsgrove, Munro, McCalliog, Knowles, Dougan, Curran, Walker (McAlle 60).
Derby County: Green, Webster, Robson, Durban, McFarland, Mackay, McGovern, Carlin, O'Hare, Hector, Hinton.
Attendance: 45,025. Referee: L. Callaghan (Merthyr).
Scoring: 0–1 Hinton (17), 1–1 Dougan (72).

Coventry City 1 Wolves 0, First Division, 30 August 1969.
Coventry City: Glazier, Coop, Cattlin, Machin, Curtis, Blockley, Hunt, Gibson, Martin, Carr, Clements.
Wolves: Parkes, L. Wilson, Parkin, Bailey, Holsgrove, Munro, McCalliog, Knowles, Dougan, Curran, Farrington (McAlle 76).
Attendance: 38,336. Referee: J. Finney (Hereford).
Scoring; 1–0 Hunt (53).

**Wolves 1 Tottenham Hotspur 0, Football League Cup second round,
3 September 1969.**
Wolves: Parkes, L. Wilson, Parkin, Bailey, Holsgrove, Munro, McCalliog, Knowles, Dougan, Curran, Wagstaffe.
Tottenham Hotspur: Jennings, Beal, Knowles, Mullery, England, Collins, Pearce, Greaves, Chivers (Pratt 76), Want, Morgan.
Attendance: 34,017. Referee: L.P. Baldwin (Middlesbrough).
Scoring: 1–0 McCalliog (8).

Wolves 3 Nottingham Forest 3, First Division, 6 September 1969.
Wolves: Parkes, L. Wilson, Parkin, Bailey, Holsgrove, Munro, McCalliog, Knowles, Dougan, Curran, Wagstaffe.
Nottingham Forest: Hill, Hindley, Winfield, Chapman, Hennessey, Newton, Rees, Lyons, Collins, Barnwell, Hilley.
Attendance: 33,166. Referee: R. Darlington (Runcorn).
Scoring: 1–0 Curran (18), 2–0 Dougan (40), 3–0 Curran (52), 3–1 Newton (61), 3–2 Rees (67), 3–3 Newton (70).
Totals: 188 (3) appearances (171 + 3 sub Lge, 11 FAC, 6 LC), 64 goals (61 Lge, 3 FAC)